THE blackest chapter in the black annals of body snatching was written in Edinburgh in 1828. Its authors were a drunken but efficient team of murderers, William Burke and William Hare.

Burke was a trader in secondhand shoes that he peddled on the street. Hare ran a rooming house.

Burke's move into that house marked the beginning of a new and successful career for the two men. It started when, one night, one of the other lodgers in the house died. The dead man hadn't paid his rent and Hare wanted it. With Burke's help he sold the body.

Once the two saw what medical schools paid for cadavers, and that these schools would be glad to buy any other corpses they wanted to sell, Burke and Hare went into business.

From stealing a dead body to helping a man close to death cross that final threshold seemed like a short step.

Burke and Hare sometimes made it even shorter....

Body Snatchers, Stiffs and Other Ghoulish Delights

BY

Frederick Drimmer

FAWCETT GOLD MEDAL • NEW YORK

A Fawcett Gold Medal Book
Published by Ballantine Books
Copyright © 1981 by Frederick Drimmer

ISBN 0-449-13324-9

Manufactured in the United States of America

First Fawcett Gold Medal Edition: November 1981
First Ballantine Books Edition: October 1987

Contents

For Evelyn

Foreword

READER, you are not a ghoul for having picked up this book, nor am I one for having written it. Everyone is interested in death and in stories about the dead. The interest is a normal one and, I think, a sign of a healthy intellectual curiosity.

All of this book is about dead bodies and most of it is about stolen ones. The word *stiffs* originated among the body snatchers. *Stiffs'* first appearance in print was in 1859, when John Russell Bartlett, a distinguished linguist, reported in his *Dictionary of Americanisms* that it was current among resurrection men in the United States. It was slang then and it is slang now, but it has been part of the vocabulary of the medical profession and the police for generations. It implies an easy familiarity with Mr. Rattlebones and a lack of fear of him that can be salutary in everyday life.

This book provides, in chapters two through eight, a popular account of the history of body snatching as it was once practiced to supply subjects for the surgeons and medical schools of Great Britain and the United States. Of books about grave robbing in Britain there are a number, but no book, so far as I know, has ever attempted to pull together the story of body snatching in America; that, until now, has been scattered through a multitude of medical journals and histories of medical schools. My account is not a scholarly one, but I think the basic facts are here. I shall be pleased if medical people find what I have written interesting and if all readers are made more aware of the social validity of donating bodies for medical purposes as well as the serious need for them.

A few remarks about some of the other chapters in the book. So far as I know, the story of the theft of the body of that consummate artist, Charlie Chaplin, and the capture and trial of the thieves has never been told before in the United States, nor so completely anywhere else. This is also the first telling in book form of the death of Elmer J. McCurdy, the Oklahoma outlaw, and the wanderings of his cadaver, which suddenly became known to millions after turning up during the filming of a popular television series.

The Hottentot Venus has been mentioned in a specialized book and in some magazines overseas, but this is the first full-scale account of the trials and tragedy of that unhappy woman. The attempt to steal the body of Abraham Lincoln was related by J. C. Power, custodian of the Lincoln mausoleum, in 1890, and again in 1929 by Lloyd Lewis, but I haven't seen a detailed account of it published in the last half century. The story of Julia Pastrana I related once before in my book *Very Special People*. I decided to retell it here because I have discovered a good deal of new information about her and because audiences before which I sometimes lecture on human oddities find that ugliest of women most attractive.

Some additional words about Julia may interest you. After she died in Moscow in 1860, it was reported that her husband, Lent, sold her body and her child's to Professor Sokolov, the Russian anatomist, for £500. Lent soon had second thoughts, and bought both bodies back for £800. Photographs of the two bodies, nude, taken at the time of the embalming, appeared in a Russian textbook by Manssurov published in 1889.

In life Julia's prognathism and hairiness often caused her to be compared to an ape. It was as the "Apewoman" that she was being exhibited just a few years ago in Scandinavia. Curiously these unfortunate features of hers have brought her a bizarre kind of immortality in racist publications in the American South. I have in my possession a leaflet with a picture of her which asserts she was the product of the mating of an ape and a black. The picture is used to "prove" the close biological relationship between the two types. This is pure poppycock. Julia wasn't black. Her oddity was genetic, as I have pointed out. Moreover, the ape and the human being represent different species, and different species cannot mate and produce young that are fertile, as Julia was.

There are many other extraordinary adventures of the dead that I could have included here. Actually I intended to, but the book kept growing and growing, so the rest will have to wait for another time. If you, kind reader, know any remarkable stories about the dead and would care to relate them to me, I would be glad to hear from you.

F. D.

The Thing in the Fun House

SUSPENDED from a crude gibbet, the man's body swayed back and forth in the shadows. It looked real. The kind of thing you would expect to find in a "fun house," it was supposed to look real. But when you came up close to it, you could see it was only a dummy, covered with wax and fluorescent red paint that made it glow eerily in the blackness when exposed to ultraviolet light. Only a dummy; still...

The cameraman squinted through his lens at the wax figure. The time was early December 1976, and the scene, in a Long Beach, California, amusement park, was the Laugh-in-the-Dark Funhouse, where a production crew was in the process of shooting an episode of the popular TV series, "The Six-Million-Dollar Man."

"Hey, Joey," the cameraman called to his assistant, "turn the dummy a little to the left."

The assistant came forward, lifting his hand to move the dummy, but paused momentarily as he noticed its face. Something about the dummy's waxen features made him vaguely uneasy. He searched for a reason. The face, he decided, wasn't the characterless, machine-made kind he was used to seeing on mannequins. He noted the odd little slant of the nose, the bulge of the forehead, the natural-looking thrust of the jaw. The eyes weren't staring straight ahead, as he would have expected in a dummy. They were closed, like those of a person asleep.

Or dead.

"Stop looking at it and swing it to the left," the cameraman reminded him. "We have a scene to shoot."

Shrugging off his uneasiness, the assistant turned the dummy. As it moved, one of its arms detached itself and clattered to the floor.

"Another delay," the cameraman grumbled. "You'll have to glue the arm back on."

The assistant bent to pick up the limb. It was strangely heavy—much heavier than an arm of wax should have been. As he scrutinized the end where it had separated from the shoulder, a look of puzzlement came over his face. He carried the limb closer to a light and saw a round protuberance that looked like the end of a bone. Surrounding it was a substance that had the appearance of human tissue—but tissue almost as hard and dry as stone. Yet the outside was coated with wax.

Curious, the cameraman joined him. He studied the arm. With a pocketknife he scraped off some of the wax. An orange-colored area became visible. Although it had a strange leathery texture, he could tell at once it was human skin.

He cleared his throat. "We'd better call the police."

A few days later the dummy lay stretched out on a gurney in one of the autopsy rooms of the Los Angeles County Morgue. That morgue, among the biggest and best equipped in the world, is presided over by Dr. Thomas Noguchi, the county's coroner and chief medical examiner, an outstanding forensic scientist. Every year Noguchi's department investigates some eighteen thousand deaths. Every day he oversees fifty autopsies or more.

Now Noguchi was studying a report of the thing that had been found in the fun house.

Stripped of its wax, the dummy proved to be pathetically and unmistakably human. The report described it as the body of a white male five feet seven inches tall, weighing 150 pounds. According to the findings, the man had died of a gunshot wound.

Although the medical examiners hadn't found a slug inside the man, they had extracted a .32-20 copper bullet jacket, known as a gas check. They determined that the missile, after penetrating the right side of the chest, had passed downward, smashing through the sixth rib, the right lung, the liver, intestine, and pelvic muscles, where the bullet jacket was found. To produce such a wound, the .32-20 must have either been discharged from overhead or entered the body while the victim was in a prone position. The body also showed signs of incisions in the chest and abdomen. Some, in the shape of a Y, suggested an earlier autopsy; others, in the groin, were doubtless the work of an embalmer.

Laboratory tests soon revealed the reason for the hardness of the tissue and the leathery quality of the skin. Arsenic was found in heavy concentrations in various parts of the body. A metallic element, arsenic has the effect of petrifying a corpse. It was an ingredient in the first embalming patent ever issued by the United States Patent Office, and was widely used during the Civil War. Arsenic made it possible to preserve and deliver to the next of kin the bodies of thousands of soldiers who had fallen on battlefields far from home. For decades afterward it was a favorite with embalmers.

Noguchi frowned as he studied the report. He knew now how the man had died and been embalmed. But who was he? Who had killed him? And what was his body doing, coated with wax and dangling in a fun house?

Meanwhile, the macabre discovery in the fun house having triggered nationwide curiosity, newspapers were clamoring for more information as police investigators went looking for answers. It was learned that the mummy (as the medical examiners were calling it) had previously belonged to a concession in the amusement park called the Hollywood Wax Museum. Displayed in an open coffin, it was billed as "The Thousand-Year-Old Man." When the wax museum failed in 1971, the mummy was acquired by the fun house manager. "I was sure it was papier-mâché," he said.

An earlier owner, the investigators discovered, was Louis Sonney, of Entertainment Ventures, Inc. After acquiring the mummy in the 1920s from a carnival operator, Sonney poured colored wax over the body and added it to the gallery of dummies in his crime show. The body, the carnival operator had informed him, was that of an Oklahoma bandit named Elmer J. McCurdy, said to have been tracked down by a posse and shot.

The investigators contacted the authorities in Oklahoma, and facts began to bob to the surface promptly. It was learned that not only had there been a McCurdy, but a good deal was known about him. He had shown up in Oklahoma in the early 1900s, coming from either Colorado or Kansas, where he had killed a man. He specialized in robbing trains and banks. He was also a proficient safecracker. And he had served a sentence in the Oklahoma Territorial Penitentiary. (Oklahoma was a territory until 1907, when it was admitted to the Union.)

McCurdy, the record revealed, was a rather mysterious character. Although he worked with a gang and had many aliases, he was hard to trace for other reasons. There was, for example, nothing particularly striking about his appearance. He did have a fondness for drink, but so did plenty of others in the shifting population of old Oklahoma. Only his *modus operandi* set him apart from other criminals. With each new job he changed his confederates. And while his activities were confined to southern Kansas and neighboring northern Oklahoma, he was constantly on the move.

McCurdy's procedure was to drift into a town and find some kind of temporary employment. Then he would keep his eyes and his ears open until he found a bank or a train that promised to be easy and profitable to loot. Once the plum had been selected, he would recruit local criminal talent to help him pluck it. After pulling off the robbery and splitting the plunder, he would disappear. When his money was spent he would pop up somewhere else and start all over again.

In September 1911 McCurdy turned up in Pawhuska. A small town northwest of Tulsa, Pawhuska was the capital of the Osage Indian nation. He soon learned a Missouri, Kansas, and Texas train was scheduled to arrive in Oklahoma early the next month with thousands of dollars of government money for the Indians. After finding two confederates, he made his plans.

On October 4, 1911, at one in the morning, as train No. 29 was puffing along east of Pawhuska, McCurdy and his two companions suddenly climbed into the cab of the engine and, brandishing guns, ordered the engineer to bring the train to a halt. The bandits uncoupled the passenger cars, then had the engineer move the mail and express cars farther down the line. There McCurdy ransacked them.

Instead of the thousands in greenbacks he had expected, however, all he found was forty-six dollars. That and a shipment of liquor were all the valuables No. 29 was carrying. Either the shipment of money had been delayed, or McCurdy had robbed the wrong train.

Their tempers frayed, the robbers gulped down the contents of some bottles of beer and prepared to depart. When McCurdy stepped down from the train he lugged two jugs of whisky with him.

After a brief ride together, the three bandits split up, taking off in different directions into the Osage Hills.

As soon as the robbery of No. 29 was reported in Pawhuska, Sheriff Harvey Frease began to round up suspects. On October 6 he learned someone resembling the leader of the bandits had been seen nearby, at the place of a man named Sears. The sheriff mustered a posse of three—two deputy sheriffs, Bob Fenton and Dick Wallace, and Fenton's brother, Stringer, a detective for the railroad—and sent them out to the Sears ranch. There they picked up one of the two whisky jugs, empty, and the information that McCurdy had left, and headed for Charlie Revard's place on the Big Caney River.

Late that night the posse rode up to the Revard ranch.

Yes, said Revard, the man they were looking for had dropped in just a few hours earlier. He had placed a jug of whisky on the table and invited the dry-mouthed ranch hands to share it with him. After about an hour, soggy with drink, he had asked for a place to sleep. Revard had told him to bed down in the barn.

It was 2 A.M. when the officers silently approached the barn. A barbed wire fence, some trees, and stumps separated them from their quarry. The hayloft, they noted, commanded a clear view of the terrain they would have to cross to get to it.

They decided to wait until dawn.

At 7 A.M. the officers called on McCurdy to come out and give himself up.

There was no reply. Then a bullet whistled by. It wasn't close, but it was close enough for Bob Fenton to know it had been meant for him. He dived for cover.

His brother, Stringer, was the next target. Three shots were fired at him. All missed.

The next bullet was aimed at the third member of the posse, Dick Wallace. It was wide of the mark.

"He must still be pretty boozed up," one of the officers said. "But there's no point in taking chances."

Hiding behind trees and stumps, they pumped bullets at the opening in the loft. From time to time they could see McCurdy's gun barrel shine in the morning sun, and a bullet would fly by.

The battle went on for nearly an hour, and ranchers from the sparsely settled neighborhood gathered around, drawn by the sound of gunfire. Positioning themselves out of range, they waited for the outcome.

"He hasn't fired a shot in fifteen minutes," one of the officers finally said. "Maybe we got him. Or he could have run out of ammunition."

"You might be right," another replied. "But it could be a trick."

The son of a rancher was listening. He was just a boy. "Let me go out under a white flag and ask him to give up. He wouldn't shoot at a kid."

The three conferred. They decided that the bandit, if he still had any ammunition left, wasn't likely to waste it on a child. A cloth was tied to a stick and the boy walked out into the open, waving the makeshift flag of truce in his right hand.

"I got no gun," he called out, holding up his empty left hand. "The sheriff says for you to surrender."

The dark opening in the loft was silent. The boy looked at the law officers. They waved him on.

The youngster moved up to the barbed wire fence, found a small hole in it, and wriggled through. He disappeared through the open door of the barn.

The three law officers waited, the muzzles of their rifles centered on the opening in the loft.

In a few minutes the boy came running out of the barn. "He's up there on a pile of hay," he said. "He don't talk none."

When the deputies found McCurdy he was lying motionless, his face buried in the hay, a jug of whisky beside him. Spent shells lay scattered around. He had run out of ammunition. They turned him over and saw the large bullet-hole in his chest.

Rewards amounting to four thousand dollars—no mean sum in those days—were being offered for McCurdy. After the body had been identified, the Fentons and Dick Wallace could almost feel the crisp new bills of the reward money between their fingers. But the money, the three soon learned, had been offered for the bandit's "arrest and conviction." So the lawmen were obliged to content themselves with congratulations in place of cash.

Meanwhile the sheriff and the undertaker still had a dead body on their hands. Descriptions of McCurdy were dispatched around the region in the hope that some relative might come forward to claim the body and provide for its burial.

But after a few days the undertaker was compelled to embalm the remains. He decided to see if he couldn't earn a few pennies for his labors. McCurdy, hardened by the arsenic embalming fluid, was stood up against the wall in a back room, dressed in the clothes he had been shot in. He was billed as "The Mystery Man of Many Aliases" or "The Oklahoma Outlaw." Thus did the devious fellow who in life had been a skulker and a hider in the shadows become, in death, a local celebrity. Indian children, dusty cowpokes, oil-field workers, overalled farmers, and neatly dressed townspeople waited in line outside the door of the funeral parlor, only too willing to pay a nickel apiece for the privilege of feasting their eyes upon an authentic outlaw.

Five years slipped by while McCurdy stood in his corner and kept the peace. Although no one came forward to claim him, periodically carnival operators passing through Pawhuska offered to buy him. The undertaker turned them all away; he was not, he declared, in the business of selling human flesh.

One day he was greeted by an angry-faced stranger.

"What you're doing here is an abomination," the stranger cried. "Elmer J. McCurdy is my brother. I intend to take him back to Kansas and give him a decent burial in the family plot. We've been trying to find him for a long time."

McCurdy had been a sturdy source of income for the undertaker—not to mention an in-the-flesh advertisement for his talents. Of course he wanted to keep the body, but he knew he didn't have a legal leg to stand on. Regretfully he watched the stranger carry the mummified body into the street and carefully load it on a wagon.

A few months later surprising reports began to arrive in Pawhuska. People who were well acquainted with the mummy of Elmer J. McCurdy said they had seen it recently in Texas, Kansas, and thereabouts. McCurdy was not resting peacefully with his deceased kinfolk in Kansas; he was in fact jostling around the country with a traveling carnival. The self-styled brother who had claimed his remains was evidently no brother at all, but a shrewd carnival operator who had thought up a ploy for getting a profitable exhibit free of charge!

*   *   *

An impressive sheaf of reports flowed into the office of the Los Angeles County coroner after the discovery of the mummy in the fun house. Noguchi also received photographs of McCurdy taken before and after his embalming, complete with his name, the photographer's, and the date.

Most curious of all was a call from Fred Olds of the Oklahoma Territorial Museum in Guthrie, Oklahoma. Olds told Noguchi he was convinced the body was McCurdy's, and he requested permission to bring him back to Oklahoma and bury him.

During his life Elmer J. McCurdy had been a robber and a fugitive. All that Oklahoma had felt it owed him then was a bellyful of lead—or, at best, a quick trial, followed by a prison term or the gallows. But after sixty-five years he was no longer an object of fear or retribution; he was a part of the gory, glorious fabric of Oklahoma's history. Like the Dalton gang, the Doolins, and Belle Starr, he had become a minor folk hero, villainous but romantic. In the best tradition of the Old West, he had died with his boots on. He was, they said, The Bandit Who Wouldn't Give Up.

So far as Coroner Noguchi was concerned, Oklahoma was welcome to relieve Los Angeles County of the honor and the expense of McCurdy's burial. "If you can prove that it's McCurdy," he told Olds, "he's yours."

For three months Olds and other history-minded Oklahomans gathered information about Elmer McCurdy and how he had met his end in the Pawhuska shoot-out. When they had finished, a committee of them went to Los Angeles to confer with Dr. Noguchi and his experts. The Oklahomans came with an expert of their own, Dr. Clyde Snow, pathologist of the Federal Aviation Administration office in Oklahoma City.

Not a single scrap of evidence escaped scrutiny. Sections of the mummy's tissue were sent to the Paleopathology Association, a medical group that specializes in examining the remains of those long dead. The description of McCurdy in his old prison record and the old photographs were screened for similarities to the mummy.

The ages checked out—McCurdy would have been thirty-three at the time of his death, and the mummy was that of a man in his early thirties. The hair color and eye color of the two were identical. The heights matched. The examiners were interested in traces of a scar they found on the back of the mummy's right wrist; McCurdy's prison record mentioned such a scar in the same location. The bullet wound in the mummy also matched the one found in McCurdy when his corpse was brought in to Pawhuska. And bunions—the mummy had enormous bunions. So had McCurdy.

With the passing of time a mummy's face can change considerably from what it was in life. The face of the corpse didn't look too much like McCurdy's in the mug shots from the Oklahoma prison records or the pictures taken after his death.

To pin down the facial identification, Dr. Snow adapted a method used in identifying the bodies of people badly burned or mangled in air crashes. Called the superimposition technique, it consists of combining, in a single photograph, a picture of the skull with one of the head of the person whose skull it might be.

Two video cameras were circuited into a single monitor. McCurdy's profile in the photograph taken after his embalming in 1911 was enlarged, and one camera was aimed at this. The other was focused on the mummy's head in profile.

The two heads appeared on the screen of the monitor, one superimposed on the other. The similarity in bone structure was striking. Not proof positive, but good supporting evidence. The estimated bone measurements also matched.

Another problem—establishing the year the mummified man had died—had to be solved purely by deduction.

In the novels of Earle Stanley Gardner and other detective story writers, the coroner often determines the exact time the deceased met his end. That kind of accuracy is rare in real life. With a body long dead, an approximate date is generally the best that can be hoped for.

The mummy had been embalmed with arsenic—and a majority of the states had outlawed the use of arsenic by embalmers by 1920. Arsenic was once a favorite with murderers. If, after being used to kill a victim, arsenic was also employed to embalm him, the evidence that it had been used as a poison could be masked, making it easy to miss the true cause of death. The year 1920, then, provided the medical examiners with one limit for the date of the mummified man's death. The .32-20 bullet jacket found inside the mummy furnished another. Bullets of that type weren't made before 1905. So the death had probably occurred sometime between 1905 and 1920—which agreed with Pawhuska's record of the shooting of McCurdy in 1911.

"In addition to the physical findings of our examination," says Snow,

> we had the testimony of the several carnival and amusement park entrepreneurs who, at one time or another over the years, had exhibited the mummy. When pieced together, it provided a virtually complete documentation of Elmer's six-decade odyssey, which took him from the funeral parlor in Pawhuska to the fun house in Long Beach. Considering both the physical and documentary evidence, we were able to conclude beyond reasonable doubt that the mummy was indeed the late Elmer J. McCurdy.

And so four months after the discovery of the thing in the fun house, Coroner Noguchi had all of the information he needed to close case 76 14 812, Doe, John, 255, fill out a death certificate in the name of Elmer J. McCurdy, and send him on his way.

On April 14, 1977, the outlaw came home to Oklahoma. It was his first trip in a jet airplane. The law requires that a body must be embalmed if it is to be accepted by a commercial carrier. Stone-stiff McCurdy had no trouble satisfying that requirement.

Rain was falling, seven days later, when McCurdy set out for his last adventure. It was to take place in Boot Hill Cemetery, an old territorial graveyard outside Guthrie, Oklahoma's first capital. (Old outlaws were buried there because the federal marshal had his headquarters in Guthrie.)

The funeral was conducted with a dignity and style that would have tickled the old-time train robber. McCurdy traveled in an elegant hearse of bygone days, pulled by a pair of cream-colored palominos, and furnished with glass panels and somber velvet curtains. His coffin, simple and old-fashioned, had a cross on its lid. Clip-clopping along on horseback with him was a reverent escort drawn from the ranks of the Oklahoma Territorial Posse of Westerners, a group devoted to keeping alive the traditions of the old frontier. Phaetons, buggies, and antique motorcars traveled in the procession. Many people walked.

"I guess," says Fred Olds, who had played such a big part

in bringing Elmer home, "it was the only funeral where I had a good time."

Around the site selected for McCurdy's last resting place were the graves of Oklahomans of earlier times—outlaws like Bill Doolin and Charles Pierce, who had punched out their names in the state's history with bullets. McCurdy's tombstone, tall and dignified, was already in place. ("It would have made Elmer proud," says Olds. "Outlaws almost never got even a rock for a grave marker. Bill Doolin rated a buggy axle for years. One grave was marked by a gun barrel until it was stolen last year.")

A preacher dressed in an old black frock coat, string tie, and slouch hat delivered Elmer's funeral eulogy. Slowly the flower-topped coffin was lowered to the bottom of the hollow oblong with ropes that had been used in hangings. Then a big cement truck pulled up and sloshed a gray flood of concrete on top, at the behest of Dr. Jay Chapman, Oklahoma's medical examiner.

Elmer J. McCurdy had been caught in the glare of publicity ever since his discovery in the Laugh-in-the-Dark Funhouse. He had even appeared on an NBC newscast. As a property he had multiplied in value—so much so that more than one carnival operator might be tempted to dig him up and take him on the road again. And even a ripsnorting reprobate like McCurdy, the medical examiner had ruled, was entitled to a sleep and a silence at the end of the trail.

The body snatchers! they have come
    And made a snatch at me;
It's very hard them kind of men
    Won't let a body be!

Don't go to weep upon my grave,
    And think that there I be;
They haven't left an atom there
    Of my anatomy!

—*Thomas Hood*

IN the dim yellow light cast by the covered lantern the two dark-smocked figures dug steadily. Every now and then they gulped heartening swigs of whisky from a pewter flask. Minute by minute the hole grew deeper. All around, the faces of the angels on the headstones frowned. The pair had been working a long time, spelling one another in the hole, when a hollow sound came from below. The wooden shovel had struck wood.

The toiler in the pit smiled and nodded at his companion. The other, spreading the shoveled dirt neatly on the canvas by the grave, smiled back.

It was hardly an occupation for smilers. The dangers, the smells, the dreadful sights were nothing to smile about.

Tonight, however, was a special night for the diggers. It would bring them not only money but revenge.

Money they needed desperately. But here, at the newest, deepest grave in the quiet cemetery of Penicuik, ten miles from Edinburgh, all they could think of was revenge. Revenge on their partner, Andrew Merrilees.

Of all the scoundrels who stole bodies for medical students

to cut up in their anatomy classes, Merrilees had the blackest reputation. "Merry Andrew" the students called him. But there was little merriment in Merrilees, with his gaunt, greedy face and his idiot leer, so like that of the skulls he sold to them.

After this night's work Merry Andrew would think twice before he lied to his partners or cheated them out of another pound.

Yet these two were hardly less black-hearted than Merry Andrew. The one in the hole, Mowatt, was called the Mole because he was so skilled in burrowing his way down to the Things. The other, a deaf mute, was known as the Spoon because he was proficient at lifting—especially the Things he found in coffins.

A last shovelful, and a third of the coffin lid was laid bare. The Mole climbed out; the Spoon climbed in. He placed the ends of two iron hooks (with ropes attached) under the lid edge. He clawed his way up again. They spread heavy sacking over the hole to deaden the inevitable sound.

The two ropes pulled taut. And tauter still.

Crack! The coffin cover split apart.

Instantly the Spoon was back in the hole. He pushed aside the splintered wood and thrust his hand inside the box, groping until his fingers touched the icy neck. The Mole had already lowered a rope. Jerking up the head by its long hair the Spoon slipped the noose around the neck and pulled hard.

He was up and out in an instant. They tugged at the rope, maneuvered, tugged again.

When they had the Thing on the grass they stripped it naked and flung the graveclothes back into the hole. Then they quickly refilled the grave with earth and smoothed the surface.

The Spoon bent over, lantern in hand, inspecting. He nodded, satisfied that not even the sexton would find the grave any different from the way he had left it that morning.

The Spoon squatted by the Thing. He held the lantern close to the face he and the Mole knew so well, and grinned again.

For it was the body of Merry Andrew's sister they planned to sell. It would end up on Dr. Knox's dissection slab in Surgeons Square. And they would be ten fine guineas richer.

The Spoon grabbed the Thing's chin. Dirt-crusted fingers

pushed back the pale lips. In the dim lantern light the dead woman's teeth gleamed.

Even. White. Good, good. The teeth should fetch ten or eleven shillings more from the dentist.

They sighed contentedly and began to pull a sack over the naked white body.

So busy were the Mole and the Spoon that at first they didn't see it.

The apparition had risen silently from behind a nearby headstone. It stood there motionless, a great white shape, wavering ectoplasmically in the night breeze and watching.

The Mole and the Spoon were bending over to lift the sack when the ghost emitted a shriek, a frightful, eldritch shriek out of another world.

Their blood turned to hard crystals of ice. Still stooped over, they froze.

The specter shrieked once more and hurtled toward them like a comet, its white tail flaring behind it.

Somehow, in the back of their minds, they had always known it could happen.

The sack thudded to the dank ground and, blind with fear, the two men tumbled and stumbled over the graves and into the blackness.

When the white billowing form came to the sack, it paused. Suddenly it changed shape, widening and sinking down to the Thing and enfolding it. Then it shot up to its giant's height again and turned to pursue the thieves. It reached the highroad just as the grave robbers were about to jump into the donkey cart they had borrowed for the trip to Penicuik.

"Stop, thief!"

They spun around, saw the great white figure with the Thing held to its bosom.

Like startled alley cats they disappeared into the underbrush.

A convulsion, sudden and violent, now shook the apparition. Whiteness billowed at its feet.

It had a mouth now, with jaws like an ogre's, leering and cadaverous. It chuckled. "The Spune maun dae wi'oot its parritch this time!" ("The Spoon must do without its porridge this time!")

Gently, Merry Andrew laid the Thing in the cart. He pulled open the sack and looked down at the gaunt dead face.

The instant he looked, it changed.

The gray hair turned brown. The thin cheeks grew round. Rosiness flooded the lips. It was the face he always saw, young and beautiful and full of love for him.

His eyes, in their big black orbits, swam with tears.

He kissed the cold mouth goodbye.

Then, tying the sack's end, he leaped up to the driver's seat and headed the cart for Edinburgh and Surgeons Square.

The years between 1800 and 1832 (when this strange incident took place) were the heyday of the body snatchers in the British Isles. Hundreds of grave robbers stalked the cemeteries of England, Scotland, and Ireland, pulling freshly buried bodies from their tombs to sell to the medical schools.

London in the 1820s had close to a thousand students working in a dozen bustling dissection laboratories in hospitals, private schools, and universities, learning the fundamentals of anatomy. Edinburgh had as many students again. With few exceptions stolen bodies were the only ones their professors could obtain for them.

In Germany, Austria, France, Italy, and Holland the authorities had long since opened their eyes to the facts of life— and death. They had recognized, by law, that a real body was the best textbook of anatomy; that it was better to dissect the dead than to mutilate the living. The remains of friendless persons who died in hospitals, poorhouses, and prisons were turned over to the medical schools. That was considerably more useful than feeding the cadavers to the worms, and cheaper than burying them at public expense.

But not in Great Britain. (Nor, for that matter, in America.)

In Britain old beliefs and traditions died hard. The awe and respect that everyone felt for the dead, reinforced by the teaching of the Church of England, continued to impede dissection long after the other countries of Western Europe had learned how to deal with the problem. British and American medical pioneers like John Hunter, Robert Liston, Sir Astley Cooper, William Shippen, and John Collins Warren had to rob graves, or pay others to rob them, so they could have subjects for their own research and for their students to study. Only by defying the law and tradition were they able to advance medical science as much as they did.

In London, as early as the 1500s, the Corporation of Surgeons insisted every prospective surgeon needed to attend two courses in dissection. King Henry VIII ruled that every year the bodies of four executed criminals be turned over to the surgeons.

Even in the sixteenth century four bodies were far from enough. Surgeons and their students discreetly provided themselves with additional subjects for dissection. That could well be what William Shakespeare had in mind when he asked that these lines be placed on his tomb in Stratford-on-Avon:

> Good friend, for Jesu's sake forbear
> To dig the dust enclosed here.
> Blest be the man that spares these stones
> And curst be he that moves my bones.

Later George II ordered that the bodies of murderers in London and Middlesex be dissected. The law, however, was not intended primarily to provide bodies for dissection. Its chief object was to discourage crime.

It didn't. Instead, it fostered a widespread belief that dissection was a particularly horrible kind of extra punishment. Surgeons and medical schools came to be hated and dreaded by the lower classes.

Since the surgeons needed more bodies than the law provided, they sometimes were forced to take extraordinary measures to get them. One was to bribe the hangman and his beadles to turn over to them the bodies of executed felons not granted them by the law. Students or surgeons' assistants would also attend public executions and fight for a criminal's body with his friends and relatives. A London magistrate, Henry Fielding (who, incidentally, wrote the classic novel *Tom Jones*), gives a grim description of such carryings-on, even in the presence of a strong guard, at a mass hanging in the 1700s:

> As soon as the poor creatures were half dead, I was much surprised before such a number of peace officers to see the populace fall to hauling and pulling the carcasses [to shorten their dying agony] with so much earnestness as to occasion several warm encounters and broken heads. These, I was told, were the friends of the persons executed, or such as, for the sake of tumult, chose to appear so, and some persons sent by private surgeons to obtain bodies for

dissection. The contests between these were fierce and bloody and frightful to look at, so that I made the best of my way out of the crowd.

Most of the bodies dissected in the medical schools—nine out of ten, in fact—were stolen from graves. Students dug them up as they needed them. Often a demonstrator of anatomy would go out with his charges to make sure they left the grave just as they had found it; otherwise they might bring the wrath of the locals down upon the school.

Sometimes doctors would get bodies for their own purposes. If someone with an anatomical peculiarity or an unusual disease died, they were interested in learning more about his condition—or in adding a diseased organ or an unusual skeleton to their anatomical collections. Occasionally a country doctor—or even a great surgeon like Sir Astley Cooper, president of the Royal College of Surgeons of England—would have a difficult or untried operation to perform, and need to test it on a dead body before risking it on a living one. Sir Astley was also interested in examining the cadavers of former patients; he wanted to see how operations he had performed years earlier had stood the test of time.

For the students, robbing graves might have had an element of adventure; it probably also appealed to their urge to tweak the nose of tradition. In later life many a distinguished medical man who had stolen bodies in his youth took a certain pride in relating his experiences as a gentleman body snatcher.

The famed Scottish surgeon Robert Liston, for one, saw nothing shameful in telling at length how he and others had lifted the body of a young sailor. Liston had read a report of the sailor's burial, which mentioned, incidentally, that the youth's tragic drowning had driven his sweetheart out of her mind. Determined to get the cadaver for the dissection laboratory, he rounded up a few fellow students and set out for the burial ground at Rosyth.

After rowing across the Firth of Forth the young men made their way to the deserted churchyard. Suddenly in the dark they saw a ghostly figure. It was the demented girl Liston had read about, strewing flowers on her lover's tomb. So the students waited impatiently until the girl went away.

After they had dug up the body and pulled a sack over it, Liston picked up a flower from the grave and fixed it in his buttonhole. (No doubt he wanted his friends to believe the grim job didn't oppress him as much as it really did.)

The students had rowed just a short distance from the shore when they heard a terrible scream. The heartbroken girl had returned and discovered her sweetheart's open grave.

Leighton, another surgeon of the early 1800s (we're indebted to him for an account of the incident at the start of this chapter), told the story of three students of the celebrated Edinburgh anatomist Monro. Learning a farmer's wife had died in a nearby town, they set out in a rented gig to steal her cadaver. After they had broken open the coffin they realized they had forgotten to bring along a sack in which to take away the body.

The biggest and strongest member of the party volunteered to carry the dead woman. Holding her on his back by her shroud, he stumbled along toward the gig. The burden was a heavy one and it began to slip down. He felt the dead woman's knees brush the back of his legs. The feet touched the ground and the body jumped. He thought he heard the dead feet shuffling behind him.

It was his first grave-robbing expedition. "By God, she's alive!" he screamed.

Dropping the body, he raced after his friends. All three, thoroughly frightened, jumped into the gig and rattled away.

The next day the farmer passed by the burial ground and saw his wife's body lying by the roadside. He became convinced she had been buried alive—a common fear in those days—and somehow had clawed her way out of the grave, only to drop dead from the exertion.

Besides the gentlemen (the surgeons and students), there was another class of body snatchers—the scoundrels. These were the men who, like Merrilees, Mowatt, and the Spoon, robbed graves for a living.

Professional grave robbers were a tough, vicious lot, given to treachery and drunkenness. They often had criminal records. Many stole bodies only part of the time; their main occupation was housebreaking, picking pockets, or robbing people on the streets or highways. In 1828 there were some two hundred men engaged in grave robbing in London alone, most working at it part-time. Edinburgh, Dublin, and other big cities with hospitals and medical schools also had their gangs of body snatchers.

The grave robbers were organized in gangs. They invented

and honed to perfection all the dirty tricks and duplicity later made famous by gangs dealing in another kind of illicit merchandise—the American bootleggers of the 1920s.

Competition between gangs of grave robbers was fierce. Hijacking was common.

Often a gang would steal into a graveyard to collect a fresh corpse, only to find another gang busy digging it up. The gangs would go at each other with spades and crowbars, the tools of their trade, until the stronger group drove the weaker one away. For the victors, getting the body wasn't enough. If they recognized the members of the defeated gang, they would purposely leave the grave a mess. Then they would send an accomplice to denounce them to the police.

Body snatchers seldom missed a chance to take revenge on rivals or put them out of business. When they saw a competitor with a loaded wagon (what would he be transporting but bodies?), they would follow him to his destination. Then they would report to the police both the surgeon who had bought the bodies and the man who had sold them. The surgeon would have his purchases seized. The seller would be whipped publicly or jailed. The rivals could now, in the lingo of the bootleggers, "take over his territory."

Once two well-known body snatchers, Murphy and Patrick, bribed a gravedigger named Whackett to give them exclusive rights to a private burial ground near Holywell Mount. The collaboration was a great success. As he worked, Whackett simply placed markers to point out the new graves. When he went home in the evening he would forget to shoot the bolts on the gate. Occasionally the thieves came away with as many as six bodies in a single night.

One day two rival body snatchers, Holliss and Vaughan, learned about the deal Whackett had made. They confronted the gravedigger and threatened to expose him unless he offered them the same kind of arrangement.

Enraged, Whackett ran across the street to a public house, where a crowd of laborers was drinking.

He pointed out of the window to Holliss and Vaughan. "See those two men? They're body snatchers. They've offered me a bribe to let them rob the graves in the burial ground."

No one was more hated by the working classes than the body snatcher. Holliss and Vaughan had to run for their lives. They were good runners. After they had made their escape, they had only one thought: Get even. Stopping at a police office, they found a magistrate holding court.

"All the tombs in Holywell Mount burial ground have been robbed," they told him and the others in the room. "It's Whackett, the gravedigger. He's selling the dead to the body snatchers."

The courtroom dissolved into a mob, which rushed out into the street and headed for Holywell Mount, picking up new adherents along the way.

The mob reached the cemetery. The gates were locked. Whackett peered out at them, then disappeared.

Smashing down the gates, the mob poured inside. Its members dug up some of the freshest-looking graves and discovered empty coffins in them.

They found Whackett in his hiding place. Carrying him to one of the opened graves, they kicked him into it, then began shoveling dirt over him.

Whackett didn't dare to climb out. He couldn't stay in the rapidly filling grave either. Constables arrived just in time to save him.

That hardly soothed the angry mob. Whackett's house was on the burial ground. They pushed in the door and broke every stick of furniture inside. They found Whackett's wife and children cowering in a corner, tied them up, and dragged them through a pond, leaving them gagging and retching and covered with black slime.

Grave robbers lived a dangerous life and they developed a colorful vocabulary to go with it. "I'm a bloody body snatcher!" roared the murderous John Bishop when the police asked him his trade, and that, in general, was what the grave robbers called themselves. The surgeons who dealt with them preferred to call them (and occasionally themselves) "resurrection men" or "resurrectionists," or, when they were speaking more formally, "exhumators." Because the grave robbers frequently carried off their quarry in sacks, they were also known as "sack-'em-up men."

Resurrection men spoke of a body as a "thing." Things came in different sizes. A "small" was a body under three feet in length. This class was broken down into "large small," "small," and "fetus." Smalls sold at so much per inch.

Body snatchers sometimes said they were "going out to look." That meant to look for funerals. A funeral was a "black." When they saw one, they would follow it to see where the body was buried. A grave they described as a "hole," and a cemetery as a "crib." If body snatchers waited too long after the funeral, they would find the thing was "bad"—decomposed, and therefore unsalable.

Prices were high in the palmy days of the body snatchers. Earlier, in the 1750s, surgeons could buy a body for as little as a guinea (a trifle more than a pound, which was, in fact, more than a skilled craftsman earned in a week). By the 1820s London and Edinburgh had so many schools of anatomy, all clamoring for bodies to dissect, that the price had shot way up. An adult "thing" often brought nine or ten guineas. In times of shortage or peak demand anatomists had to pay as much as sixteen or twenty guineas or risk losing their students to the schools that would.

It was not uncommon for the gangs, at the height of the school season, to raise their price and threaten to cut off an anatomist's supply if he refused to pay. The anatomist could not easily afford to turn them down. Once the anatomists tried to resist. They organized themselves into a group (they called it the Anatomical Club) and told their suppliers they would pay just a single set price and no more. But new schools kept appearing. The newcomers paid higher prices and the club members' supply dwindled. The united front dissolved.

How much did a body snatcher earn? Probably in the neighborhood of several hundred pounds a year. That wasn't bad money in those days.

Body snatchers who managed to stay sober and work hard and astutely at their trade did much better. "When I go to work," testified Ben Crouch, one of the sharpest of them, to a parliamentary committee in 1828, "I like to get those of poor people buried from workhouses, because instead of working for one subject you may get three or four." (A number of coffins were buried in the same workhouse grave.) Crouch saved enough money to buy a hotel after he quit. Another body snatcher left a sizable fortune to his heirs. Others had extensive investments in real estate.

But not most. Most were too careless or shiftless to hold on to their money. Many were alcoholics. They went to work only when the gin and ale ran out.

Body snatchers worked under contract. They made a deal with a surgeon to supply him with subjects at a fixed price. (Later they might raise it.)

The resurrection men loaded their arrangement with "extras." One was a bonus that had to be paid in advance. This they called a "douceur." It was common, at the start of a lecture series (the usual school season ran from October to May), to see a rough-looking character like Ben Crouch in a hospital or an anatomy school hunting around for the lecturer. "Fifty pounds down [the douceur] and nine guineas a body" was the way he might have put his proposal. When the lecture series was over, the body snatchers had to be paid "finishing money" to tide them over till the next series began.

Joshua Brookes, surgeon-owner of a prominent anatomy school, once decided to deny his suppliers' demand for a bonus. That night two badly decomposed bodies were dumped near the entrances to his prestigious establishment. Some young ladies stumbled over one of the corpses and became hysterical. Their screams caused a crowd to gather. Only the prompt intervention of the police saved Brookes and his school from an attack by the mob. Other schools were not always so lucky.

Body snatching was a risky trade that could land its practitioners in jail. If it did, the anatomy teacher was expected to help the body snatcher and his family. The teacher had to put up money for the man's bail, pay him a stipend while he was locked up, and contribute to his wife's support. Sir Astley Cooper, known as "the King of the Resurrectionists," paid out hundreds of pounds to his suppliers while they were imprisoned. He also used his influence, which reached up to the prime minister and the King, to get lighter sentences for his people.

The contract demanded by the gang was an exclusive one. If a teacher dared to purchase a subject elsewhere, his regular suppliers might teach him a painful lesson. Joshua Brookes once bought a body from an outsider. Almost immediately the police were knocking at his door; his suppliers had tipped them off that he had a stolen cadaver on his premises. Another method the gang had of teaching the teacher was to force its way into his dissection room and make mincemeat of any body he had bought from another source.

Astonishing as it seems, in English law for a long time it was not a serious offense to steal a dead body. "The carcase that is buried belongeth to no one," the law said. A corpse wasn't property; the man who stole one wasn't robbing anybody. There was no statute prohibiting body theft, and many judges were unwilling to punish it.

In 1788 body stealing was finally made a misdemeanor. Even so, prosecutions were scarce and convictions were scarcer. In all of England in 1823, when body snatching was at its height, there were just fourteen convictions. Unless the offense was flagrant, the punishment was light—a few months in jail, a fine, or sometimes a whipping. Many cases were dismissed. Magistrates recognized that the British army and navy needed surgeons, and dissecting the human body was an indispensable part of a surgeon's training. Even heads of government like George Canning and Robert Peel tacitly authorized the justices to connive with the resurrectionists.

Dead bodies were one thing, property another. The theft of property valued at five shillings or more was punishable by death. A ring on a dead woman's finger, a shroud, burial clothes, or a coffin was the property of the heir or executor of the deceased. To steal any of these could be a hanging offense. Professional grave robbers were usually careful to strip the body and throw the burial garments or other belongings back into the grave (as we saw the Spoon and the Mole do at the start of this chapter). There were, of course, always some exceptions.

Gangs had informants and helpers. Of these the most valuable were the men who worked in the burial grounds. For a share in the profits, gravediggers and sextons (who often collected twice, since they might also be paid by relatives of the deceased to protect the graves) would keep the thieves posted on who was to be buried where and help them with the digging. Cemetery workers who lost their jobs—and that was the least they could expect if it was discovered that graves in their care had been disturbed—often became new recruits for the gang.

Body snatchers, to escape detection, had to know how to work fast and efficiently. It was important not to leave any traces of their activity in the graveyard. If they did, a strong guard would be posted and the cemetery would be out of bounds to them for a long time.

The perfect time for the robbery was the night after the burial. The ground was still loose and easy to dig. Around the grave it would have been trampled during the funeral, making less noticeable any signs left by the thieves.

Weather was important. After a rain the digging was difficult. Nor was it wise to dig up a body when snow lay on the ground. On the other hand, falling snow would cover up any indications that grave robbers had been at work.

Other things could reveal a tomb had been tampered with. A dead person's relatives might make a pattern on the grave with flowers, stones, clamshells, sticks, or the like. Then they would come back day after day, anxious to see if the objects had been disturbed. Body snatchers had to watch for these patterns. If they saw any suspicious-looking objects they would gather them up and, after finishing their job, carefully restore them to their previous positions. Some relatives might scatter ashes on a grave and later inspect them for footprints. Experienced resurrection men were careful to leave no traces.

The professionals knew how to get their "things" without digging out the entire grave. Techniques varied, but a standard one was to dig down over the head of the coffin, making a hole about three feet square. Spreading out a canvas sheet by the grave, the men piled the earth on the sheet so as not to leave any telltale soil on the grass. They also avoided using metal-bladed shovels, for they might make noise as they struck stones. One gang in Scotland used flat wooden shovels shaped like daggers.

At regular intervals fresh men relieved those who had been digging, so the work proceeded rapidly. The entire job, on a grave six feet deep, might take an hour. A shallow grave could take just fifteen minutes. The men wore smocks over their clothing to keep it clean. Earth-stained clothes could attract the suspicion of the police.

When the thieves had uncovered about a third of the coffin they forced hooks or a specially made crowbar under the lid and broke off the exposed part. During this operation a tarpaulin or sacking might be spread over the work area to muffle the sound. Sometimes the thieves would make a tent with the tarpaulin. To cut down chances of being seen they used a lantern with a shade over it. One man climbed down into the grave to tie a rope around the cadaver's neck or under the arms, and they hauled it out of the coffin. After they had pulled a sack over the body, the robbers restored the grave to its original condition.

Finally the sack was heaved over the churchyard wall. Anyone abroad in the early hours would hardly pay attention to anything so commonplace as a man with a sack on his shoulders or a wagon moving through the dark streets. Local constables were frequently paid to turn the other way.

Not all the merchandise the body snatcher sold came from graveyards. He had other sources of supply. Two favorites were the workhouse and the hospital. There the bodies of people who died without relatives or friends could always be obtained if one knew how.

The resurrection man had connections in these places. Whenever a dead body remained unclaimed they would let the thief know. Promptly afterward the body snatcher—or, better still, a woman (often his wife or a prostitute in his pay) —would call. This person, dressed in black and showing signs of deep grief, would identify himself or herself as a relative of the deceased and request permission to remove the body for burial. Was the hospital or the parish likely to ask for identification? Hardly. It was glad to be spared the cost of another pauper funeral. These "relatives" were experts at disguise. They could appear at a hospital time and again without being recognized.

In the poorer districts of the cities the body snatcher could always find an undertaker with an itchy palm. Shortly before a funeral he would quietly remove the body from the coffin and substitute a sack of earth or wood of equal weight. Once the lid was screwed down, who would be the wiser?

Resurrection men often stole bodies from private homes. They would scan the newspapers for death notices, hang around the house of the deceased, and, when they saw the family go out, break in and remove the corpse in a sack or hamper. A London police officer named Glennon reported in 1828 that he had personally recovered more than fifty bodies stolen from private homes.

A newspaper account that someone had committed suicide or met death by mischance would be read with great interest by the literate body snatcher. When the coroner arrived, days later, at the place where the inquest was to be held, he often discovered the body had disappeared mysteriously. Or else a resurrection man might appear at the inquest and say he was a relative. And the body would be turned over to him, with no questions asked.

In 1799 a young American medical student was taking a course in dissection at a London hospital. (Many early American physicians were trained in London or Edinburgh.) He was especially curious about resurrection men, for back home he himself had dug up a corpse or two to dissect, to the horror of his staid father. In December John Collins Warren (later Harvard's second professor of anatomy) wrote home to Boston:

> Dissection is carried on in style; twelve or fifteen bodies in a room; the young men at work on them in different ways. The people called resurrection-men supply us abundantly. An odd circumstance happened some time since. A hungry beggar got some bread and ate it with so much avidity as to suffocate himself and fall down in the street. One of the resurrection-men, passing, immediately claimed the man as his brother, took him to the dissection-room of St. Thomas's, and secured a good price.

There was no end to the ruses practiced to get hold of cadavers. One of the most daring of the body snatchers was William Clarke. In 1826 he rented a house at the edge of a graveyard close to Bath. In four or five months Clarke resurrected forty-five bodies and shipped them to his London clients by coach, in hampers. When he was caught and sentenced to a heavy fine and a year in jail, he pleaded he deserved better treatment, avowing he had supplied four corpses for surgeons to make trial operations on before they performed the actual one—on George IV, King of England!

In 1830 we see Clarke again, back at his old trade. He had learned that a four-year-old child had died at the home of one Mary Hopkins, a nurse who had been caring for it. Next morning he was on her doorstep, inquiring about renting her cellar. The nurse's son, then out of a job, was in the room and Clarke said it was a shame; he would do his best to find employment for the boy.

Soon after, he called again, and again he showed special concern for the nurse and her family.

"By the way," he said, "I understand you've had a death lately."

"Yes, sir. A poor little girl is departed."

"Poor little dear. I should like to look at the innocent."

The nurse led the kindly gentleman to the parlor. He gazed sadly at the tiny body in the coffin.

"We must all come to this." He brushed away a tear. Then, to cheer both the nurse and himself, he went out and bought a bottle of strong drink. After one glass the nurse was yawning. Clarke took his leave.

A little while later he was back. The street was empty.

Peering in through the parlor window he saw Mrs. Hopkins dozing in her chair. From under his coat he drew a hooked stick. He thrust it into the room. The little body lay in the coffin directly below. He hooked his stick securely inside the child's funeral clothes.

A glance at Mrs. Hopkins. Still sleeping soundly. A glance up and down the street. Still empty.

Using both hands, in one movement he raised the body out of the coffin and lifted it toward the window.

Dear, valuable child! He gave her a quick hug.

He was good at making packages. Quickly wrapping up his little treasure, he tucked her under his arm and, whistling a happy tune, headed for the surgeon's house.

IT'S the most famous skeleton in the whole world. You can see it for yourself in the handsome old building of the Royal College of Surgeons in Lincolns Inn Fields, London, if you obtain permission. It stands in a glass case, splendidly illuminated, in the middle of the Hunterian Museum, the prize of the collection.

And well it might be. Charlie Byrne's skeleton is one of the tallest human skeletons anywhere—7 feet 8¾ inches high. Near it you can see his slipper and his glove. The slipper is fifteen inches long. The glove, measured from the wrist to the tip of the middle finger, is fourteen inches long—nearly twice the length of your own.

Because Charlie Byrne's size was so phenomenal, medical men had their eyes on him for most of his short life, coveting his gigantic skeleton for their anatomical collections. Charlie knew it, and he did everything he could to keep his body out of their hands after his death. But then—

It's a strange story.

Charlie was born in Littlebridge, Ireland, in 1761 or thereabouts. Like most giants—and dwarfs—he was the child of parents of normal height. He wasn't particularly big at birth. Soon after, however, he began to grow at an alarming rate. No one in those days could tell why. The townsfolk, of course, had their own explanation. Charlie, they said, had been conceived while his parents were locked in an embrace on top of the tallest haystack in Littlebridge.

By the time Charlie was nineteen he was reportedly eight feet tall. A youth that size attracts a good deal of attention. In the neighboring village of Coagh lived Joseph Vance, a man with a sharp eye for a penny or a pound. Vance told Charlie he could make him rich if Charlie would take him on as his manager. The young giant agreed. And so the two set out, traveling from city to city, from fair to fair, exhibiting Charlie. Sometimes Charlie appeared under his own name; more often he was billed as O'Brien, who, Vance claimed, was a descendant of Brien Boreau, a king of ancient Ireland. Popularly Charlie was known as the Irish Giant.

After exhibiting young Charlie in Ireland, Vance took him to Scotland. In Edinburgh one morning a watchman was astonished to see a gargantuan figure crossing the North Bridge. The figure filled a pipe and then, holding it to the flame of one of the tall lamps, began to puff. "He didn't even have to stand on tiptoe," the astonished watchman recounted.

In April 1782, Charlie came to London. On street corners and in marketplaces people picked up handbills and read:

> To be seen this, and every day this week, in his large elegant room at the cane-shop next door to late Cox's Museum, Spring Gardens, Mr. Byrne, the surprising Irish Giant, who is allowed to be the *Tallest man in the world*; his height is *eight foot two inches* and in full proportion accordingly; only 21 years of age. His stay will not be long in London, as he proposes shortly to visit the Continent.

Charlie wasn't as tall as advertised—but that's advertising. He became enormously successful. From eleven in the morning till three in the afternoon, and from five to eight in the evening, the "elegant room" in which he was exhibited was crowded. People paid half a crown, a high price for those days, to stand under the giant's arms, try on his big boots, and listen to Vance's lecture about the big man.

The newspapers lionized Charlie. "His address is singular and pleasing," they said, "his person truly shaped and proportioned to his height and affords an agreeable surprise." They were so moved they quoted Shakespeare: "Take him for all in all, we shall scarce look on his like again."

Silas Neville, one of Charlie's visitors, writing in his diary, drew a less flattering portrait. "He stoops, is not well-shaped, his flesh is loose, and his appearance far from wholesome. His voice sounds like thunder, and he is an ill-bred beast...."

Or so he seemed to the genteel Mr. Neville. Probably, though, Charlie was more ill than ill bred. A giant's lot often is not a joyous one. In Charlie's day it wasn't likely to be a long one, either.

Basically there are two kinds of giants. One is the healthy, normal kind, born to a tall mother and father, who inherits their tendency to tallness, and improves upon it. Or he may come of a race of tall people, like the Watusi of East Africa.

The second kind of giant is the abnormal one—the pathological type. Charlie was a giant with an unhealthy pituitary gland. The pituitary, a gland about the size of a pea, is located at the base of the brain. It produces an important secretion called growth hormone. A normal pituitary secretes just the amount of hormone you need for normal growth. An abnormal pituitary, on the other hand, may produce too much or too little. If you don't have enough growth hormone you could be a midget. Too much and you're likely to be a pituitary giant.

For Charlie Byrne the world was not an easy place to live in. It was a world in which things were made for average-sized people. For poor Charlie everything was too small.

Wherever the giant turned he felt awkward, overgrown, out of place. He couldn't sleep in an ordinary bed. Ordinary chairs would creak or crack under Charlie's weight. He couldn't fit his knees under the average table. When he entered a room he had to stoop or he might bang his head against the top of the doorway. Indoors he had to look out for chandeliers. Going up or down steps he might lose his footing because the treads were too small.

Love plays an important part in the lives of most people. It couldn't in Charlie's. Girls either found him ridiculous because of his awkwardness or frightening because of his size. He himself felt drawn to them but he was painfully shy.

Once he received an invitation from the famous James Graham, a mesmerist whose remarkable treatments were the rage of London. A self-styled doctor, Graham at the time was offering to restore potency to the impotent in his fabulous Temple of Health and Hymen. There he had introduced a unique feature that, he promised, would light hot fires in cold ashes. He called it the Celestial Bed and he wanted Charlie to help him popularize it with the public.

Before a man and his mate climbed up on the satin sheets

of the Celestial Bed, Dr. Graham would offer him his magic potency elixir (alcoholic content unstated). As he lolled in comfort, sensuous music would ravish his ears. Soon he would feel the tingling of new excitement (stimulated by electrical currents). And then there was the ultimate promise of "superior ecstasy" and a "fruitful union." (As an added help the bed could be tilted.)

The price for all this? £50, breakfast in bed included.

Charlie was invited to try the Celestial Bed free of charge—with the lady he loved best.

Poor, clumsy, big-limbed Charlie couldn't accept. It wasn't because the bed wasn't big enough. As his manager explained to the press, the Irish Giant was "a perfect stranger to the rites and mysteries of the Goddess Venus."

Charlie, like many other pituitary giants, was sexually underdeveloped. He had other medical problems, including a special susceptibility to infections in his legs. In his day (and up until fairly recently) his disorder wasn't understood, and nothing could be done to help it.

A life situation like Charlie's hardly makes for a sunny disposition. A person apart, he was shut out from many of the comforts and delights the rest of mankind enjoys. If he took to drink and appeared rude at times, it was easy to understand why.

One day as Charlie, in his exhibition room, looked down at the procession of people parading beneath his long, outstretched arms he found himself staring into a remarkably bright pair of light blue eyes under shaggy red eyebrows. They belonged to a short white-haired man with strong, attractive features. His clothing was sober in color but elegant.

"I must speak to you on an urgent matter," the little man said with an emphatic shake of his head. "As soon as possible."

After the audience had filed out, the little white-haired man remained behind. He hooked an authoritative finger in one of Charlie's big buttonholes.

"My name is John Hunter. I'm a surgeon at St. George's Hospital."

Charlie did not need further explanation. He knew why the surgeon was interested in him. Towering over this mite of a man, he began to tremble. Just as he had trembled the time he stood before the skeleton of Cornelius Magrath in the museum in Dublin....

Every son of Erin had heard the story of Corney Magrath, but no one remembered it better than Charlie Byrne. Cornelius Magrath, like Charlie, had been an Irish giant. Just about the same height as Charlie was, and just about the same age. And like Charlie, he had traveled in England and elsewhere, exhibiting himself for a livelihood.

In 1760 Corney returned home to Dublin. He was only twenty-three and he was gravely ill.

Many in the city followed the course of his sickness with interest. Professor Robert Robinson, the surgeon at Trinity College, was more interested than most. The dissection of a giant's body, he believed, could be of prime importance to medicine. And a gigantic skeleton like Corney's, properly displayed, could make Trinity's medical school the talk of all Ireland.

On May 20, 1760, Corney died. While the parish priest was closing the giant's eyelids, Professor Robinson was addressing his anatomy students at the college. He had heard, he said, that some of them were contemplating the theft of Corney's cadaver, and begged them to put the thought out of their heads.

"But," Surgeon Robinson continued, and his tone grew even more earnest, "if you should be so carried away with your desire for knowledge that thus against my expressed wish you persist in doing so, I would have you to remember that if you take only the body there is no law whereby you can be touched, but if you take so much as a rag or a stocking with it, *it is a hanging matter.*"

Later Corney's friends and relatives held a wake for him in his lodgings, over a public house. Neighbors and well-wishers dropped in to lament the giant's early death and drink a mournful dram to his memory. Not all were known to the family, but if you had a moist eye and a dry throat you were welcome. Soon not a soul could see straight. Except for a few medical students who had found it a simple matter to enter the house in disguise—and lace with laudanum the whiskey that was passing around so freely. Sleep came to the unwary soon enough.

Before long one of the students signaled from a window. Other students came up to the house at once, carrying an enormous door.

Tiptoeing among Corney's sprawling, snoring friends and relations, the students stripped off the giant's shroud and carried him downstairs. Outside they lowered the great mass of a man onto the door and covered him with their scholars' gowns. Then up went the door on their shoulders and away went Corney to Trinity as fast as they could carry so weighty a burden.

When Corney's friends awoke from their drugged sleep and saw his body was gone, it didn't take them long to figure out what had become of him.

The provost of Trinity was shocked to hear their accusation. "Poor Corney! I didn't know he was dead. Wait while I go to see Professor Robinson."

He was back in a moment, wagging his head. "Those students! The professor warned them to leave the poor man in peace. Now the body's already dissected. Would you permit me to offer you some compensation for this tragic misfortune?"

They would and they did.

And so poor Corney (or rather his skeleton) was laid out to wait for Judgment Day, not in a coffin but in a glass case in old Trinity College.

Charlie Byrne himself had stood there right in front of the skeleton, measuring himself against Corney's meager seven feet eight inches. He'd looked into the black pits where once Corney's eyes had been and he'd shuddered.

Now, as Charlie stared down at Surgeon Hunter, the giant could feel the panic shooting through him, just as he had then.

The surgeon had been scanning Charlie's bloodshot eyes, his poor color, his acromegalic chin. "Mr. Byrne, I won't mince words. Giants like yourself don't live very long. I put it to you: You have just a year or two to live. At the outside."

Charlie tried to pull away.

The steel-blue eyes held him like a trap.

"If medical science knew more about your condition and its cause, we could do something to correct it. I ask you to help. When you die, will your body to me. An autopsy could provide valuable information. It could enable me to aid others like you who are still unborn."

Charlie's lips quivered. He shook his head from side to side, speechless.

"Is money a consideration? I'll be happy to pay you anything within reason. Even a little beyond reason."

The giant found his tongue. "Keep your bloody money!

You'll never have my body! When I die I'll take care I'm buried where you can't find me!"

"Think. You owe something to humankind.... Well, you and I will speak of this matter another day."

Charlie didn't hear. He had run out the door and down the steps as if he were being pursued by the devil himself.

As the months went by, time and again Charlie would feel someone looking at him in a special way and discover the surgeon in his audience. He could see the eyes probing, diagnosing. *I put it to you: Now you have just one year to live. At the outside. Now you have just nine months to live. At the outside.*

And again he would flee from the exhibition room in mindless terror—a great overgrown child trying to escape from a nightmare that he feared would soon come true.

Every medical man in London knew John Hunter. They knew that when he made up his mind to have something, he would go to almost any length to get it.

They told stories about his dogged ways. Once, for example, a Dr. Clarke had a specimen the surgeon wanted for his studies. "I positively must have that preparation," he told Clarke.

Clarke refused to give it to him at any price.

"Well, then, take care I don't meet you with it in some dark lane at night, for if I do I'll murder you to get it."

And many believed he would do that or worse to satisfy his lust for knowledge. Who else, after all, was so determined —and so contemptuous of danger—that he would inject himself with the spirochete of syphilis because he wanted to study the course of that dread disease at first hand!

Hunter, in that day, was England's leading surgeon. When he was born in 1728, surgery could hardly be called a profession; it was still a trade practiced by barbers. Hunter's incandescent curiosity, his ceaseless experiments, his painstaking dissection of innumerable cadavers, led him from one significant medical discovery to another: such as a method of ligating aneurysm (a dilated, diseased artery) that still saves lives today; such as fundamental insights into the nature of syphilis (the first chancre, where the germ enters the body, is known as the Hunterian chancre); such as pioneer work in the study of the blood, inflammation, gunshot wounds, the physiology of digestion, the grafting of body parts, toxicology, the repair of tendons.

A teacher as well as a doer, he trained a whole generation of surgeons who influenced the course of medicine in Great Britain and America. One of his most devoted pupils and collaborators was Edward Jenner, father of vaccination. To Jenner, once, in a few words Hunter enunciated the method on which modern science is founded. "Don't think, try; be patient, be accurate." And again: "Why think? Try the experiment."

Relentless, driven, Hunter spared neither himself nor others. He was paid large sums of money but kept little of it. His passion was science, and on it he spent almost every penny he could get his hands on. He built an extraordinary private museum of thousands of objects. Expertly prepared specimens showing the development of the brain and spinal marrow from the crustacean up through the mammal; examples of diseases in the various organs of the body; plant and animal specimens, minerals, mummies, freaks—every type of scientific phenomenon imaginable found a place in his astonishing collection.

Now it was to be Charlie Byrne's turn.

Charlie's skeleton, Hunter had decided, belonged in his museum. And what the determined little surgeon wanted he usually got.

Of Hunter the father of scientific surgery, Charlie knew nothing. All he knew was that he had to get away from the inexorable surgeon. In hope of escaping he changed his place of exhibition. When the surgeon didn't show up again he began to breathe more easily.

One day after Charlie's exhibition a servant in livery came up to him.

"Mr. Byrne, my name is Howison. I am in the employ of the surgeon Mr. Hunter of Earl's Court. He wishes you to know he continues to be interested in acquiring your mortal remains. He begs you to name your price."

Charlie moved again. But wherever he went, Howison turned up to remind him of the surgeon's offer.

Giants were in vogue with the nobility. They used them as porters, to stand at their gates or their doors in gold-laced uniforms and assist their guests. Even the King of England employed giants in this role. When one of the equerries of George III offered Charlie the post of porter at St. James's Palace, he accepted. Perhaps he wanted a change. Perhaps

trundled the bulky thing into the
nto the dissection table.
on how steady the surgeon's hand
he reached for his scalpel. For the
vas greater than any he had ever
a lay a kidnapped cadaver, right
ile his wife and two small children
airs. A dissection took time....
nds were to discover the body was
f the undertaker? Rally a howling
:ould come banging and smashing

too long. He would have to work
n. He bent over Charlie's cadaver.
, he snipped, he tugged. Like a
a chicken.
d bubbled in a great copper vat.
ment of Charlie into the cauldron.
, until there was no room for more.
ater turned red. From time to time
re armbone, a long femur, a fibula.
of Charlie to boil away, until, fi-
akings of a magnificent skeleton.
 assemble it. The angry mob and
bursting in. Separated bones were
y corpse. The surgeon could afford
r.
ated the huge skeleton. He didn't
it in his museum. A few times a
ened for inspection by physicians
ferred to wait before his latest ac-
ed.
ned it in vague terms to a friend.
he wrote Sir Joseph Banks (the
around the world with Captain
ould make no particular observa-
to be able to show him."
of Hunter's dearest possessions.
ained it, England's most celebrated
painted by England's most cele-
hua Reynolds and John Hunter
decided to show, at the surgeon's
npublished anatomical researches.

he hoped that John Hunter or his servant Howison wouldn't dare approach him at the royal palace.

The giant didn't stay in his new post very long. No one knows why he left. But it's altogether credible that one evening, standing at the royal portals, he found himself looking down into a familiar pair of steel-blue eyes. For John Hunter happened to be surgeon extraordinary to His Majesty.

Charlie went back to exhibiting himself. By then he had saved some money and he was deathly afraid it would be stolen. His only security, he decided, was to carry his savings with him wherever he went. Who, after all, would dare to pick the pocket of a giant?

One night in April 1783, when Charlie's growing bones were aching more than ever and the loneliness was too much for him, he stopped in at the Black Horse, a public house, for some gin and sociability. As usual his fortune traveled with him—close to £800 in two banknotes, in a little pouch sewed inside his breeches.

Whenever the giant appeared in a pub a crowd would gather around. The overgrown boy enjoyed the attention and the flattery. And if his glass became empty, someone was sure to put a fresh, full one in his hand. So it was on this particular evening, and after a while he lay down in a corner to sleep it off.

He awoke with a start. The candlelight, the noises, the people—slowly he fitted them together and remembered where he was. But where was his hat? His greatcoat?

He asked. No one knew.

His enormous hand groped for the little pouch inside his breeches. It was gone, and with it every penny he owned.

Bellowing like a bull, Charlie ran about the pub, asking who had taken his money. The crowd that earlier had found him interesting now found him unpleasant and troublesome. They thrust him out into the pelting darkness of an April storm.

Charlie was soaked to the skin when he reached his lodgings in Cockspur Street. Exhausted, befuddled, he sat on the steps and wept. A cleaning woman found him there in the morning, unconscious and feverish.

The giant was seriously ill. Some friends, sons of Erin like himself, took care of him. One of them, hoping to cheer him up, told him everyone in London was praying for him and hoping he would soon be well. Charlie was so weak he could barely pay attention. But he pricked up his ears when his friend told him that a kind gentleman had sent his servant in livery every morning to inquire about Charlie's condition. And who was the gentleman?

"A Mr. Hunter. Of Earl's Court."

The nightmare had returned. A fit of trembling took hold of him. The giant finally succeeded in collecting himself. "Come closer. All of you."

They leaned forward to hear the hoarse, failing voice.

"Lads, you all remember Corney Macgrath. Swear, when I'm dead, you'll take my body out on the Irish Sea. Swear you'll weight my coffin and drop it to the bottom. I don't want any bloody body-snatching surgeon to cut me up with his bloody knives. Swear."

He looked around at the four hands raised in the air. His trembling stopped.

Soon afterward, on June 1, 1783, Charlie died. The unhappy giant was only twenty-two.

In life Charlie had attracted wide public interest. Dead, he was more popular than ever—especially with medical men. "The whole tribe of surgeons," reported one journal on June 7, "put in a claim for the poor departed Irish giant and surround his house just as Greenland harpooners would an enormous whale."

But Charlie's friends stood guard faithfully. He was safe—for the time being.

A week later another news report caught Londoners' eyes. It related the story of Charlie's deathbed request.

> In consequence of which the body was shipped aboard a vessel last night in order to be sunk in 20 fathoms of water. The body hunters, however, are determined to pursue that valuable prey...and have therefore provided a pair of diving bells with which they flatter themselves that they shall be able to weigh the hulk gigantic from its watery grave.

Diving bells? The story sounds exaggerated. But if it was true—and if the divers had located the giant's coffin—they would have been greatly disappointed.

Charlie's last journey, at the start, at least, was uneventful. An undertaker conveyed the oversized coffin toward the

Was there any other object, asked Reynolds, that Hunter would particularly like to include?

In the upper left-hand part of the picture, one can see what he chose: part of Charlie Byrne's great skeleton.

After Hunter died in 1793 the Crown bought his museum and presented it to the Royal College of Surgeons. Through the years many physicians have inspected it and lingered in front of the giant. One of these, in 1909, was the eminent American brain surgeon Harvey Cushing. Byrne, Cushing surmised, was probably a pituitary giant. But surmising isn't proving, and Cushing was a scientist. To establish the facts he obtained permission to saw off the top of the giant's skull.

Cushing probed around inside the skull. In the bone itself he found what he was looking for: signs that it had contained an abnormal growth—a tumor—on the pituitary gland. The tumor had overstimulated the gland, making it produce an excessive quantity of growth hormone. Charlie, it will be recalled, was of normal size at birth. A mishap in infancy, however, could have caused the tumor to develop.

John Hunter's magnificent collection comprised 13,682 exhibits. The Royal College of Surgeons added to it over the years, until it had grown to 63,536 specimens by May 1941.

On the night of May 10, German bombers flew over London and dropped their deadly eggs. It was one of the heaviest air attacks the English capital suffered in World War II. A dense cloud of smoke blanketed the entire city. The House of Commons was destroyed. The Hunterian Museum was gutted. The roaring flames devoured two thirds of the museum, including thousands and thousands of the specimens Hunter had labored so long and intensely to collect.

And Charlie Byrne? He survived, having been evacuated to a place of safety. The surgeons weren't taking any chances with the most famous skeleton in the world.

4   The Sicilian Fairy

NEXT to the towering skeleton of Charlie Byrne in the Hunterian Museum stands another one, grinning like him with the secret wisdom of the dead. This skeleton is less than twenty inches high.

The two, the skeletons of the Irish Giant and the Sicilian Fairy, share the same glass case. If they had known each other in life, in a circus or a carnival, they might have shared the same exhibition stand. Giants and midgets often did, and just as often were the best of friends.

Little Caroline might have set her foot, three inches long, next to Charlie's fifteen-inch one. She might have placed her baby hand in his giant paw. How they might have laughed at the contrast, those two, the long and the short of it!

But they never met in life. Only in death.

Caroline was born in Palermo, Sicily, in about 1815. At birth she measured only seven inches in height. She weighed just a pound. That she was alive at all was a miracle.

Caroline was the daughter of a musician named Crachami. Her parents migrated to Ireland, where her father took the name of Lewis Fogle and found employment in the orchestra of the Theatre Royal in Dublin. The health of the tiny girl was a source of constant anxiety. Still she reached her ninth year, a bright and happy child when she wasn't ailing.

For what happened next, we have only her father's word

to go on. One of the actors in the theatre, a man named King, told Fogle he had a brother-in-law, a physician named Gilligan, who might be able to help the sickly girl. The Fogles brought her to him.

The doctor examined Caroline. "Our Irish climate is too inclement for the little sprite." His face lengthened. "She can't live long if she remains here. You must take her away immediately. In England, in the south, she will find the air much more congenial."

To the Fogles the words were like a sentence of death for their daughter. "How can we afford to take our little girl abroad, doctor?"

The doctor pondered. Caroline, he said finally, was an extraordinary child; he had conceived a great liking for her. He was planning a trip abroad at that very moment; what would her parents say if he offered to take her to England with him and give her his personal medical attention? If they would allow him to exhibit her for a short while when he reached London, that would help him defray the expenses. If her health didn't improve in England, he would take her with him to the Continent.

It was an offer the worried parents couldn't refuse.

With Caroline in his charge, and with his wife and his brother-in-law in his retinue, Dr. Gilligan sailed for Liverpool. There he at once began to exhibit the miniature girl. In his advertisements he called her the Sicilian Fairy or the Sicilian Dwarf. She had been born, he told the press, in Palermo, to an Italian woman. Abnormal children, the world believed in those times (and even much later), were the result of some frightening experience their mothers had gone through during pregnancy. Caroline was so tiny, the doctor said, because her mother had been frightened into fits by an accident with a monkey.

Who, in fact, was the man who called himself Dr. Gilligan? Was he actually a physician—as he had told the Fogles so convincingly that they had entrusted their daughter to him? Or had he simply masqueraded as one in order to steal their daughter from them so he could exhibit her?

We'll probably never know. But we do have a curious piece of evidence from Charles Mathews, a noted English actor, who saw Caroline on exhibition soon after she arrived in Liverpool. The dwarf's exhibitor said he was a native of Palermo and he spoke with an Italian accent. He was

attired in a strange garb, had a tall athletic figure, and formed an admirable contrast to the tiny proportion of his "daughter," as he called her.... Her voice was pitched in the highest key of childish treble, indeed so thin, and comb-like, that it hardly reached the ear of those to whom she spoke. Her "papa," however, considerately repeated all she said, for the satisfaction of her patrons, adding many particulars not mentionable to ears polite.

Mathews was for a while completely alone with the pair. He was such an appreciative listener that the showman dropped his guard and eventually his Italian accent.

The English actor knew an Irishman when he saw one. "When you say you were born in Palermo," he asked archly, "do you mean Palermo in the County of Cork?"

The man scratched his head. He rubbed his cheek with his hand. Finally he winked. "Och. I see your honor's a deep 'un!" He put his finger to the side of his nose and lowered his voice. "Sure, you're right; but don't *peach!*"

Mathews, out of the courtesy due a fellow actor, kept the Irishman's secret at that time. It might have been better for Caroline if he hadn't.

Gilligan moved on to Birmingham and Oxford, showing the midget in both cities. In April 1824 he came to London. He engaged an elegant suite for himself and company in Duke Street in the house of a fashionable tailor named Dorlan. He hired an exhibition room for Caroline in Bond Street.

The little girl was a big hit in London. Everyone had seen dwarfs and midgets before, but never one so charming and unaffected as Caroline. Or so minute. Her forefingers were less than an inch long; her feet, three inches; she didn't even reach up to the knee of the average person. The Sicilian Fairy was, according to the *Times*, "unquestionably the most curious of all the dwarfish candidates for public favour that have visited the metropolis."

For an extra shilling Caroline's "father" allowed visitors to pick up the baby-sized girl and kiss her. Charles Mathews had been offered the privilege free of charge as a bribe but had declined it. One of those who took advantage of the offer was a writer for the *Literary Gazette*. "I shall visit her again and again, for she is to me the wonder of wonders. I took her

up, caressed, and saluted her; and it was most laughable to
see her resent the latter Freedom, wiping her cheek, and
expressing her dislike of the rough chin."

The *Literary Gazette* man came back to see her in May.

> She was lively and interesting, sat upon a small tea-
> caddy with infinite grace, and listened to music with ev-
> ident pleasure, beating time with her tiny foot, and waving
> her hand just as any boarding-school Miss in her upper
> teens, and conscious of the beauty of her movements, would
> do.... Weak diluted wine and biscuits she relished much,
> and patted her stomach, saying "good, good," as children
> are sometimes taught to do.... She walked a few paces,
> and expressed many various feelings, of like and dislike,
> both to persons and things, of impatience, enjoyment,
> mirth—the latter prevailing.

The tiny girl was, for the time being, in good spirits and
apparently in good health.

Surgeons and scientists came to see and examine little
Miss Crachami just as they had Charlie Byrne forty years
before. One of those who clucked the most over her was Sir
Everard Home. Home, like John Hunter years earlier, was
surgeon to the King of England. He also held the important
office of president of the Royal College of Surgeons. He was,
moreover, the brother-in-law of the late John Hunter. (Home
allegedly took secret advantage of the relationship. He had
inherited piles of Hunter's brilliant but unpublished studies
and, stealing the ideas, it is said, presented them as his own.
Then he burned the papers, once almost burning his house
down in the process.)

Sir Everard was as impressed by Caroline Crachami as
John Hunter had been by Charlie Byrne. Perhaps the thought
occurred to him that it would be a grand coup if he could
acquire her skeleton and set it up as a counterpiece to Charlie
Byrne's in the Hunterian Museum. The tiny girl was so delicate and fragile that he very likely wouldn't have long to
wait.

Meanwhile Home told his patient, George IV, about the
Sicilian Dwarf and her attractive ways, and His Majesty invited her to visit him at the palace. Gilligan happily com-
missioned his landlord, the tailor Dorlan, to make her a splendid gown for the occasion. Little Caroline performed for the

frivolous, novelty-loving King and his nobles, and they were delighted.

If Gilligan had ever seriously intended to seek the congenial air of the English countryside for Caroline's health, he showed no sign of doing so. He kept the miniature maiden in rainy, smoggy London from April into June. Business was very good.

Caroline developed a bad cough. Even in June the weather was unfriendly. Pale, thin, she continued to appear in Bond Street. Gilligan insisted.

Her parents? They were in Ireland, going about their business. They hadn't had a word from Dr. Gilligan since he had left.

Early in June the condition of the tiny girl was worse than ever. Still she did the best she could; that last day she performed for at least two hundred patrons. Then she collapsed. Gilligan carried her out to his carriage. When the carriage stopped at the house in Duke Street, the child was dead.

Less than a week later, on June 14, a distraught man with an Italian accent appeared at the police office in Marlborough Street. He identified himself as Lewis Fogle-Crachami, a native of Sicily, long-time resident of Dublin, and the father of the girl known as the Sicilian Dwarf. To the presiding magistrate, F. A. Roe, he recounted at length the story of how he had entrusted his ailing child to a certain Dr. Gilligan, who brought her to England. After months without any word from the doctor, Fogle had read in an English newspaper that his daughter was dead. He had set out at once for London to take charge of her remains.

Arriving in the city, Fogle related, he had gone to the exhibition room in Bond Street, where, according to the newspaper, his daughter had been displayed. There he had been directed to Gilligan's lodgings. In Duke Street all he had found was the special little bed his daughter had slept in and the gown Dorlan, the landlord, had made for her visit to the King. Gilligan and company, Dorlan explained, had decamped the day after the child's death, leaving an unpaid bill of £25.

Dorlan had said something more—something that disturbed Fogle profoundly. While Caroline was alive, members of the Royal College of Surgeons had told Gilligan that if the child died he should bring her body to them; the college would be interested in it for dissection. "They said," Gilligan had told Dorlan, "they'd pay me £500 for her."

Could the honored magistrate advise him, Fogle asked, how he might find Caroline's remains? Wouldn't a warrant for Gilligan's arrest be in order?

Magistrate Roe had been listening attentively and asking questions. When Fogle-Crachami finished, the magistrate declared he couldn't issue a warrant. That would be going beyond his authority. (Oddly enough, he didn't even suggest directing an inquiry to the Royal College of Surgeons—although he observed that if they had gotten her, the great likelihood was she had been dissected already.)

No, Magistrate Roe declared, another channel would have to be investigated. Where had the girl resided? In St. James's Parish? It was to the officials of the parish that the father should address his inquiries. And the worthy magistrate sent Fogle off with every wish for success in his search.

In St. James's Parish the officials were willing to assist the foreign gentleman but didn't see how they could. They would know what had become of Caroline only if Dr. Gilligan had given them notice of her death. Then, as the law required, they would have held an inquest. But they had received no notice from Dr. Gilligan, and they didn't know where to find him.

The law had proved unhelpful. Fogle now began to search for Caroline himself. He started in the anatomy schools, which were then flourishing in London. One of the first he visited was Brookes's school in Blenheim Steps, the biggest in the city.

"Yes, yes, a dwarf." Joshua Brookes drew his lips together. "I saw the body a se'nnight ago. The man who offered her wanted too much. One hundred guineas! Have you tried any of the other schools?"

But neither at the other schools nor the public hospitals, where Fogle was shown the bodies being dissected, did he find the one he was looking for. He went back to Dorlan in Duke Street for counsel.

The tailor reminded Fogle of Gilligan's remark about how interested the members of the Royal College of Surgeons had been in Caroline. "Sir Everard Home—the surgeon who got your daughter the invitation to the palace—Gilligan knew him well. He might have gone to Sir Everard to sell the body to the Royal College."

"Where can I find him?"

"His office is in Sackville Street. Wait, I'll come along and show you the way."

At the big house in Sackville Street Fogle was shown in to the surgeon's office.

"Caroline Crachami—" he began.

"Ah, you've come from Gilligan to inquire about the payment for the dwarf's body. Sorry. Tell him the surgeons haven't held their meeting yet, so I can't say how much they'll vote him for it."

"I am not from Gilligan. I am her father. Gilligan stole her body."

"Oh. You don't come from Gilligan?"

"No. He stole her body."

Hastily the surgeon explained that Gilligan had called almost a week earlier with a small package. He had unwrapped it, revealing a pathetic little corpse.

The surgeon recalled the conversation:

"Would you be interested in the remains of the Sicilian Dwarf for purposes of medical research?" Gilligan asked. "Would you care to make an offer?"

"Not I. But perhaps the Royal College of Surgeons would. If you wish, you may leave the body here and I'll present it to them. It will be up to the college to vote whatever payment they consider appropriate."

"Good enough. I must leave town for several days. I'll send a friend to pick up the money."

It was that friend that Sir Everard had taken Fogle to be.

The surgeon assured Fogle he had assumed Gilligan to be the child's guardian, with the legal right to dispose of her body.

Fogle's face was buried in his handkerchief. "Please—I must see my little one again."

The surgeon nodded. "I'll write you an order to the Royal College telling them to let you view the body." He scribbled on a sheet of paper.

Fogle took the paper. He made no move to depart.

Sir Everard picked up his pen again and wrote. "I've drawn a draft on my banker to pay you ten pounds." He held out the paper. "Please accept it with my sincerest regrets."

Fogle looked at the draft. *But Gilligan told Dorlan they would pay £500 for the body,* he thought. His weeping redoubled.

The surgeon was tapping on his desk. "I assure you His Majesty will hear of this unhappy event. He was fond of your little girl. He too will be deeply grieved."

In the end Sir Everard had to lead the weeping Fogle to the door, where Dorlan was waiting.

It was a long walk from Sackville Street to Lincolns Inn Fields and the Royal College. Dorlan and Fogle were out of breath when they arrived. Fogle presented the order from Sir Everard to the porter. The man returned at once with the head surgeon.

The surgeon took Fogle's hand. "I'm fearfully sorry. You come too late."

He led Fogle into a large operating room. In the middle was a table; students and surgeons in blood-stained garments were clustered around. Hastily they drew a sheet over the thing on the table as Fogle and the surgeon approached.

Fogle pulled back the covering. A convulsion of sobbing shook him. *"Dio, Dio, che sciagura!"* He clasped the little body.

The men in the room stood speechless in a circle, watching.

After a while the head surgeon laid a hand on Fogle's shoulder. "Believe me, sir, we are most regretful. Come, now, torment yourself no longer."

Fogle didn't hear. He wept tempestuously, clutching the little form.

"I promise you, no one shall touch the body further." The surgeon pressed some banknotes into Fogle's hand.

Fogle's sobbing faded to a whimper. Gradually he allowed the students to free the body from his grasp. The surgeon guided him out of the room. At the street door he accepted the surgeon's offer of a carriage.

Fogle gripped Dorlan's hand. "I go back to Dublin to tell the terrible news to my wife. Poor Caroline. Poor Caroline." Shaking his head, he climbed into the vehicle.

The surgeon watched Fogle and the carriage disappear around the corner. Then he turned and strode back into the operating room.

The students had already resumed the dissection.

THE three medical students—they were quite young, barely in their teens—crouched behind the shrubs across from Blackfriars.

The lane was dark, except for the constable's oil lamp and the light of the moon.

The cemetery gate rattled as the constable tried it. He held up his lamp and leaned forward, peering between the iron rods. Then, satisfied, he ambled on.

"Weel now, laddies, it's over the wall we go," whispered the redheaded boy.

He was always the first. They passed the shovels, the rope, the crowbar, the sack to him, then clambered over themselves.

The three were newcomers in Glasgow. The medical school was a small one. When the students needed a body, they went out themselves and got it.

"Gae to Blackfriars," their anatomy lecturer had said. "A puir auld body will be buried there this day. But be cannie, boys, be cannie." He winked. "Mind the patrols. And the spring gun."

They had winked back, and off they went. But *what's a spring gun?* In their excitement they had forgotten to ask.

The redheaded boy had watched the burial that afternoon. He led his classmates directly to the grave. The earth smelled damp and fresh. The mound was heaped high with flowers.

"It's here we dig. At the head o' the grave."

The redhead raised his shovel. He stepped forward into

the flowers. It was a long step forward. *The first step,* he thought, *from being a farmer's son in the Highlands to a man of science, a fine surgeon in Glasgow.*

He was warm with the promise, the excitement of it all.

Something in the flowers went unnoticed. He pressed his foot against it.

Live fire rocketed into his belly. So powerful was the charge, it flung him five feet.

Anxious hands turned him over. They felt two heartbeats. Then none.

Smoke was drifting from the foot of the grave. His friends found, hidden in the flowers, the heavy hot-barreled blunderbuss and, tied to the trigger, the trip wire his foot had pressed against.

They couldn't leave him there. It would bring the police to them. To their school.

Nor could they carry him home. He lived in a lodging house in the middle of town. Through all those streets... And the patrols. Yet they knew they must.

They passed him over the wall. They propped him up against it. They wiped the boy's face clean. They closed his eyes and pushed his hat down over the golden-red locks. One of them tied his own left ankle to the dead boy's right. The other tied his own right ankle to the dead boy's left. The cloak of one of them hid the bloodied body.

One on each side, they lifted him up and swung his arms over their shoulders. They braced and embraced him between them. Live legs and dead legs moved forward together. His head, sunken upon his chest, wagged from side to side. He looked a little alive. They staggered along....

Up ahead they saw somebody. *The constable!*

They reeled, laughing boozily. He came toward them. Throats cracking with fear, they sang a drunken song. He came to them all the same.

He lifted up his lamp. He stared hard at the one in the middle. "The chiel' looks unco ill i' the face. Tak' him hame wi' care."

They did. The way was long and slow.

Exhausted, they finally reached his room and placed his bloodied body flat on his bed.

"His fowling piece. Where is it?"

"In the closet."

They laid it by him.

How shocked his landlady would be in the morning when she found her handsome laughing young redheaded lodger dead by his own hand!

Like the unfortunate medical student of Glasgow, anyone who meddled with a grave during the heyday of the body snatchers took his life in his hands. People who had just lost a loved one might use any means in their power to protect the grave. They knew they couldn't place their trust in the graveyard watchman or in the bolts and locks of cemetery gates.

Only if a body was protected until it had putrified could a mourner be sure it would rest in peace.

People resorted to a startling range of ingenious devices and measures to fight off the body snatchers. The spring gun was popular. The firearm chosen was usually a heavy one, like the blunderbuss. A short gun with a large bore and a bell-shaped muzzle, it fired a load of lead slugs that were supposed to spread out as they traveled. As a rule the gun was concealed on the grave. Wires placed close to the ground ran from the trigger to different parts of the grave, where they were anchored by pegs. If anyone pressed against a wire, the gun went off with a deafening blast.

But seldom with a deadly one. Not many body snatchers were killed by spring guns. The weapons were dangerous at close range, but only if the robber tripped a wire and was caught in the direct path of fire. Often he escaped harm. Even so, the gun could be effective. The bang it made was big enough to frighten any amateur and summon a patrol if one was within earshot.

Professional body snatchers hated spring guns. They quickly learned how to deal with them. Once they had made up their minds to rob a grave, they would send a female accomplice, dressed in black, to the burial ground. She would arrive toward evening, when she wasn't likely to be noticed. Strolling meditatively around the new grave, the woman would locate the trip wires and detach them. Or else she would make a rough sketch that showed the location of the gun and the pegs. That night the thieves would lift the gun and wires. After finishing their ghoulish job they would put them back in place.

To the professionals, at least, spring guns were not a great menace. More potent weapons were needed to deter the body snatchers. In Scotland a father had a bomb attached to the top of his child's coffin. Trip wires led to the bomb from the four corners of the lid. The device would explode the instant anyone tampered with the cover. The gravedigger filled in *that* grave with considerable care.

The best way to protect a tomb was to keep watch over it in person. It wasn't a pleasant job, especially in bad weather. You had to stand guard night after night for several weeks. But when a gang of body snatchers found a band of armed men guarding a grave, they would usually slink away. If they started a fight, they knew the ruckus would wake up the neighborhood and bring the police down on them.

Sometimes a nervy or distraught widow would insist on keeping vigil alone by her husband's grave. Naturally she was taking her life in her hands. The only sure way to keep from being jumped by grave robbers was to be backed up by reliable men carrying firearms and in sufficient force. A Bristol diary of the years 1831–32 tells of a man who tried to protect a tomb single-handed against a gang of body snatchers. They attacked him with a shovel. His fingers were cut off.

Once in a while a gang would be so drunk or desperate it might attack even a strong body of watchers. In Ireland in 1830 at the Glasnevin churchyard, a group of men were standing guard over the grave of a friend who had just been buried. On the second night some of the sack-'em-up men appeared. When they saw the armed guards they retreated. Three nights later, however, they returned in force.

The men protecting the grave watched the body snatchers climb over the wall.

"Go away!" they shouted. "Go away!"

The body snatchers replied with a volley of gunshots.

"This brought on a general engagement," reported a newspaper.

The sack-'em-up gentlemen fired from behind the churchyard wall, by which they were defended, while their opponents on the watch fired from behind the tomb-stones. Upwards of 58 to 60 shots were fired. One of the assailants was shot—he was seen to fall; his body was carried off by his companions. Some of them are supposed to have been severely wounded, as a great quantity of blood was observed outside the churchyard wall....

During the firing, which continued for upwards of a quarter of an hour, the church bell was rung by one of the watchmen, which, with the discharge from the firearms, collected several of the townspeople and the police to the spot.

One of the most effective devices developed to protect the newly buried was the mortsafe. This consisted of riveted grids of iron, somewhat like gratings, that were firmly anchored over the graves. Mortsafes looked like cages, and they were, except to the most determined grave robber, impregnable. Some can still be seen in old burial grounds in Great Britain. (During World War II, when the British ran short of scrap metal, patriotic ministers suggested the mortsafes be turned in to the government and melted down. Respecters of tradition protested vehemently. The old mortsafes are still in place.)

New structures made of stone blocks also began to appear in cemeteries. These were the public vaults. Bodies were stored in them for several weeks, under lock and key and often under guard, until decomposition occurred. Lookout towers sprang up, from which a watchman could keep an eye on the burial ground at night. Since a watchman could be corrupted, these devices weren't always effective.

In 1818 undertaker Edward Lillie Bridgman solved the problem for the well-to-do: he invented a wrought-iron coffin. The box was fastened with iron clamps and had no movable parts. Reportedly no one could open it from the outside.

The wrought-iron coffin was bound to cause trouble. Not just for the body snatchers (who couldn't break it open without a sledgehammer—a very noisy process at best). Ministers and churchwardens were appalled by it. Unlike the traditional wooden coffin, it positively refused to decay. Church officials foresaw an early and a permanent crowding of their burial grounds. Many refused to admit the wrought-iron coffin.

Undertaker Bridgman was a persuasive man as well as an inventive one. He talked a Mr. Gilbert into joining him in a fight to the finish against the antiwrought-iron forces. Gilbert's wife had just died. The widower agreed to have her placed in one of Bridgman's coffins and, if a cemetery refused to bury her, to bring suit against it.

Gilbert applied to St. Andrew's Church in Holborn for an interment in its cemetery at Gray's Inn Lane.

"No iron coffins," said the church.

Gilbert sued.

Three months passed. The case still hadn't come to trial. Mrs. Gilbert still hadn't been buried. Bridgman persuaded her husband it was time for action.

Black plumes nodding on black horses, the lady's funeral cortege moved solemnly to Gray's Inn Lane and stopped at the gate.

"Whose funeral? Mrs. Gilbert's? Sorry. No wrought-iron coffins." The sexton refused to open the gate.

The funeral party traveled to St. Andrew's. It halted in front of the church. Mrs. Gilbert's weighty coffin was unloaded and deposited near the door. The church officials didn't like that, and said so.

Bridgman had a model of his coffin ready. He took it out and proceeded to demonstrate its virtues to the church officials. The church officials weren't interested. They called the police.

Bridgman scuffled with them. He was beaten and carried off to the police station.

The minister suddenly noticed the cause of all the trouble, the wrought-iron coffin, resting near the church door. The box was quickly carted away to the charnel house of the parish.

It was September before Bridgman came to trial for his disorderly behavior at St. Andrew's. He was acquitted. In November his patient friend Gilbert heard the London court rule on his suit against the church. Iron coffins were deemed completely within the law. The two men looked on triumphantly as the grumbling sexton of St. Andrew's buried Mrs. Gilbert safe and sound in her iron box.

Bridgman now had the official recognition he craved. He advertised widely. In 1822 he was declaring:

...many hundred dead bodies will be dragged from their wooden coffins this winter, for the anatomical lectures (which have just commenced), the articulators, and for those who deal in the dead for the supply of the country practitioner and the Scotch schools...let each one about to inter a mother, husband, child or friend, say: shall I devote this object of my affection to such a purpose; if not, the only safe coffin is Bridgman's PATENT WROUGHT-IRON ONE, charged the same price as a wooden one, and is a superior substitute for lead.

Iron coffins, despite what the advertisement said, were costly; their price was £31. Also on the expensive side was the burial safe, introduced later in America. This was a cage that enclosed the coffin and was lowered with it into the grave.

You could choose less expensive measures. You might simply bury a coffin very deep, below the water table, so the body would decay more rapidly. You might fill the coffin with quicklime. You could have wooden planks laid lengthwise over the coffin in the grave. Resurrection men would then have to dig up the entire surface of the tomb to get at the body. (This wouldn't stop them, but it made their work harder.) You could also cover the grave with a massive flat tabletop tombstone.

All of these things were tried, and more. Churches raised the walls of their burial grounds six or eight feet higher than before. Spikes were mounted in the mortar on top, or broken glass embedded in it.

People formed protective associations to patrol the grave-yards and the areas around them. One of these associations, which protected the Glasgow High Churchyard, had two thousand members. Angry patrols might exact their own measure of revenge. If grave robbers had been preying on a cemetery, the patrol would lie in wait for them after a new burial. When they showed up, members of the patrol would beat them bloody before turning them over to the police.

But still the grave robbing went on.

And on.

London and Edinburgh were the chief medical centers of the kingdom. Cadavers flowed to them steadily from less important cities. At the University of Dublin bodies were often in short supply because they brought a better price in Edinburgh. Packed in barrels, boxes, or other containers just like the ones used in ordinary commerce, the cadavers usually reached their destinations safely.

Now and then, when the body snatchers were overconfident or unlucky, a shipment would be found out. One in hundreds.

In October 1826 George Leech, a carter in Liverpool, was approached by a tall, stout man of respectable appearance.

"What is your charge for carting three casks from Hope Street to George's Dock passage?"

"Two shillings."

"That's quite agreeable."

They went together to the Hope Street address. Upstairs was a private school operated by a Dr. McGowan, a clergyman. Leech's customer had his business in the cellar.

When they arrived, two men were busy moving the first of the casks up into the street. Leech helped them carry up the second and third casks. They heaved them into his cart.

"Here's the shipping note," Leech's customer said. "The casks contain bitter salts. Set them down on the dock by the smack *Latona*. They're to be forwarded to Edinburgh. Be very careful when you lay them down."

Leech drove to the dock and deposited the heavy casks by the *Latona*. He handed the shipping note to a sailor and left.

The casks remained on George's Dock overnight. In the morning the *Latona*'s mate brought some deckhands to load them on the vessel. A horrible stench made the men draw back.

The mate examined the invoice. "Bitter salts? Hardly." He headed for the office of the shipowner's agent. The police were summoned.

At the Liverpool mortuary the contents of the casks were inventoried. The invoice hadn't been entirely wrong. The casks did contain bitter salts. But packed in the salts were eleven dead bodies that had been pickled in brine.

The police located Leech. "I don't know the customer's name. He looked respectable enough. So did the others."

He led the constables to the house in Hope Street. The cellar was padlocked. One of the constables forced the door with a crowbar.

The smell inside was overpowering. They found four big casks like the ones Leech had taken to the dock. Some sacks, full and heavy, lay on the floor. On the wall hung mud-stained smocks, jackets, trousers.

One of the constables bent over. "Here's something." They examined it. "A large syringe," the report would say, "of that description used for injecting the veins and arteries of the dead bodies used for anatomization."

The casks and sacks were opened. Men and women. Boys and girls. Pickled and fresh. Twenty-two of them.

Surgeon Dawes did the post-mortems. "The bodies were all in a perfect state," he observed. "Those in the casks appeared to have been dead six or seven days, and three men found in the sacks appeared to have been dead only three or four days. There were no external marks of violence, but there was a thread tied round the toes of one of the women, which is usual for some families to do immediately after death. I have no reason but to believe they died in a natural way."

The Reverend Dr. McGowan, who kept the school over the cellar, was interrogated. "I let the cellar January last to a Mr. Henderson. He told me he carried on the oil trade. I knew nothing about any dead bodies being there."

Where had the bodies come from? The Liverpool Workhouse Cemetery, the authorities decided, had supplied most. Some were putrid. "They are extremely dangerous to handle," observed the coroner. He ordered them buried immediately in the parish cemetery, in the casks, just as they had been found.

It was hardly a coincidence that the season for anatomy lectures was just beginning in Edinburgh.

Good detective work trapped two of the three body snatchers involved. Each was sentenced to a year in prison. Henderson, their chief, was never captured.

Bodies weren't the only wares the resurrectionists sold. Healthy teeth brought a good price from dentists, who used them to make dental bridges and plates. (Porcelain teeth had been invented as early as 1776; however, they did not win acceptance until 1830 or later.)

Some body snatchers pulled the teeth from cadavers before turning them over to the anatomists. If a resurrection man dug up a corpse and found it too badly decomposed to sell, he pulled out the teeth, then reburied it. The teeth of young soldiers lying dead on the battlefield of Waterloo continued to sparkle long afterward in the mouths of elderly Britons in Manchester and London.

The teeth the dentists bought were known as the "canines." They weren't just the two canine teeth in each jaw, but the incisors as well—the four teeth in between. (The back teeth of dentures were ordinarily made of wood.)

A number of ghouls got rich by robbing the mouths of dead soldiers. No one on record, though, ever pulled off as impressive a dental coup in a single night as Murphy the body snatcher.

A long-faced man applied one day to the sexton of a religious meetinghouse that had a burial vault for its congregation. The man was dressed in black. His eyes appeared red from weeping.

"Sir, my poor dear wife has just died. We're strangers in London and I'm going out of my mind trying to find a burial place for her." He blew his nose. "We are of your faith. Could you accommodate my darling in your vault?"

The sexton was moved. A shiny half-crown changed hands and he was moved even more. He opened the vault. "Step inside, sir; have a look around by yourself."

Lamp in hand, Murphy the body snatcher walked up and down the dusty corridors. Some of the burial compartments were closed by flimsy locks, others just by latches. In one corner a ladder led to a trapdoor in the ceiling. He climbed up, drew the bolts, and raised the door. He was looking out at the back of the meetinghouse. When he pulled down the door, he didn't bother to push the bolts back in place.

Murphy returned the way he'd entered. He found the sexton. "Thank you very much. I'm sure my Betsy will be happy there, with all those good people. I'll return tomorrow with the payment."

But he returned sooner. That same night, in fact. Quietly raising the trapdoor, he climbed down and lit his lamp. From his bag he drew a stout metal clipper. He snapped off the first lock. He jimmied up the lid of the dusty coffin. A skull laughed up at him. He laughed back. It was a young one, with good, healthy teeth. He went to work with his awl.

When Murphy climbed out of the trapdoor some hours later, rattling inside his bag were the front teeth of the entire deceased membership of the congregation. His net for the night's work was £60.

How do we know so much about the gruesome deeds of the body snatchers? Much of our information comes from their friends the surgeons, who were fascinated by their stories. One of the most extraordinary records of their macabre doings, however, can be found in a curious little work known as *The Diary of a Resurrectionist*. This document, in the col-

lection of the Royal College of Surgeons, matter-of-factly records the day-to-day affairs of a major gang of body snatchers
in London during the years 1811–12. The diarist was Joseph
Naples, a member of the gang.

Naples, the son of a stationer and a bookbinder, had a
better education than most who followed his trade. He was
described by a surgeon who knew him as "a civil and well
conducted man, slight in person, with a pleasing expression
of countenance and of respectful manners." As a youth he
had served in the Royal Navy. Later he found employment
as a gravedigger, a job in which he made friends with body
snatchers and worked with them.

In 1802 a stolen body was traced to Naples and he was
sentenced to two years in prison. Put to work picking oakum,
he wove a rope with it and climbed over the prison wall. It
was his misfortune, later, to fun afoul of a rival resurrection
man, Ben Crouch, who denounced him to the police. Naples
would have drawn an additional sentence, but he had a powerful friend, Sir Astley Cooper. In later life Naples worked
in the dissecting room of St. Thomas's Hospital in London,
where Sir Astley lectured.

Here are a few random excerpts from Naples' diary:

> We all lookᵈ. out [watched to see the funerals that were taking
> place and where they went], at Home all night. . . .
>
> At night went out and got 10, whole [the whole gang] went to
> Green [a cemetery] and got 4 . . .
>
> Met together me & Butler went to Newington, thing bad [the
> body was decomposed and therefore unsalable]. . . .
>
> Met at St Thos., me & Jack went to Tottᵐ. got 4 adts. Ben and
> Bill got 6ᵃᵈ1·1ᶠ at Pancrass took Tottenᵐ. to Wilson, Panˢ. to Barthol.
> [got 6 adults, 1 small, 1 fetus from St. Pancras Cemetery; these were
> taken to St. Bartholomew's Hospital; the four adults from Tottenham
> were delivered to the surgeon Wilson]. . . .
>
> Intoxsicated all day; at night went out & got 5 Bunhill Row. Jack
> all most buried.
>
> Remain'd at Barthʷ. packing up for Edinboro, sent 12 to the
> wharf for the above place, at home all night.
>
> Went to St. Thomas's, sold the extremities. At night Tom & Bill
> got drunk at the Rockingham Arms, at home all night. . . .
>
> Met and settled £108 13s. 7d. each man's share £18 2s. 3d., at
> home all night. . . .

Naples mentions a number of the gang's other members in these excerpts. Ben is Ben Crouch, the leader, who had earlier denounced him to the police. A big, muscular man with a taste for fine clothes, Crouch had made a name for himself as a prizefighter. He drank less than the rest of the gang, and he was always sober on the nights when they settled accounts, so he was able to get more than he was entitled to. Later, with Jack Harnett (the "Jack" of the diary), he dealt in teeth. The two followed the British army in Spain and France, selling food and drink. For extra income, after a battle they would pull the teeth of dead soldiers and steal their valuables. Saving his money, Crouch bought a hotel in Margate; when people learned about his past, however, he was obliged to sell it and leave. He ended up poor and friendless.

Unlike most body snatchers, Jack Harnett, Crouch's partner, managed to hold onto his money. When he died he left his family £6000. His uncle, Bill Harnett, another member of the gang, was highly valued by Sir Astley Cooper. Bill, like Crouch, had been a boxer. He died of consumption after exacting a promise from his doctor that his body wouldn't end up in a dissection laboratory.

Butler, a small, plump, hearty man, had worked as a porter in a hospital dissection room before becoming a grave robber. There he had developed an exceptional skill in mounting skeletons. Later he robbed the Edinburgh mail, was captured, and sentenced to death. To while away the time before he went to the gallows, he put together the skeleton of a horse. His work so impressed two visiting Austrian archdukes that they persuaded the Prince Regent to grant him a pardon.

At least two women were known to have practiced the trade. They were Scottish nursemaids. Their names were Jean Waldie and Helen Torrence.

The two women had promised some surgeons to secure a body for their laboratory. When a child died in the neighborhood, they tried to get the job of keeping the traditional death watch over it. They planned to pry open the sealed coffin and steal the body.

The dead child's parents declined their services, however. Not wanting to disappoint the surgeons, the nursemaids lured a young boy into their home and smothered him. The boy was eight or nine years old. He must have been small for his age. Torrence carried his body in her apron to one of the surgeons.

"Two shillings. Take it or leave it," the surgeon said.

The nursemaids haggled with him. At length they settled for the two shillings plus some extras. Sixpence for transporting the body. And another sixpence for beer. It was possibly the lowest price ever paid for a body.

The crime was found out. The court showed as much mercy to the two women as they had to the boy. In 1752 the nursemaids said their prayers for the last time as they felt the nooses tightening around their necks.

Torrence and Waldie are the only resurrection women (as Sir Walter Scott called them) on record. But they were not the only body snatchers who murdered to provide "things" for the surgeon.

6 Burke's the Butcher, Hare's the Thief

THE blackest chapter in the black annals of body snatching was written in Edinburgh in 1828. Its authors were a drunken but efficient team of murderous Irishmen, William Burke and William Hare.

Burke has left us three mementos. The first is his death mask. The second is his skeleton. (After he was hanged and dissected, his bones were mounted. Both mask and skeleton can be seen today in the Anatomy Museum of the University of Edinburgh.) The third is a word. When Burke was finally arrested and found guilty, "to burke" instantly became the standard way to describe how he and Hare killed their victims.

Of Hare nothing remains but his evil reputation. He got off scot-free.

Professional body snatchers usually sprang from the lower elements of society. Burke and Hare were no exception. William Burke was born in County Tyrone, Ireland, in 1792. As a youth he spent six years in the military. Then he resigned, took himself a wife, and gave her some babies. He used a quarrel with her father as a pretext for walking out on her and the children. In 1818 he moved to Scotland. For a while he worked as a laborer on the Union Canal. To ease his loneliness he took up with Helen McDougal, a homely hank of a woman with a character as loose as his own.

Some nine years later we find Burke and his common-law wife, Helen, in Edinburgh. He has become a trader in secondhand shoes, which he buys cheap, cobbles, and peddles in the streets. A short, well-proportioned man, he is light of foot: he can dance an Irish jig with the best of them. His voice is soft, his eyes are hard, and his manner is full of guile. He has a sociable nature that's especially likely to emerge over a jug of toddy. It was probably over one of these that, in 1827, he made the acquaintance of his future partner, William Hare.

Hare, heavier and more muscular than Burke, had a sullen, brutal nature. He had come to Scotland from Ireland about the same time as Burke, and also worked on the canal. Meeting a man named Log who kept a tramps' lodging house in a seedy section of Edinburgh known as the West Port, he stayed with him till they had a falling out. Perhaps the quarrel was over Mrs. Log; when Log died Hare returned and took his place in the widow's bed. Soon after, Burke and his woman settled in the house. The Burkes and the Hares became fast friends.

On November 29, 1827, one of Hare's lodgers, an elderly ex-soldier named Donald, died. The landlord felt like crying; the old man owed him £4. How could he hope to collect his money? The only way, he decided, was to sell Donald's body to an anatomy school.

Hare had never disposed of a corpse before, so he asked his countryman, Burke, to lend him a hand. A small difficulty: the parish undertaker had already nailed down Donald's coffin cover. When the room was empty they pried up the lid, removed the body, and replaced it with a bag of bark, which was buried with all fitting solemnity.

That evening the two men went looking for the lecture theater of Alexander Monro. They asked a youth for directions. He must have been a student of Dr. Robert Knox, for he sent them instead to Knox's lecture hall at 10 Surgeons Square. There they learned the doctor, Edinburgh's most successful teacher of anatomy, would be glad to buy what they wanted to sell.

After dark the two men lugged Donald's body in a sack to Knox's premises and received £7 10s. for it. Knox exhibited no curiosity about how they had come by the body. Every year he spent seven or eight hundred pounds to keep his classes supplied with cadavers. If he felt anything about his latest purchase it was pleasure because it was so nice and fresh. His assistants told Burke and Hare they would be glad to see them again when they had another body to dispose of. These words weren't wasted on the two hungry Irishmen.

From stealing a body to helping a man close to death cross that final threshold can seem but a short step. That winter a miller named Joseph, who lived in Hare's house, fell ill of a fever. Lodgers slept three or more in a bed, and Hare and his wife worried that the man's illness might keep prospective tenants away. The ailing miller, Hare expected, would put up little resistance—especially after he had a stiff drink.

Again Burke's help was enlisted. The smaller man held a pillow down on the victim's face; Hare, with his heavier weight, lay on top of Joseph in a last, silencing embrace. A feeble struggle and the miller lay still. Anticipating their full pockets, Burke and Hare hired a porter to carry the body for them on their trip to 10 Surgeons Square.

Stiffs, the two men learned, brought more in the winter, when the schools were in full session and the demand for subjects was brisk; this time Dr. Knox paid them £10. Again the doctor raised no questions about how they had come by such a fresh corpse. Neither did his assistants. They had learned never to say anything that might embarrass their suppliers.

The second victim was also a lodger in Hare's house. A poor peddler, he was confined to his bed by jaundice. As Burke later described it, the pair "got above him and held him down, and by holding his mouth suffocated him, and disposed of him in the same manner."

By chance or design Burke and Hare had hit upon a method of murder perfectly suited to their purpose. Suffocation left no marks on the body. (Or at least none that could be detected in those days.) The victim looked as though he had died a natural death. Drunkenness was widespread among the poor of Edinburgh, and constables often found alcoholics lying dead in the street after they had rolled on their faces and smothered.

So far Burke and Hare had limited their homicidal solicitude to sick lodgers at Hare's place. Now success made them bolder.

Abigail Simpson was an elderly beggarwoman who used to call regularly in Edinburgh to collect a small pension. On a visit in February 1828—her last—she had the misfortune to come under the greedy, questing eye of William Hare. He invited her to his lodging house. He didn't have to ask her twice.

In the dingy West Port hovel drinks were passed around freely. Hare planned to kill the old woman that night, as soon as she became tipsy. By the time she had had enough to drink, however, he himself had had too much.

The next morning Burke was available to help.

The pair notified Dr. Knox's assistants they had acquired another subject. After dark, carrying Mrs. Simpson in a tea chest between them, they lurched along to the rear of nearby Edinburgh Castle. A porter was waiting there to relieve them of their burden. They accompanied him to 10 Surgeons Square and collected their money.

By now Burke and Hare were congratulating themselves: they had hit on a fine new way to make a living and it paid better than anything they had ever done before. They preyed only upon the poor, the weak, the witless, the unwanted. With the glittering promise of free drink, bed, and board, it was easy to lure these innocents to Hare's place. Although as killers Burke and Hare weren't particularly skillful or imaginative, they seldom had any trouble subduing their victims—particularly after anesthetizing them with alcohol. And after the poor souls had disappeared? Neither the police nor anyone else showed any serious interest in finding out what had become of them.

That spring Burke and Hare separately murdered two women whose names are unrecorded. Now that their blood money was coming to them with some regularity, they established a set way to divide it. Out of every £10 paid them, Hare kept £6. Burke got the rest. Mrs. Hare, as custodian of the slaughterhouse, expected an honorarium. Burke agreed to pay her £1 per body out of his share. (Neither she nor Burke's woman, McDougal, took part in the murders. They might help to lure the victims and get them drunk, but they slipped quietly from the scene before the main action began.)

In their new affluence Burke and Hare bought better clothing, and so did their womenfolk. Burke, the cobbler, gave up cobbling. They all spent more of their time in drunkenness. To explain their sudden prosperity, they said they had come into an inheritance.

The neighborhood knew better. Even in the dark the comings and goings of Burke and Hare, with their heavy sacks and their tea chests, didn't escape the sharp-eyed residents of the West Port. The two, they surmised, had set themselves up as grave robbers. In that squalid section of Edinburgh it was almost as acceptable a profession as any other.

On April 9, 1828, Burke and Hare murdered Mary Paterson. Mary, a strikingly attractive, bold-mannered girl of eighteen, was an orphan. She was also a streetwalker. If she vanished from the red-light district of Edinburgh, few would wonder what had become of her. But one who would was her close friend, Janet Brown, a girl of the same age and calling.

After a distressing stay in a police station Mary and Janet were released early on the fatal day. They immediately headed toward a spirit shop for the warm consolation of a gill of whisky. On the premises, enjoying his morning dram, was Burke. He sized them up at once. Pretending he had taken a fancy to the girls, he bought them more to drink. Then he invited them to have breakfast with him at his lodgings. As an added inducement he bought each girl a bottle of whisky.

Burke's lodgings—or so he called them—were really a one-room hovel belonging to his brother Constantine and family. By the time Burke and the girls had finished breakfast and drunk their whisky, Mary Paterson was adrift in a stupor. One look at her told Burke she was as good as in his tea chest. Janet, however, still had command of her senses. First he took her to a tavern. Then he brought her back to drink some more. Mary was snoring in her chair.

As Burke poured Janet another glass, who should burst in on them but his mistress, Helen McDougal. She was intensely jealous of any young woman her man paid attention to, and she splattered him and Janet with abuse. He beat McDougal without mercy. Janet made up her mind to leave. Burke was reluctant to let her go, but he finally agreed when she promised she would return a little later.

In twenty minutes Janet was back. Burke was no longer there (having left for Surgeons Square to make arrangements for the next delivery). The two Hares were waiting to greet her.

Janet looked around for her fellow prostitute. "Where is Mary Paterson?"

"Stepped out with Mr. Burke—they will soon return."

Determined to finish the job Burke had begun so well, Hare poured drinks for all. Janet sipped hers.

Under a sheet on the bed just a foot away lay her friend, still warm but lifeless. A few minutes more and Janet was to be stretched out beside her.

Just then there was a knock at the door. Grumbling, Hare opened it. It was someone sent by a worried friend to call for Janet. For the second time that day the girl's life had been saved by an interruption.

During the months that followed, Janet wondered why Mary never came back. Constantine Burke, when questioned, insisted she had gone off with a packman. *Why doesn't she send for her belongings, then?* Janet wondered. Like others in her profession, she knew better than to go to the police for help.

What, then, *had* become of Mary? On the afternoon of the murder her body was carried to 10 Surgeons Square in a tea chest. As Burke, Hare, and their porter walked through the streets, a pack of boys began to follow them.

"They're carrying a corpse!" the boys chanted. "They're carrying a corpse!"

How can they know? Burke asked himself, greatly agitated.

But no one paid the scantiest attention to the children. The chest reached Knox's establishment safely, and the ghouls pocketed £8.

Mary had been dead just four hours. Her body was cold now, but rigor mortis hadn't set in. Looking at the cadaver stretched out on the floor, Knox's assistants commented on its voluptuous form, its youthful beauty. Knox was just as impressed as they were. He said he would have an artist of his acquaintance make drawings of the body. (He did.)

"She's as like a girl I've seen in the Canongate," said a student, "as one pea is like another." He had been with Mary only a few days earlier.

Now he noticed that her long golden hair was tied in curl papers, and he realized she hadn't been buried. "I want to know how she died."

"She killed herself with drink," Burke replied. "I bought her from an old hag in the Canongate. If you don't believe me, come with me and I'll show you the house."

"His explanation was feasible," wrote an ex-student years later. "It rested on the whisky tendency of all such women—

and Paterson's body smelt of liquor when brought in—their reckless life and exposure, and their frequent abandonment when at death's door."

Knox kept Mary's cadaver in alcohol for three months. When it was laid out for dissection, reports of its loveliness of face and form spread far beyond the lecture hall.

Meanwhile Burke and Hare kept a steady supply of subjects moving to the doctor. Of all their murders, none was more audacious than that of a youth of eighteen known as Daft Jamie. The boy, whose real name was James Wilson, was tall and strong, but he had a weak mind and deformed feet. Daft Jamie was a familiar figure in the streets of Edinburgh. When he was twelve his mother had given him a severe thrashing and he had run away from home. From then on he slept in doorways, ran errands, and lived off handouts.

How daft was Daft Jamie? The people of Edinburgh had many tales to tell of his simplemindedness. None was more typical—or touching—than the story of the kindhearted man who saw Jamie wandering about the icy streets of winter without shoes or a hat and decided to make him a present of both. Jamie's gratitude was boundless. Still he showed not the slightest interest in putting them on.

He was asked why not.

"I dinna want to wear them in sic hard times as these," he replied.

Jamie was decoyed to the lodging house by the artful Mrs. Hare. Burke poured him a drink. One was enough, for the boy soon became drowsy. He accepted an invitation to lie down.

Hare stretched out on one side of Jamie. Burke sat on the other. When Jamie seemed to be fast asleep Hare clamped his hands over the boy's nose and mouth.

His breath cut off, Jamie awoke in an instant and flailed at the iron hands.

"Hare and him fell off the bed and struggled," Burke said later. "I then held his hands and feet. We never quitted our grip till he was dead."

Daft Jamie brought the murderers £10. Several of Knox's students and assistants said they recognized him. Dr. Knox insisted they must be mistaken.

Jamie was too well known a character in the city not to be missed. When word reached 10 Surgeons Square that inquiries were being made about his disappearance, the body was hauled from the alcohol. The head and deformed feet were cut off and Jamie was promptly dissected.

Of the six anatomy lecturers in Edinburgh, Knox was far and away the most popular. Every year his classes were more crowded. In 1828 he had an enrollment of five hundred and four students—more than any other lecturer throughout the British Isles. His demonstrations, he advertised, were performed on "fresh anatomical subjects." Thanks to Burke and Hare, they could hardly have been fresher. "We were always told to get more," Burke said.

That October the partners made plans for expansion. Burke was to go to Glasgow or Ireland, taking another man with him, and open a branch of the business. Then they would ship the subjects to Hare for delivery to Dr. Knox. The future looked bright for the bloody pair.

On October 31, 1828—Halloween—Burke was taking his morning dram at his favorite spirit shop. A woman, frail and aging, came in to beg. To Burke she looked like a highly qualified candidate for a tea-chest trip to Dr. Knox's. Drawing her into a conversation, he learned her name was Madgy Docherty. She was an Irishwoman and she was in search of her son.

By coincidence Docherty had been the maiden name of Burke's mother. With a gush of warmth he imparted this exciting piece of information to the old woman, insisting she had to be a distant relative of his. The least he could do under the circumstances, he said, was to offer her free bed and board under his roof until she found her son. Would she be willing to come with him now and have a nip with him and his good wife?

The beggarwoman was very willing.

Burke by this time had moved from Hare's lodging house to a room he had sublet close by. There he led old Madgy Docherty and introduced her to Helen McDougal. Then out he went to buy some whisky and to notify his business associate, Hare, without whom no party could be complete.

"I've got a good shot in the house for the doctor," he said. "Shot" was the word they used for an intended victim.

Burke had living in his room an ex-soldier, James Gray, with his wife and child. No doubt he had plans for them. But old Madgy would be a much easier shot, and to take care of her he would have to get them out of the way.

"You and your husband have had a difference," he told Mrs. Gray. "I won't have my house made a boxing house. You must get out of the house directly."

But he offered to pay for the Grays' lodging for that night. Mrs. Hare, who was present, said she had a bed available. The couple went off with their child, Mrs. Hare, and Burke. When they got to Hare's lodging house the bed Mrs. Hare showed them hadn't been made. Burke made it for them.

The scene was now set for Burke and Hare's Halloween party.

That evening Burke was at his most winning. In the apartment of a Mrs. Conway, a neighbor, he sang old Irish songs and danced the Irish jig, and his delighted kinswoman joined him. Hare was there, and Mrs. Hare, and Helen McDougal. McDougal had brought a bottle. It was passed around freely.

By eleven o'clock Burke, Hare, their wives and old Madgy had said goodnight to the Conways and gone back to Burke's place to continue the party.

After a while the neighbors heard sounds of scuffling and screams of "Murder!" "Police!"

One of them went out to get a constable, without success. When he came back everything had quieted down.

Next morning the Grays came back to Burke's; he had invited them for breakfast. Mrs. Docherty was nowhere to be seen, and McDougal told them she had to throw the old woman out because she had become too friendly with Burke.

Breakfast finished, Mrs. Gray went toward the bed. Her child's stockings were missing, and she thought she would find them in a pile of straw that lay at the foot of the bed.

"Stay away from there!" Burke had never spoken to her in that tone before. He threw whisky on and around the bed, on himself, and up to the ceiling.

To Mrs. Gray his behavior appeared exceedingly odd. How could he waste something he valued so highly? When he explained he simply wanted to empty the bottle so he could get more to drink, it seemed odder still.

Twilight had fallen before Mrs. Gray had an opportunity to satisfy her curiosity. Poking around in the straw by the bed, she touched an arm as cold as snow. Horrified, she pushed away the straw and saw the naked body of Madgy Docherty. She and her husband grabbed their few possessions and rushed out of the place with their child.

Outside they ran into Helen McDougal. Gray asked her

about the corpse. McDougal begged him not to tell anyone what he had seen. "If you'll be quiet it will be worth ten pounds a week to you."

"God forgive my husband should be worth that for dead bodies!" cried Mrs. Gray, and the couple hurried to a nearby police station.

At 8 P.M. there was a knock at Burke's door. Opening up, he saw the police. Although they made a thorough search, they could find no dead body on the premises. But they did find fresh blood on the bed and on the straw near it. They also discovered Mrs. Docherty's clothing.

The circumstances were distinctly suspicious. Denying everything, Burke and McDougal were placed under arrest.

Early the next day the constables paid a visit to No. 10 Surgeons Square. In the cellar they came upon a tea chest, from which they extracted a body that fitted the description of Madgy Docherty. From there they went to Hare's house and took him and his wife into custody.

All four of the suspects were led in to view Docherty's body at the police station. Again and again they swore they had never seen it before, and persistently denied that they had any knowledge of the dead woman. The denial only served to strengthen the suspicions against them. Witnesses had already testified they'd seen Docherty in the company of the suspects on Halloween.

The coroner convened an inquest. The statements of witness after witness left no doubt the Hares and the Burkes had been involved in the slaying, some as direct participants, some as accessories.

But here Scottish justice found itself up against a stone wall. While the evidence against the accused was overwhelmingly convincing, it was purely circumstantial. No one had seen the murder committed; there was no direct proof of the guilt of any of the accused.

Even the autopsy findings were inconclusive. They revealed no signs of violence. According to the police surgeon himself, experience told him the old woman had died of suffocation. On the other hand, he was completely unable to *prove* that murder had been done or how it had been done.

Scottish jurors were notoriously hard customers. Although in other places accused criminals were convicted on circumstantial evidence, in Scotland jurors had refused time and again to find a defendant guilty without hard and fast proof,

such as the testimony of an eyewitness. There was no point
in trying the accused unless such proof could be presented to
them.

All the evidence indicated Burke had taken the greater
part in the killing. Approaching Hare, the prosecution promised him immunity if he would testify against his partner.
Hare leaped at the offer. Mrs. Hare was included in the immunity, since a husband couldn't testify against his wife.
Although the authorities had evidence of a string of murders,
they were able, in the end, to prosecute Burke and McDougal
for just one, the last.

No trial in the history of Scottish crime ever aroused
greater excitement. The press had been running one terrifying story after another about the grisly deeds of Burke and
Hare. People were so wrought up that the authorities expected trouble. To prevent it, they brought in three hundred
extra constables to reinforce the police. As an added precaution infantry and cavalry troopers were placed on alert.

The trial began on the morning of Christmas Eve. Every
available space in the courtroom was taken. All through that
day and night and into the following morning the proceedings
went on—with interruptions only for meals. Burke and
McDougal were defended by some of the most brilliant lawyers in Scotland.

Witness after witness testified. Finally came the one for
whom everyone had been waiting. Hare took the stand.

The prosecutor, Sir William Rae, questioned Hare about
the events of Halloween, when the Burkes, Hares and old
Mrs. Docherty, after drinking liberally at the Conways', had
returned to Burke's place.

"Had you a fight then?"

"Yes."

"Now, where were the women during this?"

"They came in betwixt us to separate us."

"Now, when you were fighting, where was this old person?"

"She was sitting at the fire, and she got up and desired
Burke to sit down, and she said that she didn't want to see
Burke abused."

"Did she run out?"

"Yes, she ran out twice to the entry, and cried out for the
police."

Helen McDougal, Hare related, went out and brought her
back. The men were still struggling when Hare accidentally

pushed Docherty and she fell. She raised herself on her elbow—she wasn't able to get up, being drunk—and begged them to stop fighting. At this point Burke knocked Hare down.

"What did Burke do next?"

"He stood on the floor. He then got stride-legs on the top of the woman on the floor, and she cried out a little, and he kept in her breath."

"Did he lay himself down upon her?"

"Yes, he pressed down her head with his breast. She gave a kind of cry and moaned a little. He put one hand under her nose and the other under her chin, under her mouth."

"Did he continue this for any length of time?"

"I could not exactly say the time; ten or fifteen minutes. He said nothing and got up off her. She wasn't moving; I couldn't say whether she was dead or not. Then he put his hand across her mouth and kept it there two or three minutes."

"What was [sic] you doing all this time?"

"I was sitting on the chair."

"Now, during the time this man was lying on her, where was McDougal and your wife?"

"When they heard the first screech, they left the foot of the bed and went into the passage."

"Did they come in again when this was going on?"

"They didn't come in till this was all over, and her covered over with straw."

Early on Christmas morning the judge charged the jury.

It took them fifty minutes to reach a verdict. Burke was guilty. The charge against McDougal was "not proven." But that didn't mean they had found her innocent. "They have not pronounced you *not guilty* of the crime of murder," Lord Justice-Clerk Boyle said sternly.

She turned in disbelief to Burke. "Nelly," he said, "you are out of the scrape."

But he was in it, up to his neck. He heard His Lordship sentence him to an early hanging. No one could have appreciated better than Burke the irony of the judge's further order—"that, as required by statute, your body should be publicly dissected and anatomized. And, I trust, that if it is ever customary to preserve skeletons, yours will be preserved, in order that posterity may keep in remembrance your atrocious crimes." Burke was then admonished to seek heaven's forgiveness for his crimes.

Burke's fate was now sealed. What of the other members of the gang?

McDougal was released from jail the night after Christmas. The following day she went to a tavern. She was recognized and almost lynched. The police came to her aid, whisking her off to the shelter of a jail, but the mob quickly laid siege to it. Later, dressed as a man, she escaped from a back window. After close calls with other infuriated mobs she made her way to Australia, where she died in 1868.

The Hares were kept in jail while the public prosecutor considered whether they could be brought to trial for some of the other murders, particularly that of Daft Jamie. Finally he decided they couldn't.

Mrs. Hare was released on January 19, 1829. After a number of narrow escapes from angry crowds—the cry "Hare's wife! Burke her!" rang in her ears repeatedly—she was shipped off to Ireland by the police. She was never heard of again.

On February 5, 1829, Hare was set free. Muffled in a cloak, a hat pulled down over his eyes, he was put on a mail coach headed south. When it pulled up at Dumfries he was recognized and a crowd of eight thousand packed the street. The police rescued him and took him to a jail. The mob assaulted the lockup, but early the next morning, with a guard of militia, Hare was smuggled out and made his way across the border into England.

Almost nothing reliable is known of him afterward. It was said he was blinded by a vengeful mob and ended his days a beggar in London, feeling his way along the streets with a dog and a cane.

Burke prepared for his end like the good Christian he had never been. Much of his time he spent in prayer and meditation, with an occasional complaint that Knox still owed him £5 for Madgy Docherty. "Since I'm to appear before the public I'd like to be respectable," he whined, chained to the wall of his cell by his ankle. "I haven't a coat and waistcoat that I can appear in, and if I got the £5 I could buy them."

He made a full confession. He and Hare, he said, had killed sixteen people. He couldn't remember the names of all of them, but he could recall such details as these:

When they [Burke and Hare] kept the mouth and nose

shut a very few minutes, they [the victims] could make no
resistance, but would convulse and make a rumbling noise
in their bellies for some time; after they ceased crying and
making resistance, they left them to die by themselves;
but their bodies would often move afterwards, and for some
time they would have long breathings before life went
away.

Burke had repented often of his crimes, he said, and during
the period he was committing them "could not sleep without
a bottle of whisky by his bedside, and a twopenny candle to
burn all night beside him...they were always in a drunken
state when they committed those murders, and when they
got the money for them while it lasted."

As for their relations with 10 Surgeons Square, the record
showed, not only had Dr. Knox seldom spoken to them, but
he and his assistants had never encouraged them to murder
anyone.

On January 28, 1829, Burke climbed the scaffold that had
been erected for him in High Street. A crowd of twenty-five
thousand, the largest that had ever assembled in Edinburgh,
had been waiting for hours in the pouring rain. All the many
windows and housetops that looked down on the scene had
been rented; Sir Walter Scott, the country's greatest novelist,
was one of the many notables watching.

Kneeling, Burke said his prayers while the crowd cried,
"Hang Hare!" He got up and stepped to the drop.

"Burke him!" chanted the crowd.

He gave a signal and the hangman released the drop. A
great roar rose from the multitude.

Forty minutes later the body was cut down. The mob
surged forward to get hold of it, but a strong force of constables
held them in check. Some lucky ones came away with pieces
of rope and shavings from the coffin.

Next day, at Edinburgh University, Burke was dissected
in public by Professor Alexander Monro. Medical students
were given tickets to attend, but a tremendous crowd had
gathered, and people were admitted till the hall was full.
Monro lectured on the brain, which, he observed, was remarkably soft. As he cut, an unusual quantity of blood gushed
from the body, making the area look like a butcher's slaughterhouse.

Meanwhile more students had arrived outside and clamored to be admitted. The police were summoned to keep order. The students grappled with them and almost overpowered them; they also smashed some windows of the anatomy theater. When the authorities agreed to admit them in groups of fifty, they finally quieted down.

The following day the general public was allowed in to view the remains. Twenty-five thousand persons filed through the theater and past the slab of black marble where the murderer lay.

Next morning another great crowd had gathered. The university authorities declined to continue the show. They were of one mind with Sir Walter Scott, who that very day was writing,

> The corpse of the murderer Burke is now lying in state at the College, in the anatomical class, and all the world flock to see him. Who is he that says we are not ill to please in our objects of curiosity? The strange means by which the wretch made money are scarce more disgusting than the eager curiosity with which the public have licked up all the carrion details of this business.

Later Burke was dissected in detail for the students' benefit. His skin was tanned, and portions of it ended up in private hands. William Roughead, the Scottish barrister-author, had "an authentic specimen of it, resembling in colour and texture a piece of an old brown leather strap." Reportedly Charles Dickens also owned a piece. Burke's skeleton, short and broad, was mounted and became the pride of the university's anatomy museum.

The drama of Burke and Hare had another actor, although for most of it he didn't appear in center stage. The name of Dr. Robert Knox was often mentioned in the testimony at Burke's trial, but he was never called as a witness. Repeatedly assailed in the press, to the people he seemed as guilty as the men who had committed the murders. Rhymes were made about his part in the affair:

> Up the close [passageway] and down the stair,
> But and ben [*out and in*] wi' Burke and Hare,
> Burke's the butcher, Hare's the thief,
> Knox the boy that buys the beef.

Edinburghers wanted him to pay as Burke had paid:

> Hang Burke, banish Hare,
> Burn Knox in Surgeons Square.

Before long the public had whipped itself into a fury over Knox's part in the affair. On February 12, 1829, a large mob marched to his house, carrying an effigy of the doctor. Hanging it from a tree, they set it on fire. As it blazed, the mob flung stones at the house and surged into the garden. The police pushed them back. Meanwhile Knox, armed with a Highland dirk, pistols, and a sword, slipped out the back.

Angry crowds laid siege to Knox's lecture theater. Whenever he went anywhere he surrounded himself with a bodyguard of students.

Finally a committee, headed by the Marquess of Queensbury, was organized to look into Knox's relationship with Burke and Hare. Knox was exonerated of all charges of wrongdoing. The group did, however, find that he had behaved in "a very incautious manner" in his dealings with the killers. His students celebrated his victory by presenting him with a gold vase, and his classes were more packed than ever.

Knox had a sharp, sarcastic tongue and took delight in belittling his contemporaries in medicine. For this reason, and because his reputation had been hurt by his association with Burke and Hare, by 1835 attendance at his lectures had fallen off markedly. His applications for various professorships at the university were turned down. Moving to Glasgow, he tried to make a comeback as a lecturer but failed. In the end he found himself an exile in London, where he built an obstetrical practice and wrote textbooks on anatomy. He was highly esteemed as a writer on anatomy and ethnology. He died of a stroke in 1862.

The anger unleashed by the Burke and Hare murders helped to arouse Parliament to the need for an act to assure a regular, legal supply of bodies for the education of Britain's future doctors. But parliaments are notoriously sluggish and opposition was strong. Before such an act was finally written into the lawbooks many more corpses were to be hauled from their graves—and innocents slaughtered.

A brutal killing in London to get a body for the anatomists provoked as much fury there as the sixteen murders by Burke and Hare had in Edinburgh—directly spurring Britain's law-makers to end the problem forever.

On November 5, 1831, James May and John Bishop, two known sack-'em-up men, came to the dissecting hall of King's College in London and said they had a body for sale.

"What kind of body is it?" asked Hill, the porter on duty.

"A boy of fourteen," replied May, who was quite drunk.

The two asked twelve guineas for the subject. After some dickering they settled for nine.

Later that afternoon they returned with a third man, Thomas Williams (whose real name was John Head), and a porter carrying a hamper containing the body.

Hill inspected the boy's corpse. His face and lips were swollen; his tongue protruded; his teeth had been gouged out. His eyes were bloodshot and starting out of his head. On his forehead was a gash. His fists were clenched. The position of the body was so grotesque, it could never have fit inside a coffin.

The porter at once suspected the boy hadn't died a natural death. He mentioned his suspicion to Partridge, the demon-strator of anatomy. Partridge took one look and agreed. To stall the resurrection men, he told them all he had on him was a £50 note; they would have to wait while he sent out for change. They seemed uneasy and offered to take a little on account and return another day for the rest.

Partridge meanwhile had sent for the police. They showed up promptly and arrested the men.

The autopsy at first showed no injury that could have caused the boy's death. One of those present was the college's lecturer on anatomy, Mayo, who happened to have a speech impediment.

"By Jove!" he exclaimed. "The boy died a nathral death."

When the surgeons examined the spine, however, they found the upper cervical vertebrae had been fractured.

"By Jove!" said Mayo. "This boy was murthered!"

At the inquest the jury brought in a verdict of willful murder. Bishop, Williams, and May were indicted.

At the trial the Crown introduced evidence to show the dead boy was an Italian named Carlo Ferrari. He had been brought to England two years earlier by a beggar master (the man had a house full of beggar boys and made his living off them). Carlo earned his keep by exhibiting white mice, which he carried about the streets of London in a cage.

Bishop and Williams (who were brothers-in-law) had met the boy at a tavern. They lured him to a house they shared in Nova Scotia Gardens by promising to help him find regular employment.

When they reached the house Mrs. Bishop, her children, and Mrs. Williams were still awake. The boy was told to stay in the privy, while Williams hurried the two families off to bed. Bringing the boy into the house, the men gave him some cheese and a piece of bread. To wash it down they provided their own version of a Mickey Finn—a cup of rum and laudanum. The boy downed it in two gulps and then accepted some beer from them. In ten minutes he was sound asleep.

With their lamb ready for the slaughter, the two men suddenly felt the need of some heartening and they adjourned to a tavern. Twenty minutes later they returned, floating on a cloud of gin and beer. The boy hadn't stirred.

Bishop and Williams carried the boy out into the garden and tied his feet with a rope. Then they lowered him head first into the well. They fastened the free end of the rope to a paling.

In a confession he made after the trial, Bishop explained at length how the victim had died.

> The boy struggled a little with his arms and legs in the water, and the water bubbled for a minute. We waited till these symptoms were past, and then went indoors, and afterwards I think we went out, and walked down Shoreditch to occupy the time, and in about three-quarters of an hour we returned and took him out of the well, by pulling him by the cord attached to his feet; we undressed him in the paved yard, rolled his clothes up, and buried them where they were found by the witness who produced them.
>
> We carried the boy into the washhouse, laid him on the floor, and covered him over with a bag. We left him there, and went and had some coffee in Old Street Road, and then—a little before two o'clock on the morning of Friday —went back to my house. We immediately doubled the body up, and put it into a box, which we corded, so that nobody might open it to see what was inside.

At the trial, however, all three defendants protested they were innocent. Bishop admitted freely he was a professional grave robber. He had resurrected a thousand bodies in the past twelve years, he said; the boy was just the most recent of them. When the Crown charged he had struck the boy on the neck to subdue him, he insisted the spinal injury was produced when he forced the body into the hamper.

In the house in Nova Scotia Gardens, however, the police had found damning evidence: the boy's cap, his bloody breeches, and the awl with which his teeth had been removed. Even his white mice were still in the house; Bishop's children were petting them. A dentist named Mills testified he had bought the boy's teeth from May for twelve shillings.

It took the jury just thirty minutes to decide all three men were guilty.

"I'm a murdered man!" cried May.

"We're all murdered men," growled Williams.

All three were sentenced to be hanged and anatomized. Shortly before the execution Bishop and Williams made full confessions. The dead boy, they insisted, wasn't Ferrari, but a boy from Lincolnshire. They also told how they had murdered a woman and a child and sold their bodies to anatomists. May, they declared, had nothing to do with any of the killings; he had merely helped them dispose of the boy's body.

Accepting their confession, the Lord Chief Justice commuted May's sentence to transportation to a penal colony. When May heard the news he collapsed. He never quite recovered from the shock.

Tens of thousands of people assembled to watch the two killers die on the gibbet near London's famous courthouse, the Old Bailey, on December 5, 1831. So enormous and so hectic was the crowd that an entire hospital ward was needed to treat those injured in the excitement. Afterward Bishop's and Williams's cadavers were turned over to the medical schools for dissection; Bishop's went to Kings College, in grim appreciation of the help Partridge, the demonstrator of anatomy, had rendered in the murderers' capture.

And May? He didn't survive his mates for long. He died on shipboard after being abused by fellow convicts.

In 1828 Parliament held hearings on a bill to provide bodies for the surgeons, and the House of Commons passed it. When it came to the House of Lords in 1829, however, the archbishop of Canterbury objected strenuously and the bill was killed. The pathetic murder of the Italian boy and the two others, coming in the wake of the Burke and Hare horror in Edinburgh, swept away any further objections. A new bill was quickly introduced and on August 1, 1832, it became law.

From that time on any body that relatives or friends didn't claim—and there were thousands of such bodies in hospitals, almshouses, morgues, and elsewhere—could be turned over to the medical schools. After dissection the remains had to be given reverent burial. The act also provided that the bodies of executed murderers would no longer be anatomized—erasing the shame associated with dissection in the minds of the poor.

An incredible era had come to an end. The ghastly problem that had dogged the training of physicians was solved once and for all. With it went the fear and anguish that had tormented the hearts of almost every family that lost a loved one. By a stroke of the pen the body snatchers had been put out of business in Britain.

But not in America.

In America body snatchers continued to haunt the burial grounds and rip the dead from their graves right into the twentieth century.

7   The Body Snatchers Stalk America

BY 9 A.M. the three hundred grumbling, growling men had reached Castleton. Up ahead they saw the buildings of the Vermont Academy of Medicine shining in the morning sun. At a command the men broke ranks....They surrounded the academy buildings like a tightening noose. So tight no one inside it could get out.

They had loved and respected Mrs. Penfield Church.

If her body was there they would find it.

And the ghouls who had stolen it.

Shrouds of vapor floated up from bitter mouths as Dike, the Hubbardton sheriff, chose his committee.

The old dean was waiting inside. Dike unfolded the search warrant. "We want to see the dissection room. And fast, sir."

The dean fumbled in his desk drawers. "I'm terribly sorry. Afraid I've mislaid the key."

A plump student, wrapped in a great cloak, hesitated near him, pale, big eyed. "Sir?"

The dean looked up, nodded. The youth went out.

"Ah, here's the key after all."

Inside the room the sharp smell of brine, alcohol, brimstone chemicals; the dissection slab still wet from washing.

She wouldn't be far away.

Cupboard and closet doors banged open. Drawers creaked. Feet clomped around inside the enormous fireplace. Eyes squinted up the chimney.

Nothing.

One man, more inquisitive than the rest: "See that loose board in the wainscoting?"

Nervous, callused fingers tore it off....Then the board next to it....Then, faster, another....The sick, sweet odor of death seeped from the darkness inside.

Faces twisting, they lifted the body out. Nude. A woman. Mrs. Church? No one could be sure. Not even her moaning husband.

Raw-edged with tendrils of tendon, artery, vein, trachea, a gaping red pipe the neck....No head.

Sheriff Dike retched. "I demand to see the head."

"Can the students have disposed of it?" The dean pursed his lips. "They'll have to find it. But how hard will they search, sheriff...knowing you'll take some of them off to jail?"

The sheriff, finally understanding: "All right. No arrests. I promise."

The plump student, somehow not so plump as before, had joined the group. The dean nodded to him. They watched the youth tramp out, disappear into a barn, reappear. Under his arm a bundle, bulky, cloth wrapped. He bore it in to them. "Sheriff..." He held it up.

Gingerly Dike peeled off the wrapping. A groan went up from the men of Hubbardton.

Tender hands carried her out to the cart...hands that soon knotted into fists that shook and shook at the shining school buildings until they shrank in the distance and the brown hills swallowed them up.

In southern Vermont they call it the Hubbardton Raid. It happened on November 29, 1830.

The raid ended better than most. The school at Castleton survived. Mrs. Penfield Church was restored to her grave.

If the lady wasn't all in one piece she was all in one place. Her friends and relatives could take comfort in the thought that they knew at least where she lay.

That was more comfort than many others could take. In thousands and thousands of graves all over America the dead were—and often no one ever suspected it—literally the departed.

Listen to Dr. Claude Heaton, writing in the *New York State Journal of Medicine*: "At this time [the 1840s] in the City of New York and the surrounding country not less than six or seven hundred new-made graves were annually robbed of their tenants."

In Ohio alone, declared Dr. Frederick C. Waite, close to five thousand graves were robbed in the 1800s. In New England Waite estimated several thousand graves were robbed during the same period.

Body snatching was bigger and better by the late 1870s. According to an expert the medical schools of the United States were dissecting five thousand cadavers a year at that time—most of them stolen. As late as 1883 Harvard University's medical faculty was dissecting bodies unlawfully procured.

Ten years later, in 1893, Baltimore's now celebrated Johns Hopkins Medical School threw open its doors. In that year and for years afterward the city's seven busy medical schools used large numbers of stolen bodies. In the West at the time, body snatching was common.

In the 1920s, reports Dr. D. C. Humphrey, stolen cadavers—black ones—were being shipped from state to state, just as they had been for a hundred years.

In 1922 the New York State Board of Medical Examiners charged that cadavers were being illegally snatched from the New York City mortuary and turned over to students of "naturopathy."

"The practice of body snatching," wrote Dr. Heaton in 1943, "is probably a thing of the past."

"Probably."

America was—and is—Great Britain's daughter. Along with the mother country's language the thirteen colonies inherited her laws and beliefs, lock, stock, and barrel. Neither the colonies nor the states that succeeded them were willing to grant the medical schools and doctors the bodies they needed to teach anatomy and do medical research. Only a handful of the early states had laws saying executed murderers could be anatomized, and the demand always exceeded the supply. In Massachusetts, for example, during the first thirty years of the nineteenth century the schools had to find more than a thousand bodies for themselves—somewhere.

It was the same all over the country.

As in Britain the surgeons tried to procure bodies that, presumably, no one would miss. Whenever possible the cadavers of the poor, the wretched, the unfortunate—and those with black or "red" skins—were taken.

The safest place to get bodies was potter's field. Resurrection men also sought out the cemeteries of prisons, hospitals, and almshouses; sometimes they even had arrangements by which they got the bodies before burial. When body snatchers were arrested, judges usually gave them a sympathetic hearing; they realized, just as the English authorities did, the law was lagging behind the times. Unless a public furor had been unleashed, fines were light and prison sentences rare.

Body snatching increased as the medical schools did. So did the public protest, and lawmakers kept boosting the penalties. Eventually they went as high as ten thousand dollars and ten years in jail. But judges seldom imposed the maximum punishment.

To keep themselves in cadavers, many schools depended on their graduates. These were practicing doctors, and they formed a network through the surrounding country. When someone died in a town where the graduate lived, he would quickly get in touch with his old school. Next a stranger would show up in the cemetery; he might be carrying a gun and look like a hunter. He would unobtrusively note the grave's location and how it could be reached most directly. As soon as possible after the funeral, the body snatchers appeared at night and removed the subject. In many places the grave robbers were professionals; college youths were considered too unreliable for such a risky undertaking unless they were supervised by a demonstrator of anatomy or a college porter.

The moment a corpse was brought into a school, the practice was to burn the clothing if it hadn't been returned to the grave. Then the students lifted the skin off the head and cut away scars and other distinctive markings. That made it hard for the police to identify the body if they came looking for it. Subjects were dissected rapidly. Students sometimes worked throughout the night.

If you were a demonstrator of anatomy, you probably couldn't count on finding your material close to home. The Vermont Academy of Medicine often got its subjects from Albany or Troy, New York; the cadavers were pickled in brine and shipped in barrels marked "pork" or "beef," in care of a local grocer. Harvard had agents who prowled the burial grounds of New York City. Ohio medical schools frequently got their bodies from Indiana and Kentucky. Ohio graves were robbed to supply subjects for the University of Michigan.

The coming of the railroad made it much easier to get bodies from a considerable distance. After the Civil War, agents of northern colleges could rob black cemeteries in the South and ship the cadavers to the North. In the 1880s and 1890s one New England college received several consignments a year of black bodies in barrels labeled "turpentine" and consigned to a local hardware store.

Like the doctors who outwitted the Hubbardton men, medical professors developed ingenious ways to deal with search parties. In New England, for example, many college buildings had domes or cupolas. Inside one of these the faculty might rig up a block and tackle. At the first sign of trouble, up went the corpse through a trapdoor in the ceiling. The students then shut the trapdoor and removed the ladder used to reach it. A rapid scrubdown—and the searchers would find absolutely nothing.

Some schools hid their subjects ("cadaveric material," they called them) in boxes concealed under mountainous heaps of firewood in the cellar. Others had wide fireplaces and chimneys. When the alarm was given, the students quickly hoisted the cadaver up the chimney by means of chains (ropes would have burned) attached to pulleys. Then they got a cheerful blaze going in the fireplace. Later they might have to dissect a somewhat smoky subject, but that was better than no subject at all.

Often the local sheriff was in cahoots with the medical school. Whenever practicable, bodies were obtained from burial grounds in other townships. If the constable of a neighboring town wanted to search a school for a missing body, his warrant might not open its doors to him; he might have to call on the local sheriff for assistance. The sheriff always cooperated, but not before he had warned the college it was about to be searched.

No matter what precautions they took, many physicians and certainly every early professor of anatomy in America lived in fear he would be accused of body snatching. He might even be severely manhandled or killed by angry mobs.

Take Philadelphia-born William Shippen, for example. One of the most brilliant physicians of his day, Shippen opened America's first private anatomical school in the 1760s. For his students he provided the cadavers of executed criminals, suicides, and paupers (mostly the last). Mobs attacked his school repeatedly, stoning the dissection room. They also went after Shippen himself. On one occasion he jumped out of his carriage just in time to escape a musket ball that came smashing into the seat. Shippen the body snatcher headed the medical corps of the Continental Army during the American Revolution. He also helped found the University of Pennsylvania's great medical school.

Richard Bayley, another medical pioneer, was a British army surgeon during the Revolution. At the end of the war he settled in New York City, becoming professor of anatomy and surgery at Columbia College, and city health officer. Unwittingly Bayley, through his anatomical activities, endangered not only his own life but that of every other doctor in town—triggering one of the major mass upheavals in the history of New York City.

Body snatching was no novelty in New York City. Bayley's students were directly involved in it, and in 1788 they seem to have been more active and reckless than ever.

Mostly they found their subjects in the black graveyard. In February the city's free blacks and slaves, exasperated by the medical students' constant forays, begged the common council to protect their cemetery. "It hath lately been the constant Practice of a Number of Young Gentlemen in this City who called themselves Students of Physick," they said,

> to repair to the Burying Ground assigned for the Use of your Petitioners, and under cover of the Night, and in the most wanton Sallies of Excess, to dig up the Bodies of the deceased friends & relatives of your Petitioners, carry them away and without respect to Age or Sex, mangle their flesh out of a wanton Curiosity and then expose it to Beasts & Birds...Your Petitioners most humbly pray Your Honours to take their case into Consideration.

Their Honours did—and decided to do nothing. Evidently they agreed with the New Yorker (probably a medical student) who sent a letter to the newspaper saying he believed "the only subjects procured for dissection are the productions of Africa or their descendants," as well as criminals who had been executed, "and if those characters are the only subjects of dissection, surely no person can object." (One out of ten of the city's twenty-nine thousand inhabitants was black then; two thousand were slaves, one thousand freemen.)

The letter writer was wrong. Besides the black cemetery the students were robbing potter's field—and, occasionally, "respectable" cemeteries too. The city was shocked to learn bodies had been stolen from new graves in the burial grounds of two illustrious houses of worship, Trinity Church and Brick Presbyterian Church. People of every class—but especially the most vulnerable, the poor—grew increasingly nervous about the security of their loved ones' graves.

In that tense atmosphere only two things were needed to produce a deadly outburst of violence: an ugly incident and an angry mob.

The incident began quietly at New York Hospital, off lower Broadway. There Dr. Bayley was giving lectures on surgery, and his future son-in-law, Dr. Wright Post, was teaching anatomy. Bayley had also set up a museum of priceless anatomy specimens in the hospital.

On Sunday, April 13, 1788, some boys were playing in back of the hospital. According to one report, John Hicks, Jr., a very young medical student, waved a dissected arm at them. One of the boys, his curiosity aroused, climbed a ladder leaning against the wall and asked whose arm it was.

"Your mother's," Hicks replied.

Unfortunately the boy's mother had died just a few days earlier. He ran to tell his father, a mason working on Broadway. Hastening to the churchyard, the father opened up his wife's grave. The coffin was empty except for the graveclothes. Distraught, the father returned to Broadway and told his mates what had happened. The men snatched up tools that might serve as weapons and headed with him toward New York Hospital. As they hurried along they told everyone they met about the atrocity. The crowd kept growing.

What happened when the mob—now numbering in the hundreds—reached the hospital we learn from a letter written by Colonel William Heth, a former officer in the Continental Army.

> The Hospital apartments were ransacked. In the Anatomy room, were found three fresh bodies—one, boiling in a kettle, and two others cutting up—with certain parts of the two sex's hanging up in a most brutal position. These circumstances, together with the wanton & apparent in-

human complexion of the room, exasperated the Mob beyond all bounds—to the total destruction of every anatomy in the hospital, one of which, was of so much value & utility, that it is justly esteemed a great public loss having been prepared in a way, which costs much time & attention, and requires great Skill to accomplish.

The leaders of the mob carried cut-off heads, arms, and legs to the windows and doors. Waving them to the multitude in the street they whipped up their fury. Inside the building the leaders had seized Bayley and Post and three students, who got a good mauling. The rest, including Hicks, had slipped through their fingers. The bones and half-dissected bodies were carried out into the street and burned in a huge bonfire. Later some fresh cadavers were found in another room in the hospital, infuriating the crowd still more.

Word of the disturbance reached the city's mayor, James Duane. While the throng—which had grown to two thousand—was debating how to punish the physicians and students, Duane arrived with the sheriff and a number of prominent citizens. They tried to pacify the horde, which in its rage manhandled some of them.

"But the Mayor," wrote Heth, "obtained them [the prisoners], upon a promise of sending to gaol—a measure, to which in their rage, they submitted—not reflecting, that *sending them to gaol,* would secure them from their violence & resentment."

Duane's fast thinking and talking saved the captives from lynching. Catcalling and cursing, the angry mob escorted them and the sheriff to the jail.

As for young Hicks, the cause of all the trouble, he had taken refuge in Dr. Cochrane's house, near Trinity Church. Learning his whereabouts, the rioters set out after him. On the way they saw David Hosack, who some of them knew was a medical student. They stoned him but he escaped with his life. Hicks, meanwhile, had learned the mob was after him. Soon they were raging through the Cochrane house. They didn't find their quarry. He was on the roof of a neighboring building, crouching behind the chimney.

During the evening the bodies that had been discovered in the hospital were buried. In streets and taverns small groups of men heatedly discussed the day's events. They weren't satisfied; they made plans to root out the tribe of dissecting doctors the following day.

The next day, Monday, April 14, Dr. Bayley, fearing what might lie in store for him and smarting from the loss of his precious anatomical collection, signed an affidavit in the city jail. Never, he swore, had he been involved, either directly or indirectly, in the removal of bodies from any churchyard. (The black burial ground and potter's field were, of course, not churchyards.) Neither, to his "knowledge or belief," had any of his students.

That afternoon a crowd began to gather near Columbia College, where the doctors taught. When the throng reached a good size it headed for the school.

Waiting outside the college to receive the mob was one of Columbia's most respected graduates and trustees. He had been George Washington's aide-de-camp and a heroic officer in the Revolution. He was one of the founding fathers of the new Republic. Now he hoped his name and his eloquence would persuade the rioters to leave the school in peace. His pleading only served to convince them Columbia had something to hide. They knocked Alexander Hamilton rudely aside and swept through the doorway.

Although they looked everywhere they couldn't find a single body—not even an anatomical specimen. (Everything had been removed after the attack on the hospital.) That didn't pacify them; they decided to make a thorough search of the homes of the physicians on the college staff.

At about this time Governor George Clinton of New York State, Mayor Duane, and a group of leading citizens breathlessly appeared on the scene. They walked along the street with the restless crowd, urging it not to do anything rash and promising over and over again to stop the grave robberies. Their efforts weren't wasted. The muttering mob kept its temper as it searched the houses of Bayley and others. . . . It found nothing.

Many left now, to go home or to taverns. But others kept taking their place. Riffraff and mischief makers—the city had its share of them, and they would flock to any commotion. The ringleaders began to point out what a mistake they had made to give up the doctors and students they had captured at the hospital on Sunday. The mood of the rioters became nastier and nastier. It was drizzling heavily as they turned toward the jail.

Near the jailhouse stood the city gallows, the stocks, and the whipping post. Like a great flood the crowd engulfed them. After it had flowed past, gallows, stocks, and post were gone. The bigger pieces would make good battering rams; the smaller ones, cudgels and clubs for the business at hand.

Not blind to the trouble that was building, the mayor called up the militia. They were slow in arriving. Most, in fact, never would arrive; they were there already, part and parcel of the riot pack. When Duane finally mustered a small party—eighteen in all—he sent them up Broadway to put the fear of Authority into the crowd.

Loud jeers and hoots greeted the militiamen, but the mob opened up to let them pass through. Then it let loose at them with a volley of stones and dirt. Bruised and begrimed, the irregulars withdrew. The mayor's show of force had fizzled.

Inside the jail Bayley, Post, and the three students watched the fury of the mob continue to build. They had never seen so many people in the street before. The warders fixed their bayonets.

The mayor tried again. In just a short while another detachment of militia marched up. This one was even smaller than the first, and it fared worse. Wrenching the militiamen's weapons out of their hands, the rioters smashed them, and the men ran for their lives.

By now the horde had reached enormous dimensions. How many could have been in it? Some observers guessed close to five thousand. Remember, the city's entire population was just twenty-nine thousand.

Hoarse cries of "To the jail!" "To the jail!" rang out.

The mob surged forward. The fence in front of the jail gave way and the rioters were upon the building. They shattered the windows and rammed a gallows post against the door. For the moment the bolts held.

Inside the warders brandished their firearms at the rioters. One man managed to slide in through a broken window. He was skewered on a guard's bayonet.

Darkness fell. The rain kept up. As the throng, cursing and shouting, continued its assault, the men in the rear saw a body of irregulars coming up. Governor Clinton had mustered all the militia in the city.

Only the officers had answered his call. Of the one hundred and fifty men he had been able to gather, no more than fifty carried firearms. Some gentlemen armed with swords and clubs had joined the party, and with them came not only Clinton and Mayor Duane but two of the most important men in the city—John Jay (a year later he would be named first Chief Justice of the United States Supreme Court) and Baron von Steuben, the crusty Revolutionary War general. Leave the doctors to the justice of the courts, they told the rioters; return to your homes.

At first the peacemakers could ignore the stones—there was just a flurry of them. But soon they were a bruising, painful hail, filling the air. Almost everyone in the party was struck.

John Jay reeled and fell; knocked unconscious by a rock, he had to be carried to safety.

Clinton, hit, wanted to order the militia to fire.

"No, no, wait," pleaded von Steuben, still hopeful.

A brick banged him over the eye. He tumbled to the ground, blood pouring from his face.

He had an abrupt change of mind. "Fire, Governor, fire!" he cried.

The officer in charge gave the order. Flashes of fire blazed into the wet gloom, and the street was filled with smoke and the smell of gunpowder. The soldiers had fired over the heads of the rioters. That didn't slow down the heavy fusillade of stones.

The militia fired again, this time directly into the thick of the mob.

Eight of the rioters fell, dead or wounded. The rest, enraged, closed in. The militia split into two bodies. One, about thirty strong, stayed to protect the jail; the other charged into the rioters. The mob opened up, then closed behind the soldiers. Surrounded, they fired to the rear. The men guarding the jail thought the shots were aimed at them; they fired back. It was a nightmare of confusion.

In full retreat now, the soldiers in the midst of the crowd held it off with fixed bayonets. Reaching St. Paul's Chapel they dispersed. At this time a troop of cavalry rode up and charged the rioters. Some fled into the churchyard to escape the flashing sabers.

The fighting seemed to go on and on. Men on both sides were wounded. But hot lead and cold steel have a way of bringing people to their senses. Gradually most of the rioters melted into the night.

Not all, however. Groups of the angriest and most violent

spread through the city. More vengeful than ever, they were determined to raid the homes of the doctors. On the street they encountered a man dressed in black. His clothes made him look like a physician, and they beat him and kicked him till he was a bloody pulp. One gang, coming to the home of Sir John Temple, mistook his first two names for "Surgeon" and smashed up the dwelling.

Mostly they found nobody home. The doctors had left the city with their families, to stay away until the excitement died down. All of New York's medical students had been sent out of town.

There was no third day. On Tuesday, wrote Colonel Heth, "the Militia turn'd out again, made a respectable appearance, & paraded about exceedingly—both *Horse & foot*—but it must be observd, *that the enemy were not to be heard of*. In truth, numbers who were *in the Mob on Monday evening*—turn'd out *yesterday to support government*." A regiment of artillery helped to make any more trouble unlikely.

Across the ocean, in Paris, an American named Thomas Jefferson—he was minister of the United States to France then—learned of the incident and was worried. He was afraid Europeans might think the riot was a political act, a sign the new republic was in the hands of mobs.

Governor Clinton kept his promise to the rioters. Hicks and others were indicted for body snatching. The very next year the legislature passed an act "to prevent the odious practice of digging up and removing, for the purpose of dissection, dead Bodies interred in cemeteries or burial places." At the same time the act recognized the importance of the dissection of "proper subjects" to the advancement of science and allowed the courts—at their discretion—to give the bodies of executed arsonists, burglars, and murderers to the surgeons for dissection.

But laws prohibiting grave robbing couldn't stop it. Not if they didn't provide an adequate supply of subjects for teaching and research. Caught in a vise, doctors and medical students had to go on robbing the graveyards—a practice they hated—for the ultimate benefit of the very people who opposed them.

The violence that exploded in New York City was far from isolated. Other outbursts took place in many parts of the country.

In 1807 accusations of body snatching led an irate mob to burn down the first medical building of the University of Maryland.

The first grave robbing ever reported in Ohio happened in Zanesville in 1811. A mob assaulted the inn where the doctor it believed responsible taught private students. It would have lynched them if it could have found them.

In 1839 a crowd invaded the medical school in Worthington, Ohio. Rummaging through the building, it found two bodies. Surprisingly the crowd showed forbearance. Its leaders ordered the doctors to load all the school's belongings on wagons. Then they escorted the physicians and their wagons to the county line, telling them never to come back. They never did.

Things went worse for a school in Cleveland, Ohio, in 1852. A crowd led by an anguished father waving an axe poured into the rooms of the Western College of Homeopathic Medicine in search of the body of his daughter. Policemen who tried to stop them were overpowered. Failing to find the corpse, the raging mob destroyed the school's equipment. Then it began to batter the building. So devastating was the damage that the college never returned to its quarters. Close by, at the Medical Department of Western Reserve College, students armed themselves with muskets from the local armory; when the rioters learned the situation, they turned elsewhere.

In January 1824 Dr. Jonathan Knight, first professor of anatomy at Yale University Medical School in New Haven, Connecticut, was informed that the body of Miss Bathsheba Smith had been stolen from a West Haven cemetery and that his students were under suspicion. With Constable Erastus Osborn and an attorney he began to hunt through the school for the body.

"We searched from bottom to top," Constable Osborn wrote. "I found just as I suppose usually to be found at such Institutions and concluded further search would be unavailing." Determined to be thorough, however, he gave the cellar a particularly close examination. In one place he noticed some fresh dirt. "I scratched with the end of my walking stick and the more I examined the more suspicion was created."

Under a large stone Osborn found a white bundle. It was Bathsheba, "doubled up in a heap.... The father was almost distracted but greatly rejoiced at the discovery." Dr. Knight, swearing he knew nothing about the body, had it washed and provided a clean cap and shroud. Then Bathsheba was carried through New Haven in a wagon while church bells tolled and "people were wrought up to a great pitch."

Knowing they faced trouble the medical students got firearms and shut themselves up in their school. A huge crowd began to gather, to the ominous beating of a drum. Bathsheba, meantime, was buried in her father's garden. There he could keep an eye on her.

"Attempts have been made (and some of them violent) upon the Medical College almost or quite every Night through last Week," Osborn wrote later. Several of the rioters were arrested. So was a medical assistant, Ephraim Colborn, who more on suspicion than on evidence was considered responsible for the body snatching. After narrowly escaping being tarred and feathered he was sentenced to nine months in jail and a fine.

A few months later Connecticut, which had no law forbidding body snatching, passed one. It also provided for turning over to the doctors the bodies of dead prisoners and executed criminals.

There were very few.

By now you have a pretty good idea how Americans felt toward the resurrection men. But nowhere were the public's anger and frustration more poignantly expressed than on a tombstone in Maple Grove Cemetery, Hoosick Falls, New York. The stone, on the grave of little Ruth Sprague, who died in 1816 at the age of nine, relates:

> She was stolen from the grave
> by Roderick R. Clow & dissected
> at Dr. P. M. Armstrong's office
> in Hoosick, N.Y. from which place
> her mutilated remains were
> obtained & deposited here.
> Her body dissected by fiendish Men
> Her bones anatomised,
> Her soul we trust has risen to God
> Where few Physicians rise.

The physicians' need for anatomical subjects led to many strange and pathetic incidents. The New York *Gazette* reported one that occurred in Rochester, New York, in January

1831. A thirteen-year-old boy, "while at work in a cotton manufactory, caught his leg in the gearing, and was obliged to have it taken off. While the child was lying at the point of death, the unnatural father took the amputated limb, and sold it to a surgeon for 37 1/2 cents, with which he kept himself drunk for several days."

An even stranger incident occurred some years later. Walrus-mustachioed Joseph Nashe McDowell was a brilliant lecturer on anatomy at the Medical Department of Cincinnati College before the Civil War. He was able, it was said, "to make dry bones talk." He was also very superstitious. He refused, for example, to give lectures on Fridays.

McDowell believed in ghosts, and he was afraid of them. He would not, however, allow his fear to keep him from robbing graves when he needed a subject for his lecture or for his research. Once when a girl died near Cincinnati College of an unexplained disease, McDowell became extremely interested in her case. He went to the graveyard, dug out her body, and took it back to his laboratory.

McDowell first became aware he was in danger of losing his subject—and his life—when he saw men galloping wildly around the building and shooting into the air. One member of the party was swinging a stout "hanging" rope around his head. The doctor had been careless; the dead girl's relatives had quickly found out about the theft.

Grabbing the body off the dissection table the doctor hurried up to the attic and hid it. The evidence was now safely out of the way, he thought. If only he were too! Suddenly he felt a draft and his lamp went out. . . .

Before him glowed a strange, supernatural light. His dead mother was standing in front of him. The light was streaming from her. The unearthly figure gestured toward the dissection table.

McDowell climbed on the table, pulled up over himself the sheet that had covered the dead girl, and tried to lie as still as she had.

Almost immediately the door burst open and the room was full of angry men. McDowell heard them come stamping across the room. The sheet was jerked off his body. He kept his eyes shut tight and tried to hold his breath.

"Here's a feller who died with his boots on," a voice said. "I guess he's a fresh one."

He could feel them standing around him. He could feel

their eyes examining him. It was becoming harder and harder to restrain his breathing.

Thirty seconds more... *Why don't they go away?* he screamed inside himself.... He could stand it no longer. Agony began to warp reason. *If I jump up suddenly—a dead man—it could scare them away....* Lungs bursting, muscles tensed, he was ready.

"Be still. Be still...." His mother's voice was so soft, so low, so soothing to her frightened child.

Thirty seconds more...

Unbelievably the men's heavy footfalls moved away and the door slammed.

He couldn't get enough air into his lungs. He sat up. He thanked God.

It was a story McDowell told the rest of his life.

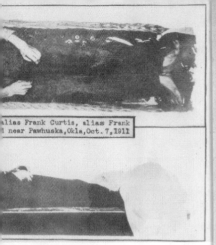

alias Frank Curtis, alias Frank
near Pawhuska, Okla, Oct. 7, 1911

oked after the posse brought him
y dressed and laid out, the body
homa Historical Society and Fred

s dead, Elmer McCurdy is finally
n Boot Hill in Guthrie, Oklahoma.
ciety and Fred A. Olds. Photo by
ociates

A HEAVY snowstorm—perfect weather for body snatchers. Behind a thick white curtain, why should grave robbers even bother to shield their lamp?

On the snowy night of January 10, 1817, someone saw a dim light in the graveyard of Chebacco Parish, Ipswich, in northeastern Massachusetts.

That was enough for the townspeople of Ipswich to suspect that the grave of Sally Andrews, who had died on Christmas Day, had been robbed. But the snow was deep. The townspeople would have to wait for the spring thaw before they could make sure.

When the snow began to melt, near Sally Andrews's grave they picked up a comb—a comb that had been buried with her. The ground was still too frozen for digging.

In April they dug. They found not only the Andrews grave empty, but the graves of seven others as well. Anguished relatives offered a reward of five hundred dollars for information leading to the arrest of those responsible for the biggest grave robbery in the history of New England.

On July 23, after looking at the empty coffins for three months, Ipswichers gave up hope that the missing bodies would ever be returned and sadly reburied the boxes in a common grave. They made a big event of it. The Reverend Robert Cromwell delivered one of his longest sermons, in which he not only condemned the robbers, but also acknowledged that dissection was not un-Christian.

The reward must have appealed to somebody. A finger was pointed at a local physician, Dr. Thomas Sewall, who trained medical students in surgery. Ransacking his laboratory the constable found parts of three corpses. They were identified as having come from the Chebacco graveyard, and in November Sewall was indicted on a charge of illegal possession of dead bodies.

A year passed before Sewall came to trial. By then his practice had been ruined. Defending him was golden-voiced Daniel Webster, one of the ablest lawyers in the country and a former member of Congress.

Even Webster's skilled pleading couldn't get Sewall off. The doctor was found guilty on two counts and fined eight hundred dollars and costs. In Ipswich he was a pariah.

Sometimes a disaster can be turned around so it becomes not an end but a beginning. Webster told Sewall to get out of Ipswich fast and come to Washington, D.C., where doctors were in demand. Sewall took the advice. With Webster's backing he was able to build one of the most successful and respected practices in the bustling capital.

Sewall never gave up his love of anatomy and teaching. In 1825 he founded the National Medical College, Washington's first medical school. He was the college's dean for nineteen years and a distinguished professor of medicine as well. What's more, the convicted possessor of stolen bodies served as personal physician to three Presidents of the United States!

The Ipswich Horror would never have happened if Massachusetts law had provided bodies for the training of future physicians. Not until 1831 were doctors able to persuade the state's lawmakers to pass a proper anatomy act—one that directed the overseers of the poor to turn over the bodies of paupers for medical study unless relatives or friends objected.

Massachusetts thus became the first state to enact such a statute—and it did so a year before Parliament passed the British anatomy act. New York followed Massachusetts in 1854 with its own "bone bill."

No other state passed a permanent anatomy act until after the Civil War. Yet by 1860 the country already had close to ninety medical schools—and dissection was part of the curriculum in every one of them.

Elmer McCurdy Davidson, kil

Top: McCurdy as he
in. Bottom: Fashiona
awaits a claimant. *Ok
A. Olds*

ELMER M'CUR

In 1977, sixty-six ye
lowered into a grave
*Oklahoma Historical
Sandra Kraus and A*

Arsenic
virtually
homa Hi

8 The Ipswich Horror, and Other Tales Bizarre but True

A HEAVY snowstorm—perfect weather for body snatchers. Behind a thick white curtain, why should grave robbers even bother to shield their lamp?

On the snowy night of January 10, 1817, someone saw a dim light in the graveyard of Chebacco Parish, Ipswich, in northeastern Massachusetts.

That was enough for the townspeople of Ipswich to suspect that the grave of Sally Andrews, who had died on Christmas Day, had been robbed. But the snow was deep. The townspeople would have to wait for the spring thaw before they could make sure.

When the snow began to melt, near Sally Andrews's grave they picked up a comb—a comb that had been buried with her. The ground was still too frozen for digging.

In April they dug. They found not only the Andrews grave empty, but the graves of seven others as well. Anguished relatives offered a reward of five hundred dollars for information leading to the arrest of those responsible for the biggest grave robbery in the history of New England.

On July 23, after looking at the empty coffins for three months, Ipswichers gave up hope that the missing bodies would ever be returned and sadly reburied the boxes in a common grave. They made a big event of it. The Reverend Robert Cromwell delivered one of his longest sermons, in which he not only condemned the robbers, but also acknowledged that dissection was not un-Christian.

The reward must have appealed to somebody. A finger was pointed at a local physician, Dr. Thomas Sewall, who trained medical students in surgery. Ransacking his laboratory the constable found parts of three corpses. They were identified as having come from the Chebacco graveyard, and in November Sewall was indicted on a charge of illegal possession of dead bodies.

A year passed before Sewall came to trial. By then his practice had been ruined. Defending him was golden-voiced Daniel Webster, one of the ablest lawyers in the country and a former member of Congress.

Even Webster's skilled pleading couldn't get Sewall off. The doctor was found guilty on two counts and fined eight hundred dollars and costs. In Ipswich he was a pariah.

Sometimes a disaster can be turned around so it becomes not an end but a beginning. Webster told Sewall to get out of Ipswich fast and come to Washington, D.C., where doctors were in demand. Sewall took the advice. With Webster's backing he was able to build one of the most successful and respected practices in the bustling capital.

Sewall never gave up his love of anatomy and teaching. In 1825 he founded the National Medical College, Washington's first medical school. He was the college's dean for nineteen years and a distinguished professor of medicine as well. What's more, the convicted possessor of stolen bodies served as personal physician to three Presidents of the United States!

The Ipswich Horror would never have happened if Massachusetts law had provided bodies for the training of future physicians. Not until 1831 were doctors able to persuade the state's lawmakers to pass a proper anatomy act—one that directed the overseers of the poor to turn over the bodies of paupers for medical study unless relatives or friends objected.

Massachusetts thus became the first state to enact such a statute—and it did so a year before Parliament passed the British anatomy act. New York followed Massachusetts in 1854 with its own "bone bill."

No other state passed a permanent anatomy act until after the Civil War. Yet by 1860 the country already had close to ninety medical schools—and dissection was part of the curriculum in every one of them.

Arsenic will do it. Old postcard shows McCurdy, turned virtually to stone, in the undertaker's back room. *Oklahoma Historical Society and Fred A. Olds*

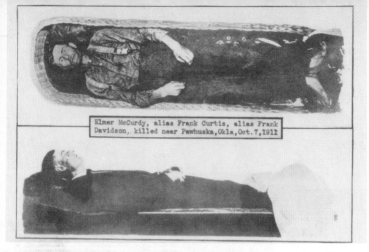

Elmer McCurdy, alias Frank Curtis, alias Frank
Davidson, killed near Pawhuska,Okla,Oct.7,1911

Top: McCurdy as he looked after the posse brought him
in. Bottom: Fashionably dressed and laid out, the body
awaits a claimant. *Oklahoma Historical Society and Fred
A. Olds*

ELMER McCURDY

In 1977, sixty-six years dead, Elmer McCurdy is finally
lowered into a grave on Boot Hill in Guthrie, Oklahoma.
*Oklahoma Historical Society and Fred A. Olds. Photo by
Sandra Kraus and Associates*

Body snatchers examining a corpse. England once swarmed with bands of tomb robbers. Another gang lurks in the rear, ready to pounce.

The human body is the best textbook of anatomy. A scene in a medical school, by Thomas Rowlandson. The highest figure is said to be the famous surgeon William Hunter. *Royal College of Surgeons of England*

The Irish Giant and the Sicilian Fairy, two celebrated skeletons at the Royal College of Surgeons in London. The bodies of both were snatched.

John Hunter, eminent British surgeon, and brother of William, in a portrait by Sir Joshua Reynolds. At upper right the leg bones of his prize specimen, the Irish Giant. *Royal College of Surgeons of England*

The copper vat used by Hunter to boil the flesh off the giant's bones. *Royal College of Surgeons of England*

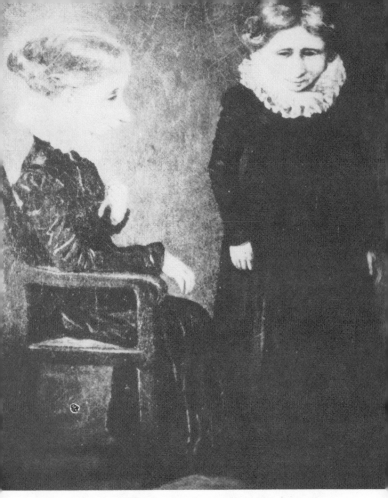

Caroline (or Carolina) Crachami, the Sicilian Fairy, in a double portrait painted from memory. She was only ten when she died. *Royal College of Surgeons of England*

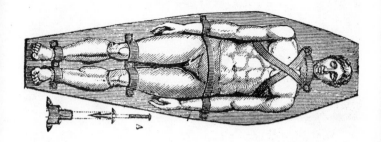

Antighoul device: The coffin was provided with a false bottom to which the body of the deceased was securely attached.

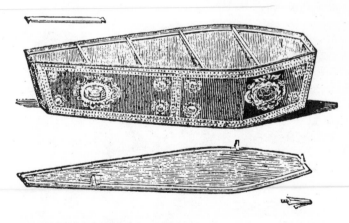

As advertised: The iron coffin developed by undertaker Edward Lillie Bridgman to foil body snatchers. The lid was fastened with the iron clamps shown. Cemetery officials and body snatchers both hated the coffin.

To protect a tomb, a cagelike device called a mortsafe often proved effective. Massive tabletop tombstones were also popular.

Helen M.Dougal.
Pannel.

W.M.Burke.
Pannel.

William Hare.
King's Evidence.

William Burke frowns at his trial in 1828; he was charged with killing to supply the surgeons. His fellow pannel (or defendant) was his common-law wife, Helen McDougal. Their smiling accomplice, William Hare, testified against them.

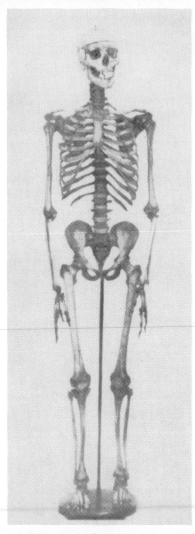
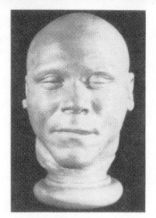

Murderers in Britain and America were often sentenced to dissection as well as hanging. Burke's death mask and skeleton are preserved at the University of Edinburgh.

Two notorious body snatchers and murderers, Bishop and Head, sketched shortly after they were hanged in 1831.

Anatomy lecture at an American medical school. By the 1870s American medical students were dissecting five thousand bodies a year—most of them stolen.

In Indianapolis the corpse of a young woman is torn from its tomb in a much-publicized incident. Body snatching in the United States continued into the twentieth century.

Dr. Martin Van Butchell on his painted pony. The eccentric dentist kept his mummified wife in his home, showed her to visitors.

The Hottentot Venus was a source of not-so-innocent merriment to the British. Here Richard Brinsley Sheridan, the playwright, measures her backside against Lord Grenville's, in a caricature by Heath.

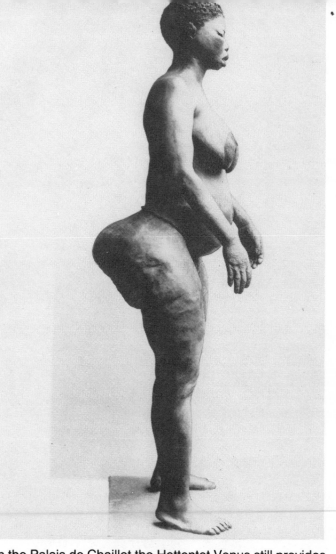

In the Palais de Chaillot the Hottentot Venus still provides amusement for Parisians. Plaster cast made at the time of her pathetic death in 1815. *Collection Musée de l'Homme*

Alive or dead? "The Ugliest Woman in the World," Julia Pastrana, could be either in this photograph. She was embalmed in 1860 in the same pose.

Old poster advertising the exhibition of the mummies of Julia Pastrana and her son. They have been widely exhibited in Europe and the United States.

Sarcophagus containing the remains of a President—object of the astonishing body-snatching attempt of November 7, 1876.

The catacomb as the body snatchers left it. Numbered panels are the crypts of the President's family.

To their shame some of the biggest states didn't enact anatomy laws until the closing decades of the century or later. Even in states that did, the laws weren't enforced. The schools frequently had to scrounge for bodies.

Washington, D.C., didn't have an anatomy act until the 1890s. Not long after Thomas Sewall founded the National Medical College a number of other medical schools sprang up in the capital. To supply their dissection labs resurrectionists carried on an active traffic in stolen bodies. Five hundred students were cutting into illegally obtained corpses "almost under the shadow of the Capitol," in the words of Dr. Thomas Dwight.

One of the most brazen—and sloppy—of the Washington-area body snatchers was a man named Janssen. His face was well known to the police, who had caught him red-handed many times. Janssen once stole the body of an executed criminal and sold it to a medical school. Then he stole the body back. He was riding with it in a hack, intending to resell it, when the police stopped him. For this offense he served a term in prison. Coming out he decided his bad name could do him some good. He appeared at a local theater and lectured on the fine art of grave robbing. His performance included a how-to demonstration with a dummy.

Janssen thus became more of a hindrance than a help to the medical schools; just the news that he had been seen on their campuses was enough to bring the police clanging down on them in search of the latest stolen body. Finally the schools put up a purse to induce him to leave the capital.

With subjects for dissection often scarce, medical students and doctors seldom passed up an opportunity to remedy the situation. Wars and times of public disorder were a boon to them.

In 1840, after a battle with the Indians outside San Antonio, Dr. Weideman, a local physician who had taken part in the fight, came home with the bodies of two Indians. "I've been longing exceedingly to secure such specimens," he said. Weideman boiled the dead Indians in a huge kettle to remove the flesh. That night he dumped the offal into Acequia Ditch, a fast-flowing stream near by.

San Antonians got their water from Acequia. When they heard what the doctor had done, many felt ill; some pregnant women even had miscarriages. The doctor was arrested.

In court Weideman protested he had dumped the remains into Acequia during the night, when no one was drawing water, and they had washed swiftly downstream. He was reprimanded and fined—and told by his fellow San Antonians he was lucky they didn't ride him out of town on a rail.

Dr. George A. Kenny, an Idaho pioneer, wanted a skeleton. Poking around in an Indian cemetery, he came upon a dried-up head. Kenny carried the head home with him and placed it in a kettle of hot water on the stove in his kitchen, to remove the flesh.

While the head was cooking, two Indian women came in to ask for food. One picked up the lid of the kettle, curious to see what was inside. What she saw sent her shrieking out of the kitchen, pulling her friend with her.

For a long time after, the Indians wouldn't go near Kenny. They were convinced he would eat them.

In October 1859 John Brown, the abolitionist, with a band of twenty-one followers, captured the United States arsenal at Harpers Ferry, West Virginia. Brown hoped his act would jolt the country into taking action against slavery. He was mistaken. The government sent Colonel Robert E. Lee and a force of marines against him and he was made prisoner.

Word of the insurrection at Harpers Ferry quickly spread through the countryside. At nearby Winchester Medical College virtually all the students jumped on board a train headed in the direction of Harpers Ferry. Near the Shenandoah River the students came upon the body of a white man. They put it in a case and took it back to school with them.

At Winchester, after stripping the clothing from the dead man, the students found in his pockets papers revealing he was John Brown's son Owen. That didn't stop them from going ahead with their work. The body was dried and added to the school's anatomy collection.

In December the school acquired the bodies of two blacks who had fought for John Brown, were captured during the raid, and hanged at Charles Town. Students subsequently dug up the bodies and brought them to Winchester. The nooses were still around their necks.

In 1862 the Civil War engulfed the Winchester area. Massive battles were fought there. By then, to Northerners, John

Brown was no longer the lawless hothead he had seemed before Fort Sumter; he was a martyr.

When the Union forces moved into Winchester, General Banks learned the college had the dried body of Brown's son. He sent troops to seize it. They burned the college to the ground.

In 1835 Harriet Martineau, an important English writer, was visiting the South. "In Baltimore," she observed, "the bodies of coloured people exclusively are taken for dissection because the whites do not like it, and the coloured people cannot resist." Even if the blacks had complained, as their brothers did in New York City in 1788, no one would have listened. Before the Civil War owners often turned over their dead slaves to anatomists. After the war black bodies were easy to obtain in potter's fields. White cemeteries were rarely disturbed.

"Were you ever shot at?" a newsman asked a resurrectionist in 1978 in Louisville, Kentucky.

"Oh, no," was the answer. "We let the private cemeteries alone."

Dissection was, in a sense, the penalty people paid for being poor or of the wrong color.

At southern medical schools the black janitor was usually in charge of getting subjects for the dissection lab. Often a couple of medical students went along to lend him a hand. The white authorities willingly shut their eyes to the nocturnal prowlers.

Richmond in the 1880s was well acquainted with Old Billy, janitor of the Medical College of Virginia. To avoid attention Billy waited for cloudy or moonless nights to go about his business, traveling with an assistant in a cart provided with sacks and digging implements. Both men were looked upon with awe by the black residents of Richmond. Everyone had heard terrifying tales of how the two stalked black people who made the mistake of being out late and alone. The janitors, so the legend ran, would sneak up behind their prey, throw sacks over their heads, and suffocate them. No one would ever see them again.

In 1884 the new superintendent of Richmond's much-robbed potter's field decided the two resurrectionists had gone far enough. With a policeman he lay in wait for them near a fresh grave.

At 4 A.M. the two janitors, accompanied by three students, made a cautious appearance and began to dig up a fresh grave. Charging out of their hiding place the officials captured all but one of them and led them off to the lockup. The judge handed out a lecture, fines, and jail sentences. While the five languished in jail, their relatives and people at the college kept them supplied with choice foods and comforts. In a short while the governor pardoned them. At its next session the state legislature passed the Virginia Anatomy Act.

It looked now as if old Billy, his assistant, and other resurrection men could put away their carts and sacks for good. But could they—really? Richmond's two medical colleges, the University of Virginia Medical School and the Medical College of Virginia, both had big enrollments. In a typical six-month period they received a meager total of thirty subjects under the act.

Wednesday, May 29, 1878, was a hard day in the life of Benjamin Harrison. An ex-Civil War general and a prominent corporation attorney, Harrison was one of Indiana's most important citizens. In ten years he would be even more important. He would be elected twenty-third President of the United States.

Right now, however, Harrison's heart was heavy. He had come back to North Bend, Ohio, his family home, to bury his father. The dead man, John Scott Harrison, had been a farmer and a member of Congress. Not only was he the father of a future President. He was also the son of a past one, William Henry Harrison, ninth President of the United States—the Tippecanoe of "Tippecanoe and Tyler too."

As the procession followed the casket to the grave, General Harrison suddenly felt the hair bristle on the back of his neck. One of the tombs in the family plot had been noticeably disturbed. Only a week before, his nephew, young Augustus Devin, had been buried there. Body snatchers, the general knew, were active all over the state. Could they have taken young Devin's body?

But the funeral had to go forward. General Harrison at least could comfort himself that everything possible was being done to assure the security of his father's remains. He looked down into the deep opening that was prepared to receive them. At the bottom a thick-walled brick vault had been constructed, with a base of stone. His father's coffin itself was enclosed within a metal casket.

After the casket had been lowered the general watched as three massive flat stones were placed on top of the vault and cemented together. The grave would have to be left open while the cement dried. A watchman had been hired to check the tomb at hourly intervals at night. He was to continue to check for a number of nights. After that no anatomist would want the body.

When the service was over the family turned its attention to young Devin's grave. Their fears were confirmed. The coffin had been broken into, and the body removed.

Not far away, in Cincinnati, was Ohio Medical College. The Harrisons had reason enough to suspect that young Devin's body was stretched out on a slab there. The school had been mixed up in grave robberies before.

The Harrisons had to move fast. The general's younger brother, John, took charge of the search. The next day, with several police officers and a warrant, he was knocking at the door of the college.

Grudgingly the college authorities admitted the search party. The men went through the dissection laboratories and the adjacent rooms. To their disappointment Devin's remains were nowhere to be found. But as the party was preparing to leave, one of the policemen pointed to an open trapdoor in the floor. Overhead was a windlass with a taut rope suspended from it; it disappeared into the darkness below.

"There's got to be something heavy at the end of that rope," the policeman said.

After a hard job of pulling they hefted into the room a large cloth-swathed object. The policeman pulled aside the edge of the cloth.

Harrison caught a glimpse of white hair. "That's an old man," he said. "We're after a young one."

The constable was still curious. He laid the body on the floor and unwrapped it.

Harrison drew back in horror. "My God, that's my father! We buried him only yesterday!"

John Scott Harrison's long flowing beard had been shaved off. His veins showed evidence of injections, a regular preliminary to dissection. Had the searchers come a day later they might not have found a trace of him.

Old Harrison's body was turned over to an undertaker. At

the same time his grave at Congress Green was examined. Digging a few feet down investigators found the lighter of the three stones had been removed from the vault top. The casket lid had been drilled through and part of it broken off, just as Devin's had. The watchman admitted he had not been as diligent as he should have been.

At the medical college the janitor was arrested for receiving and concealing Harrison's body. The faculty quickly rallied to his aid. They put up five thousand dollars to bail him out.

The recovery of Harrison's body created a national sensation. For weeks the newspapers played up new developments for their appalled but appreciative readers. Reporters had a field day when professors at Ohio Medical revealed they had a contract with a resurrectionist for an annual supply of corpses. They had no idea, they assured the press, that respectable middle-class burial grounds were being broken into; they had assumed the subjects came from potter's field.

Meanwhile where was Devin's body? One medical college after another was searched without success.

Then, from a completely unexpected quarter, came a break in the case. At the medical college of Miami, Ohio, the janitor confessed he had allowed one of the most notorious body snatchers in the country, Charles Morton, to use the school's building to prepare and ship bodies to other medical schools. The janitor revealed a large number of the cadavers had been sent to "Quimby and Company" in Ann Arbor, Michigan.

There was, it soon turned out, no "Quimby and Company." The shipments, when they arrived in Ann Arbor, ended up at the medical school of the University of Michigan.

Detectives swooped down on the school. They fished cadaver after cadaver out of vats of brine.

One, without hair, with eyes almost obliterated, was ultimately identified as Augustus Devin.

The Harrisons and Devins consequently sued the colleges involved. Moreover the case convinced responsible Ohioans once and for all that they had to put an end to grave robbing. Old prejudices die hard, however. So bitterly did much of the public oppose dissection, it took the state legislature three years to introduce and pass an anatomy act sanctioning the acquisition of unwanted bodies by medical schools.

But like many of these laws Ohio's anatomy act of 1881 was poorly drafted and enforced. The grave robbing went on.

* * *

On February 15, 1884, outside Avondale, Ohio, a cabin burned to the ground. It had been the home of an old black couple named Taylor, who lived there with an adopted daughter. Poking through the ashes the local marshal was puzzled that he couldn't find any human remains. Taylor, he knew, had a bad case of rheumatism, and the old folks never left home. The marshal thought of the Harrison body-snatching case of a few years earlier and he headed for Cincinnati.

At Ohio Medical College the marshal learned three subjects had been delivered on the same night as the fire. He asked to see them. Looking at the dead faces he recognized the Taylors. Their skulls had been fractured.

The killers weren't hard to track down. They were two black men, who confessed what they had done. One, Allen Ingalls, admitted he was a professional resurrectionist and had been digging up bodies in local cemeteries and selling them to medical schools.

If you had been out walking on the streets of Baltimore in the early 1880s you might have been approached by a pathetic middle-aged white woman asking for alms. Emily Brown's bloodshot eyes, her slurred speech, her unsteady gait suggested that she spent the pennies given her on drink—not to mention opium—and you might have turned away from her. Many did.

It was impossible to recognize in this sodden, bedraggled woman the attractive young Southern belle she once had been. The daughter of a prosperous innkeeper, Emily had been well educated. She had never married, but for many years kept house for a bachelor brother, who operated a mill. When he died his affairs were in chaos. Left with hardly a cent, she was soon reduced to begging.

Emily lodged in a squalid street known as Pig Alley. Her landlady, a Mrs. Bluxom, was a black woman who had eighteen children. The eldest was a disreputable creature named John Charles Ross.

Mrs. Bluxom had another lodger, a black man named Perry, who was partly paralyzed. Perry worked as a porter in the medical school of the University of Maryland. One of his duties there was to provide bodies for the dissection lab.

By 1886 Emily could no longer pay her meager rent. She became completely dependent on her landlady. Poor Mrs.

Bluxom didn't need another mouth to feed, but she fed it anyway.

To Perry it didn't seem fair.

"Miss Emily," he told Ross, "is a burden to herself and to your mother. It can only get worse." He paused. "You can help both of them."

Ross's eyes widened.

"The university dissecting room pays fifteen dollars for a body. And you—couldn't you use the money?"

Ross's head wagged up and down. . . .

To at least one member of the university staff the marks on the new subject suggested death by violence. He called in the police.

Meanwhile Mrs. Bluxom had reported Emily's disappearance. The police put the two reports together.

"Can you identify this?" The constable held up a well-worn dress.

"That's Miss Emily's," said one of the Bluxom girls.

"What was she doing the last time you saw her?"

"She was giving Uncle Perry a cup of coffee."

They came for Perry. "It was Ross. Ross did it," he said.

Ross admitted his guilt. "But Perry put me up to it."

The testimony of a confessed murderer isn't very credible. Perry was exonerated. Ross was found guilty and hanged.

All that Perry suffered was the loss of his job. Henceforth, though, he was shunned by his black neighbors and he lived in fear of his life.

Emily Brown needn't have died the death she did. Maryland had passed an anatomy act four years earlier, in 1882, but it simply wasn't adequate. In 1893, when Johns Hopkins Medical School opened its doors in Baltimore, the city had seven medical schools. They needed three hundred cadavers a year; the state supplied only forty-nine. At Johns Hopkins dissection was supposed to begin on November 15—but there were no subjects to dissect.

"We postponed work until the sixteenth and then the seventeenth," recalled Dr. Franklin P. Mall, "and late in the evening a subject was mysteriously left in the basement. The next day, one came from the state, and a few days later, another appeared in the basement."

The last illegal body in Maryland, according to Dr. Alan F. Guttmacher of Johns Hopkins, was acquired in 1899.

Massachusetts, it will be recalled, had blazed the way for all the states by passing its anatomy act in 1831. It didn't work too well. In the 1880s the state's medical schools were still using illicit bodies. The president of Harvard University, in 1883, warned his medical faculty that the university would not pay for bodies illegally acquired. Only after the Massachusetts anatomy act was revised in 1902—providing more bodies and allocating them fairly among the schools—did the shortage disappear.

Some states were slower than others in facing up to the facts. As late as 1913 medical students in Tennessee and North Carolina were still limited, legally, to dissecting dead criminals. Louisiana and Alabama—believe it or not—had no law whatever to provide their schools with bodies. As late as the 1920s medical colleges in Nashville were getting cadavers from resurrectionists. Bodies from Tennessee graveyards were being shipped to schools in places as far away as Iowa.

By that time, fortunately, most of the states had passed anatomy acts. Supply was at last catching up with demand. By 1943 we find Dr. Claude Heaton writing in the *New York State Journal of Medicine* that the practice of body snatching was "probably" a thing of the past.

What about the supply of bodies today? In recent years, all authorities agree, demand has once again exceeded supply. In 1963 the Committee on Medico-Legal Problems of the American Medical Association (AMA) was impelled to declare: "The supply of cadavers is again becoming inadequate in a number of areas because there are fewer and fewer unclaimed bodies." A report in the *New York Times* in 1972 indicated two-thirds of the 110 medical schools in Canada and the United States had an undersupply of subjects for their students. Nor has the supply improved significantly since then. "Medical schools are having serious difficulty," Dr. Thomas R. Forbes of Yale University asserted recently, "in obtaining enough cadavers to meet the needs of their first-year classes.... We accept nearly all bodies that are offered to us."

The main reason for the shortage, according to the AMA, is Social Security coverage. It allows a death benefit for funeral expenses. Many labor unions also supply burial benefits. And charitable organizations often bury the indigent.

Nowadays, too, people in lower-income brackets have inexpensive burial insurance available to them. Another factor, says the AMA, is "lax enforcement of Anatomy laws."

To complicate matters the demand for cadavers has soared. "Approximately fifteen thousand new students enroll in colleges of medicine in the United States each year, and almost all of them take a course in gross human anatomy," according to Dr. John F. Pauly, secretary of the American Association of Anatomists. "Most departments provide one cadaver for every four students, and therefore an estimate of 3500 to 4000 cadavers is probably realistic" as the number they require. Soon there may have to be six students to a cadaver, or eight.

"In addition to the cadavers used for the freshman courses in anatomy," Dr. Pauly continues, "most departments also teach senior electives and provide bodies for courses for students of dentistry, nursing, physical therapy, etc. Human bodies are also used by colleges of osteopathic medicine." Embalming and physical education students are others who use cadavers in their studies. Dr. Burton S. Sherman of Downstate Medical College, New York, placed the overall requirement at five thousand a few years ago. Already, at some schools where the shortage is acute, important courses like surgical anatomy or anatomy for nurses have had to be dropped.

Dead bodies have other important uses. Corneas, bones, arteries, kidneys, and other body parts are needed to save life or make it more livable. So are products from the bodies of the dead. HGH, the growth hormone, is extracted from the pituitary glands of cadavers and given to midgets—enabling many to grow taller and lead a more normal existence.

Dr. Aaron J. Ladman, professor of anatomy at the University of New Mexico, describes another vital use for cadavers:

At times there are specific needs for surgeons to use cadavers to explore new approaches to operations, and these are carried out in virtually all medical schools. Currently at our institution, several surgeons are working with the dissecting microscope in terms of transplanting skin and other organs and re-anastomosing [rejoining] the smallest blood vessels to provide enough nourishment in the experimental situation.

Dr. Ladman's school has done significant research with human bodies to help improve automobile safety, under the auspices of the United States Department of Transportation. In filmed automobile safety tests you usually see dummies strapped in the seats of cars. But dummies aren't people. Cadavers are—or were, a short while ago. What happens to their brains, their arteries, their spines, and all the other fragile equipment of the body in accidents gives us incredibly more reliable information than dummies ever can. Automobile safety experiments with dead bodies are being carried on at a number of universities in the United States. Who can quarrel with the use of bodies to learn how to make cars safer—in a country in which fifty thousand lives are lost in automobile accidents every year?

Military aviation already owes a good deal to this kind of experimentation. It developed its pilot ejection mechanism with the help of cadavers.

"The majority of human bodies used in teaching programs today," says Dr. Pauly,

come from donor programs. Persons interested in donating their bodies to science generally write to the chairman of a department of anatomy, and he or she provides them with the necessary forms. Other people make less formal arrangements by signing the back of their driver's license or some other such form. The Uniform Anatomical Gift Act now is legal in all fifty states.

Under this act you can make a gift of your body or any part of it to a hospital, school, organ bank, or physician for research, education, therapy, or transplantation. You can do this by a will or any other document (even a recorded message), to become effective on the death of the donor. The next of kin may also donate a body.

Medical schools foot the entire bill for body donations. They pick up the body and transport it to their premises. After the body has made its contribution to medical knowledge, the university will bury it or cremate it, as the donor requests (medical universities often maintain their own cemeteries), or the remains may be returned for a family burial. "Medical schools treat with respect and dignity the human remains that are entrusted to them," says Yale's Dr. Forbes.

Most major religious groups, from Catholic to Moslem, have approved body donation.

Physicians, incidentally, no longer have to go to the lengths they once did to obtain skeletons to study human bone structure. Skeletons can be bought from almost any big scientific supply house. The price of a good skeleton was recently about six hundred or seven hundred dollars. All of them come from abroad. Plastic skeletons are also available, costing a little less than the real thing.

And yet—in spite of all this—body snatching still goes on.

Things for the surgeon? No...

Things for the witch.

Today's witches are modern men and women with modern ways. They don't look or behave much different than anybody else. They don't gather on wind-blasted heaths or in ruined churches. They prefer air-conditioned apartments or steam-heated flats.

But they still cast spells.

> Nose of Turk and Tartar's lips,
> Finger of birth-strangled babe
> Ditch-deliver'd by a drab

were some of the bizarre ingredients yesterday's witches dropped into their pots to make their magic in Shakespeare's *Macbeth*. Not the black-magic practitioners of today. What they require is far less exotic, and readily available at any cemetery....

On a dark night in November 1977 three American teenagers were prowling about in New Calvary Cemetery in Queens, New York. Ignoring the fresh new graves they focused their attention on an older mausoleum and stopped to examine its heavy brass door. They agreed it was worth a try. One of the youths then reached into a sack and pulled out a sledgehammer. He pounded on the door with it until the lock gave. They pulled open the door.

The pale beam of a flashlight explored the musty, cold little room. It came to rest on the marble cover of a crypt. The head of the hammer came crashing down on the marble. Chips flew. The cover cracked. They lifted the broken pieces away.

On a shelf inside the crypt lay the casket. From other shelves holy figures looked down blessingly. The sledgehammer smashed at them. There was not enough room to open the casket and inspect the treasure, so the youths hauled the heavy box down and tugged it outside.

They pried up the lid of the casket.... She had been a woman once. Filomena Rossano had been her name. A man had loved her. She had nurtured children. But, lying in the tomb since 1953, she had become a thing of moldering bone. Shreds of a shroud covered her. Black fungus fed on her skeleton.

Under the yellow beam of light they examined the skull. That was what they were after. Weeks before, they had broken into another mausoleum and stolen another skull. It was shown to the warlock—the male witch who had already sold one for them to a coven in Manhattan.

"The jaw is gone," he grumbled. "You'd better try again. The skull must be complete."

This one was all there. *Score! Big bucks!* they exulted.

One of them grabbed the skull by the matted hair that still clung to it. Another hacked through the vertebrae that held it to the skeleton.

"She'll never miss it," they snickered.

They brought the skull to the home of a strange young woman named June, who lived in Woodside. She was only eighteen, and she already had a two-year-old child. She also had a knowledge of the ways of witches. Her friend Ed was with her. Sometimes he called himself Ed Caine, which was not his real name but a witch name derived from the biblical Cain, who killed his brother, Abel. Ed was nineteen. He seemed to know more about black magic and witchcraft than June did.

"It's a good skull. But it's covered with mildew. And there's still some hair on it. Some scalp too. We better clean it up."

Water roared into the bathtub. June scrubbed the skull until it shone like polished alabaster. But not on top. The scalp with its tufts of hair clung stubbornly to the bone.

They took the skull outside to the front lawn. They brought an axe with them. Squatting on the grass they chipped away at the tenacious scalp. One of them held the skull. Another worked the axe. The others watched.

So did a neighbor, who couldn't believe her eyes at first, then finally did and rushed to her telephone....

Even the hard-fisted, street-wise detectives of the 108th Precinct were surprised. Grave robberies they knew about. Rings, necklaces, trinkets that people insisted on burying with their loved ones, and that thieves are constantly digging for. But a skull? Hacking at a skull on a lawn? Right there in Woodside?

The blue cars flashed through the crowded streets. Suddenly the house at 61-16 Laurel Hill Boulevard, Woodside, was full of detectives.

The woman June and the ghouls in the house with her were no problem. But where was the skull?

The officers spread out through the neighborhood. On a street corner nearby one of them stopped by a public litter basket. He poked through the papers and the trash inside. At the bottom the whiteness of bone: Two skulls. One with no jaw.

By 1 A.M. the last member of the gang was in custody.

New York City has many laws against body snatching. A grave robber can be charged with anything from the felony of possession of a dead body (a violation of the public health law, punishable by up to four years in prison) to the misdemeanor of criminal trespass.

At their trials in 1978 the teenage ghouls were found guilty of a misdemeanor. One, a juvenile (fourteen), went to juvenile court, where hearings are private.

Because the woman June had no previous criminal record and because she had cooperated with the police, she was placed on parole for three years. Another, with no previous offense, received a sentence of zero to three years. Two others with criminal records received a year in prison. And for Ed Caine, the male witch, a modern extra: regular psychiatric attention.

Except for that, the sentences were just about what they might have been a hundred and fifty years ago. The big difference between yesteryear and nowadays would appear to be in the price of things. For the witches of New York City that year were paying five hundred dollars for a skull—a price high enough to have made the hearts of Burke and Hare beat faster.

The dead are the only ones who never die.

John Hall Wheelock

ON the morning of January 14, 1775, all the blinds were suddenly drawn in the big handsome Georgian house on Mount Street, a stone's throw from Berkeley Square, in London. It was as though the great mansion had closed its eyes.

The front door swung open. Out popped a strange little owl of a man in a shabby old coat and boots. The neighbors, peering out of their windows, could see he was holding a scarf. It was black.

"Poor Mary Van Butchell," they said, as he fixed the mourning scarf on the door. "Thank God it's over for her. She's rid of her suffering—and rid of that horrid little man!"

They said that, even though they knew he had given her the best of care. For Martin Van Butchell was himself a medical man, and a highly successful one.

During his wife's long illness he consulted often with his friends and teachers, the brilliant Hunter brothers, the most famous surgeons in all Britain. No one knew more about disease than the Hunters. They did all they could for the ailing woman, but her pleuropneumonia ultimately proved stronger than all their pills and potions.

"Well, black won't be any novelty in that house," the neighbors said.

Never had they seen Mrs. Van Butchell in any color but black. To a few close friends she had once confided that, before her wedding, the doctor made her choose between two colors, black and white, for her clothing. Once she made her choice, he had told her, she couldn't change it. Whereupon Mrs. Van Butchell—perhaps out of a pious turn of mind—chose black. And black she wore at her wedding and for all the rest of her life.

People wondered how Mary Van Butchell could stay married to the little man. What a queer and quirky fellow! He never, for example, allowed his wife and his children to sit down and eat a meal with him. He always ate alone. When he wanted the children to come to him he never called them by name—he whistled.

England had its share of eccentrics in the late 1700s, but few could hold a candle to Dr. Van Butchell. His bizarre ways were talked of from one end of London to the other.

To begin with, there was his appearance. He wore a faded old wide-brimmed hat like no one else in town. His boots were old and faded too, and so was his coat. From his wrist dangled a human thighbone. It was, he said, a war club from Tahiti. He used it to whack at persistent beggars or ragamuffins attracted by his odd appearance.

And then there was his pony. It was the only horse in London painted with purple spots or, sometimes, stripes. On the pony's head, above the eyes, the doctor had fixed a blind; this he would let down to keep the animal from seeing anything that might frighten it. He never trimmed the pony's tail or its mane.

He did as much with his own hair. In an age when city men wore wigs and shaved their faces clean he let his hair grow down to his shoulders; his gray-streaked whiskers reached down to his chest. The combings from his beard he offered for sale—at a guinea a hair! "Of use to the fair that want fine children," he advertised. "I can tell them how; it is a secret."

Insane? Maybe. And maybe not. People were always talking about his singular ways—and the more they talked the better they remembered to call him when they needed his services. As his reputation for eccentricity grew, so did his fortune. Surgeons came from foreign countries to learn the treatment he had developed for rupture. He was even more famous as a dentist than as a doctor. His dentistry, he boasted, was painless, and many paid large sums to be treated by him. Everyone talked about his truss and other remarkable inventions of his. If he was a quack—and many said he was—he was a gifted one.

On the fourteenth day of January, however, the talk was not of the eccentric Dr. Van Butchell but of his poor dead wife.

One lady after another of Mrs. Van Butchell's acquaintance called at the darkened house on Mount Street. They offered the doctor their condolences. They inquired about the funeral arrangements. The little doctor's utterances had always been unpredictable. Now he surprised the ladies more than ever.

"No, ma'am, there will be no burial. Not for Mrs. Van Butchell." He mopped up tears. "Thank you for your sympathy." And before they realized what was happening he was ushering them out the door.

In the afternoon a carriage pulled up. Two gentlemen hurried out. A young medical student who lived across the street recognized them and got very excited. "That's Dr. William Hunter. And Mr. William Cruikshank. They're my anatomy teachers at the school in Great Windmill Street. What can they want with the unfortunate lady, now that she's passed away?"

Later a cart stopped at the tradesmen's entrance. Great flagons of colored liquid, packages and sacks of varied shapes and sizes were carried into the house.

The next morning another cart. Delivery men moved carefully, unloading a bulky wooden chest with a lid of glass.

During the days that followed, Hunter and Cruikshank became familiar figures to the neighborhood. They came and went repeatedly. They remained in the house for hours on end. When they emerged, Van Butchell escorted them to their carriage, talking volubly, gesticulating.

The neighbors could only watch and wonder what was going on. Gradually, however, through their servants—who were friendly with Van Butchell's servants—they began to find out.

It was the dead mistress, the servants said. The doctor loved her so much he couldn't bear to part with her. And they poured out the details:

On the day Mrs. Van Butchell died she was carried downstairs to the doctor's laboratory. The next day a glass-covered chest was brought in. Mr. Cruikshank mixed up a quantity of liquid red as blood. The smell of turpentine was so strong the servants had to hold their noses. Then he injected large quantities of the liquid into the dead lady—until her white, wasted body rounded out and took on a pinkish hue.

Next morning Mr. Cruikshank and Dr. Hunter cut open the body. They did a—what was the word?—an autopsy. Both of the unfortunate lady's lungs were diseased, they said. So was her poor liver. The doctors took out her insides—her heart, her lungs, her bowels, and whatnot. They squeezed the blood out of them. They also squeezed the blood and the red liquid out of her body. The whole room was splashed and splattered like an abattoir. Then they mixed up another red mixture and injected it into her arteries.

Odors of camphor and wine and strange chemicals filled the laboratory. All the organs were washed and wrapped up. Then back they went into the body of Mrs. Van Butchell. Mr. Cruikshank threaded a needle and sewed her up like a stuffed animal.

On the fourth day Dr. Hunter and Mr. Cruikshank emptied sack after sack of plaster of Paris into the great chest. When it was half full they lifted up the dead woman and placed her on top of the plaster. "It will draw off the moisture," Dr. Hunter said.

Dr. Van Butchell was there every minute helping the surgeons. One day he opened her belly up and filled it with powders and chemicals. He was always examining her. And rubbing her skin with fragrant oils.

Dr. Hunter came back again and again, accompanied by distinguished-looking visitors. Sir This and Sir That, members of the Royal Society.

The visitors couldn't stop staring at the dead woman. "Dr. Hunter," they said, "you've preserved Mrs. Van Butchell better than the way the ancient Egyptians preserved their kings and queens. And without wrappings, too."

"She promises well," Dr. Hunter said. "Exceedingly well."

And everyone agreed that the late Mrs. Van Butchell looked beautiful.

"Yes, beautiful," confirmed one of the servants. "She's not the thin, wasted body she was when she lay dying. She's all plump and round. Her cheeks are full of roses. You would almost expect her to open her eyes any minute and speak...."

The glass-lidded chest, with Mrs. Van Butchell inside, was carried up to the doctor's sitting room. Dressed in her lacy black wedding gown, she rested on her bed of plaster of Paris. Every day it grew harder. As it hardened it crystallized, until it turned into a splendid, shining couch.

Embalming was known little and practiced less in England. It was done occasionally, as when a king or a queen died and was to lie in state, but even royal bodies had to be laid away soon enough. Not Mrs. Van Butchell, however. She looked as though she would last for ages.

London couldn't stop talking about her. Dr. Van Butchell's acquaintances and patients were eager to see her. They didn't have to ask him twice. With a sad, proud smile he would lead them into his sitting room and draw aside the curtains that covered the chest.

She became a national celebrity. Physicians traveled from all over the country to look at her. Lords and ladies, men of letters, foreign dignitaries called. Poems and epitaphs appeared in the magazines, celebrating the dead lady, her husband, and Dr. Hunter's "curious and newly invented method of embalming":

> O! lucky Husband! Blest of Heav'n
> To thee the privilege is given,
> A much lov'd wife at home to keep,
> Caress, touch, talk to, even sleep
> Close by her side...
> What a rare treasure thou hast got!
> Who to a woman canst lay claim
> Whose temper's every day the same!

Some, like poet-surgeon Sir Richard Jebb, were less than charmed:

> To do his Wife's Corps peculiar honour
> Van Budgell wish'd to have it turn'd to stone;
> Hunter cast his Gorgon Looks upon her,
> And in a twinkling See the Thing is done.

Curious tales about the "preserved lady" and her husband were rampant. So were rumors. According to one—the most popular—it was not out of affection that Van Butchell had refused to part with his late wife. Mary Van Butchell had been, they said, a woman of considerable property. Her marriage settlement had been awkwardly worded. It stipulated her husband could control her property "only so long as she remained above ground." That was just another way of saying "only so long as she lived." The shrewd doctor had chosen to interpret the clause literally—and the proper heirs could do nothing about it.

Other tongues insisted it was a clever kind of advertising, like all the doctor's other eccentricities. Even a corpse could be good for business if you didn't mind turning your home into a sideshow. Whether they were right or wrong, for months after Mary Van Butchell's death people clamored to be admitted to the house in Mount Street.

In the end the curiosity seekers became too much even for the publicity-minded Dr. Van Butchell. Taking quill in hand he wrote out a public notice. On October 31, 1775, it appeared in *St. James's Chronicle,* announcing he would not admit strangers to see his embalmed wife unless a mutual friend introduced them. Visiting hours, he declared, were restricted to from nine to one on weekdays.

Van Butchell went on building his reputation and his fortune. He became celebrated for his treatment of fistulas. He advertised he could cure something his teacher the great John Hunter couldn't: the dreaded "king's evil," scrofula. He applied for an appointment as dentist to King George III. From his lively brain poured new inventions: rubber carriage-wheels, a fire extinguisher, spring girths for saddles, cork bottoms for iron stirrups to keep the feet from slipping—even elastic braces for underwear. However, none of these would make him as famous as the late Mrs. Van Butchell.

Dr. Van Butchell had a handsome wife on a bed of plaster. In his own bed he had none....

To the big house in Mount Street there came a new maid. Her name was Elizabeth and she was a spirited, pretty girl. The doctor couldn't keep his eyes off her. Elizabeth worked as assistant to the housekeeper, whose voice he sometimes heard scolding her shrilly. The problem, he hoped, would work itself out. But it only got worse.

One day she came into his study, her cheeks wet with tears. "Sir, I give you two weeks' notice. I must leave."

The doctor asked her why, but he had already guessed; the housekeeper was treating her intolerably. He tried to persuade her to stay. She was unwilling. The thought that this sweet-faced young girl was about to disappear forever from his household was extremely upsetting to him. He would have to find a way to make her stay.

"Well, then, will you marry me?"

Overcoming her surprise, she looked the strange little man over, then made a bold decision. "Yes, sir, I will...on one condition. The housekeeper must go."

"So be it. I too must make a condition. We will order your trousseau at once. It will be all black or all white. Choose one—and that one color you must wear for the rest of our life together."

She agreed. She knew the color the first Mrs. Van Butchell wore. Unhesitatingly she chose white.

The marriage was a happy one. Soon there were more little Van Butchells for the doctor to whistle to.

In only one matter was the second Mrs. Van Butchell uneasy. The great chest in the sitting room seemed to be growing bigger and bigger. Even when the curtains were drawn on top of the glass lid they couldn't hide from her the still form lying underneath.

Finally she could stand the silent presence no longer.

"Martin Van Butchell," she said to the strange little doctor, "you will have to choose between your two wives—the living one and the dead one."

The doctor, it appeared, was not so strange after all. He bent before the tempest. The first Mrs. Van Butchell was carried out of the sitting room.

But as long as Martin Van Butchell lived, she still remained above ground. He died in 1814 at the age of seventy-nine. The following year his son, a physician, donated the body of the first Mrs. Van Butchell to the Royal College of Surgeons in London.

Saint-Fond had always heard the British were a cold, reserved people. He finally got to meet them in 1784. In spite of their reputation he found many of them warm and open. Especially John Sheldon, the brilliant young London surgeon and anatomist.

One of France's leading naturalists, Saint-Fond had come to Britain to tour and study the country. When Sheldon invited him to visit his house and examine his collection of rare objects and anatomical preparations, the Frenchman promptly accepted.

The French savant was fascinated by the endless variety of curious preparations in the Sheldon collection. Nothing, however, interested him more than a strange object the surgeon kept in a large case, under a sheet of glass, near his bed.

It was a human body. The body of a woman in her early twenties. Lustrous brown hair framed a face of rare beauty. She looked as though she was sleeping.

"Would you care to examine her more closely?" Sheldon raised the sheet of glass. She was, he explained, a Miss Johnson, who had died in 1775. "She will, I hope, last for hundreds of years." Proudly Sheldon took Saint-Fond's hand in his own and drew it down to the body until it rested on the rounded bosom. "Feel the elasticity. Remarkable, is it not?"

Repelled yet fascinated, Saint-Fond had to say yes.

Sheldon raised one of the limp arms from the case. "Observe how flexible." He bent it at the elbow. "And the cheeks—feel how soft they are. Would you believe she's been dead for almost ten years? For the first five I kept her hermetically sealed up. Since then I've opened the box a few times for a few special visitors."

Gazing down at the dead face Saint-Fond began to notice things he hadn't seen before. Although the features still retained their loveliness they looked a trifle peaked. The muscles seemed strained. The skin was drying. There was something unnatural about the coloring.

Meanwhile the surgeon was telling him how he had embalmed the dead woman. He had injected her blood vessels with spirits of wine mixed with turpentine and camphor. He had removed the intestines, dried them, and covered them with a varnish of camphor mixed with resin. He had injected her carotid arteries with a reddish solution to give the skin of the face some color. Then he had rubbed her skin with alum, like a tanner, to preserve it.

Saint-Fond felt the nausea creeping through him. He shook it off. "Who was this Miss Johnson?"

"A woman I loved. Most tenderly."

Loved! Saint-Fond almost shouted to himself. *Loved most tenderly!*

His revulsion mounted. How could a man who truly loved a woman go about the sordid business of embalming her? Even the Egyptians, who made a cult of embalming, ritually drove away the man who cut open and disemboweled the dead.

He had to remind himself that he was a man of science. "Why did you preserve her body?"

"She asked me to." Sheldon sighed. "She was my mistress. We adored each other. Then she fell ill. She coughed and coughed. When I saw the blood on the handkerchiefs I ordered her to the hospital. I did everything I could for her. I might as well have done nothing. Now and then I spoke to her about the mummies of Egypt. Of my admiration for Hunter's achievement in preserving Mrs. Van Butchell. It was the talk of London that year.

"The poor girl knew death was near. 'I'm frightened,' she said. 'I don't want to die. I don't want to leave you.'

"A terrible fit of coughing shook her. It tore my heart. The spasm passed. A strange look came into her eyes. 'You could do what Hunter did. Make me into a mummy . . . and keep me always by your side. Promise you will.'

"I promised. In a few days she was dead. . . . I have kept my word to her."

They talked on. Saint-Fond's view changed. Sheldon, he saw, wasn't cynical or cold-blooded. He was a man of deep feeling. He had fulfilled a dying girl's last wish by performing an act few men could have if they really cared for her. Ten years after her death he still kept her by his side. It was, in its way, an act of love.

THEY called her the Hottentot Venus. She was neither a
Hottentot nor a Venus—but she was one of the wonders of
the age.

Thousands upon thousands of Englishmen queued up in
Piccadilly, London, to get a look at the gigantic buttocks of
the Hottentot Venus. In Paris thousands of Frenchmen paid
their three francs apiece at the *baraque* on the rue Saint-
Honoré, hoping she would expose her fabled sex organs.

Noted scientists came with the same expectation....

One was Geoffroy Saint-Hilaire, chevalier of the Legion
of Honor, founder of the Paris Zoological Gardens, world authority on freaks. Another was the brilliant Georges Cuvier.
Secretary of the Institut National, chancellor of the University of Paris, Cuvier had been a member of Napoleon's council
of state. The French revered him as a wizard. Who else could
look at a dry old piece of bone and tell you all about the
animal it belonged to thirty million years ago?

Both of these great naturalists were bursting with curiosity about the incredible woman from South Africa, the first
of her kind they had ever seen. They approached Réaux, her
exhibitor. Would he, in the interests of science, allow the
Hottentot Venus to be examined by a committee of the nation's leading savants?

Réaux thought it over. Finally he agreed, with one proviso.
He wanted an eminent member of the group to give him a

written statement of what they found. (Nothing, he knew, would keep interest in his Hottentot bubbling like a description, written by a nationally known scientist, of what an extraordinary animal she was.) Geoffroy Saint-Hilaire promised to provide it.

In March 1815 Réaux brought the Venus to the Royal Botanical Gardens. There, in the Museum of Natural History, the foremost research center in the world, Cuvier presided like the god of science.

Short, stout, elegantly dressed, Cuvier watches as the Venus and Réaux descend from the carriage in the porte-cochere. Behind Cuvier cluster the group of professors he has invited.

Flattered by the attention of all these important-looking white-haired gentlemen, the Venus moves swiftly and gracefully toward them. Her thick lips spread in a broad smile. *"Bonjou', m'sieu, bonjou'."* She has seen Cuvier only once before but she recognizes him. Surprised, he makes a mental note: *She has a good memory.*

The great anatomist beckons her and Réaux inside. His secretary is waiting there, notebook in hand. A Dutch interpreter is waiting too; the Venus knows very little French but learned to speak Dutch at the Cape. Four artists are standing expectantly next to their easels, set up, on Cuvier's order, at four different points of vantage.

Cuvier gets right to the point. Through the interpreter he asks the Venus to take her clothes off.

Her smile wilts. But she sees the frown growing on Réaux's face. Reluctantly she begins to pull her gown over her head. Shoes and stockings come next and a multitude of undergarments.

Cuvier watches her remove her bosom support. Her breasts tumble out, ripe and full. The nipples are flattened, almost invisible in their great blackish, wrinkled aureolas.

Finally the underpants come off. Everyone's eyes are fastened on her thighs and buttocks—and the sparse woolly black peppercorn hair that covers her pubis.

She stands before them completely naked, her brownish-yellow skin shining in the pale sunlight, a sight such as none of them has ever seen before.

Excited, gesticulating, the professors walk around and around her. When the great Cuvier steps forward they know enough to fall back. The room is silent except for the scraping of the four charcoal sticks outlining her extraordinary figure on canvas.

Cuvier contemplates her. Her hips are the widest he has ever seen. He walks to the side and surveys the remarkable backward thrust of her buttocks. It is one thing to study drawings of the legendary backside of the Bushwomen, quite another to see how it juts out in the flesh. He makes a quick estimate—"more than half a foot"—and his secretary jots down the master's words.

Cuvier caresses his chin reflectively, pretending to be all detachment. But he is aware a historic moment has come, one that anatomists have long awaited. He is about to unravel the mystery—to see what is between her legs.

"Tell her to walk up and down," he orders the interpreter.

The Venus hesitates, then moves a shapely foot forward. The professors hold their breath, eyes fastened on the peppercorn triangle. Even Cuvier leans forward a little.

She walks primly and slowly, in a cramped, awkward way, her thighs held close together in an invisible clamp. She isn't showing any more of her sex than she has to, even to the luminaries of France. Alas, they cannot see what they want to see.

Their eyes follow her. The fat that accumulates on the bellies of other women is, on her, laid up on the legs and buttocks. It is so heavy on her thighs that she looks knock-kneed. The gigantic backside, a great elastic mass that trembles and quivers with every movement, appears to be rather sensitive, for it is covered with many scars and scratches.

"Are the Bushwomen's buttocks always so big?" he asks her, and waits impassively while the interpreter translates.

"No, no. They grow bigger with the first pregnancy."

How like the female mandril and the baboon, he thinks, and is delighted by the clever (but inaccurate) comparison; *their buttocks enlarge greatly when they're ready to mate.*

His eyes rest on the great breasts with their four-inch-wide aureolas. "So you have had children?"

"Yes, *baas*. I was married to a black man. I had two children." Sadness shadows her face.

Cuvier doesn't seem to notice. He is busy observing the structure of her features—the forward thrust of the jaws, the thick lips, the small chin, the heavy cheekbones, the flat nose. Every race has its own beauty; he, however, sees only the beauty of his own. ("What was most repelling about our Bush-woman," he will write later, "was her physiognomy.")

"Who brought you to Europe?"

Her eyes cloud over. *"Baas,* it was an Englishman. He told me he would help me earn a great fortune if I would come and show myself to the people of Europe. Then he abandoned me to an exhibitor of animals."

Cuvier measures her height. "Four feet seven inches tall." Except for her thighs and buttocks her proportions are nor-mal; her shoulders, her back, even the height of her bosom have a certain grace. He examines her hands and feet. *Très bien faits!*

But again and again his bias intrudes. *There is something brusque and capricious about her movements. Like a monkey. She is always thrusting out her enormous lips. Exactly what I've observed in the orangutan.*

For three days Cuvier and his colleagues study the Hot-tentot Venus. She plays her jew's harp for them and he's impressed by her good ear. She dances for them the dances of her people. She wears her native costume for them, and he notes the pride with which she adjusts her necklaces and girdles of glass beads and her other African finery.

The scientists offer her food and watch how she eats, just as they would with a new animal; they note the things she likes most, those she likes least. She is especially fond of the brandy. *She can't get enough of it,* Cuvier observes disap-provingly. At the end Réaux has to half-carry, half-push the befuddled woman to a coach.

Cuvier watches the pair drive off. Geoffroy Saint-Hilaire stands beside him. "These primitives, with their taste for eau de vie." Cuvier shakes his head. "She won't last long at this rate."

He feels more than a little bitter. She had swallowed glass after glass of the museum's fine brandy, until finally she was talking to him garrulously in a bizarre tongue full of clicking sounds. But drunk as she was, she steadfastly refused to let him pry between her legs and see her *tablier hottentot.*

He will examine it yet, he promises himself.

Who was the Hottentot Venus and what was the *tablier hottentot*—or Hottentot apron—that so intrigued the French public and the French professors?

Why—more than 160 years after her death—does the

Musée de l'Homme in Paris exhibit in Case Number 33 the skeleton of this unhappy woman and the painted cast of her dead body made by Cuvier as soon as he could get his hands on her? (Elsewhere in the museum are her brain and wax molds of her genitals and anus.)

There is ample evidence that the Hottentot Venus was not a Hottentot. Cuvier called her a Bushwoman. She probably had, in addition, some alien blood. Her race, the San, live today in the Kalahari Desert region and other parts of southern Africa. They were once (and in some places still are) great hunters, stalking the antelope and the lion with poison-tipped arrows while their women gathered wild food. Nomads, driven by hunger, they were constantly on the move, carrying with them all they owned. They lived in the bush or in rock shelters or caves whose walls they covered with paintings that today are considered treasures of art.

The San aren't black. Their skin is yellowish brown. They are short, wiry people. Their foreheads bulge. Their noses are broad, their cheekbones prominent. These physical traits they share with the Hottentots (who today are known by their native name, Khoikhoi). The San and the Khoikhoi are collectively called the Khoisan. Both groups were the earliest inhabitants of South Africa. The Bantu, the blacks of South Africa, came later.

The Dutch reached South Africa in the 1600s. By then the San had been pushed back by the Bantu from the Cape to the interior. Finding them in the bush, the Dutch called them Bosjemans or Bushmen. (The term isn't used today; it's considered derogatory.) The San put up a stiff fight against the invaders both white and black, but they didn't have a chance. Many fled to the remote wilderness. The rest bowed their heads. Some found work (or were forced into it) caring for the cattle of the Bantu and the Boer.

Large numbers of Khoisan women, like the Hottentot Venus, are steatopygous. That ornate word simply means "having a fat backside" (a feature their men find enormously attractive). Steatopygia turns up among the pygmies and occasionally in other peoples. It occurs to some degree in the men. The big buttocks, like the humps on camels, contain a reserve of fat which nourishes the body when food is scarce.

More curious still is another physical feature intrinsic in the women. This is the Hottentot apron, the sexual phenomenon that so intrigued Cuvier and his colleagues. More about that later.

European travelers and naturalists had brought back from Africa reports of the extraordinary buttocks and the Hottentot apron of the Khoisan. Their statements about the apron, based on haphazard observation, were frequently contradictory. In time the apron became part of the legendary lore of natural history, like the crocodile's tears, or the mermaid. Every scientist in Europe had heard about it—but who had seen it?

With the arrival of the Hottentot Venus in Europe, men of science at last had a chance to find out the truth for themselves. So far, however, they hadn't succeeded.

The name of the Hottentot Venus was Saartjie Baartman.

Saartjie was born on the Gamtoos River in South Africa. She didn't know exactly when, but it was probably about 1788. When she was around ten she and her family were brought to the Cape by Dutch farmers. Her father had been a drover of cattle; he was murdered by the Bushmen, she said, when he went upcountry. After she had become famous, a clergyman of the London Missionary Society found the house she had lived in and made a drawing of it. The dwelling was a typical native Cape shack—they call it a *pondokkie* there—just two miles from the Cape.

It was an age when enterprising, money-hungry Westerners were penetrating deeper and deeper into Africa in search of natural wonders to bring back home. Hippopotamuses, elephants, giraffes, apes were great rarities in the West. So were some of the people of Africa. In 1807 a Hottentot boy had been exhibited in France. But a Hottentot woman? Europe was still waiting to see the first one.

Destiny chose Saartjie Baartman. In March 1810 young Saartjie was approached by an English surgeon named Alexander Dunlop. He had already acquired the skin of a camelopard (as they called a giraffe in those days) that he knew would bring a good price in England. But a girl like Saartjie—with her incredible backside (and her Hottentot apron)—would, he had decided, bring him much more.

Dunlop told Saartjie he could make her rich if she would come to Europe and let him exhibit her there. She would see great cities more wonderful than she could imagine and be welcomed by lords and ladies in their glittering salons. Dunlop would pay all of her expenses, give her money, and at the end of two years pay her passage back home. Would she go with him?

Would she go with him? A San woman's prospects on a Boer farm were dismal. Saartjie had already lived with a man, borne him two children, and seen them die. Times were hard and her man had deserted her. Many San women were abandoned by their men; the choice then was to starve or become a prostitute. And now here was this fine white man, clinking the coins in his purse in front of her. Would she go with him!

Soon Saartjie was gathering her belongings—her kaross of antelope skin (which a San woman lived in by day, slept on at night, and was buried in when she died), her digging stick, her treasured amulets and beads. The Europeans, *baas* Dunlop had told her, had never seen a San woman before. She would wear her best costumes for them, she would sing and dance for them, and they, in appreciation, would shower her with gold and jewels. Of course, Dunlop told her only the bright things. The black things he had in mind for her she would find out in time.

London boasted a number of private museums in 1810. The newest and most successful of them was called the Liverpool Museum. Its proprietor was a prosperous silversmith and jeweler, William Bullock. Possessed of a deep love of natural history and art, Bullock had accumulated outstanding collections in both fields and was constantly adding to them.

One day Alexander Dunlop appeared on the doorstep of the Liverpool Museum at 22 Piccadilly. He had a bale with him. Unwrapping it, the surgeon showed the naturalist-showman the magnificent camelopard skin he had brought from Africa. Bullock was tempted to buy it until he heard the price.

Dunlop called again. This time he offered Bullock an even more valuable exhibit. "I have a Hottentot female who will soon arrive from Africa. She's a handsome woman with an enormous backside, the like of which has never been seen in Britain. She is also endowed with the—ahem—Hottentot apron you've undoubtedly read about. In two years she'll have to be returned to the Cape. But by then she's certain to have made a fortune for the man who exhibits her."

Dunlop's new offer was a package deal—the woman and the camelopard skin together. Bullock was intrigued, but he had never exhibited a human being before. He was also something of a humanitarian and he didn't exactly like the way

Dunlop spoke of the woman. It smacked of bondage.

Dunlop called a third time. They finally agreed on a price for the skin. Bullock asked about the Hottentot woman. Dunlop shook his head. "I've sold most of my rights to the profits from her exhibition to a man named Hendrick Cezar. Now I've begun to regret it."

Bullock remembered all of this with complete clarity when the time came, some months later, to set it down in a deposition for the Attorney-General.

In due course Saartjie finds herself in London. Her days are a turmoil of hope and worry as she prepares for her first confrontation with the Englanders. She has seen the hall at 225 Piccadilly, with its curious stage setting. Vaguely she begins to understand the odd performance her exhibitors—Dunlop and the South African Hendrick Cezar—expect her to put on there. She lives with them nearby in a house in York Street.

Someone has come up with the stage name under which she'll become famous: Saartjie, the Hottentot Venus. An advertising campaign is in the making. She has sat (or rather stood) for a picture that will be used to present her to the British public, and she doesn't know whether to laugh or cry at how she looks in it.

One thing is certain: the public won't cry. In the print they will see Saartjie dressed, or, really, undressed, in her "native costume"—virtually in the nude. She's posed sideways to provide a titillating view of her backside and thighs. Their size is vastly exaggerated. Her breasts are bare. The beads and bangles she wears only serve to set off her nakedness; so does the mantle of antelope skin hanging at her side.

Saartjie can be pleased, at least, with the artist's representation of her face. Her features are small and winsome, her expression demure. On her cheeks are some savage daubs of paint and from her lips hangs a small pipe, the constant companion of the Cape woman. Overall she's a curiously shaped, somewhat attractive, definitely comic figure of a woman.

Copies of the print (bearing the name of Hendrick Cezar as publisher) are being sent out to journalists and reviewers with an invitation to a preview performance. Signs are going up in the center of the city. Men have been hired to march about the town carrying sticks with placards advertising the forthcoming appearance of the "Wonderful and Surprising Hottentot Venus."

In September Saartjie's show opens. An eager, curious crowd packs the hall to behold the woman with the incredible rump. They don't see everything they've been led to believe they will—but they do have an uproarious time.

Saartjie doesn't. She can't understand why Dunlop and Cezar make her do such humiliating things on the stage. Or why they allow the audience to touch her. She can't understand the strange words the shopkeepers' apprentices and the idlers in the audience hurl at her. Their crude gestures, however—their screeches, their catcalls, their howls of indecent laughter—need no translation.

To a few in the audience there is nothing comical about Saartjie's appearance. Unlike the others, they do not see a laughable freak with exaggerated sexual characteristics. Instead, with rising anger, what they see is one of God's innocent, helpless children being abused and degraded like a slave or a captive animal. Especially appalled by the display is a man named Zachary Macaulay. (Only a handful of people know his name nowadays. Yet his life helped to change the lives of millions.)

When Saartjie appeared in England slavery was already illegal. Since 1772 a slave became free simply by setting foot anywhere in the British Isles. In 1807, just three years before she arrived, the slave trade itself had been banned in the empire. No ship could clear a British port on a voyage for slaves or land them in a British colony.

Zachary Macaulay had been a banner bearer in the battle that made the slave trade illegal. Victorious, he continued to fight. He helped found the African Institution—an organization dedicated to the abolition of the slave trade in Europe and to the education of black people.

This heroic man (the father of the historian Lord Macaulay) had in his youth worked as the manager of a plantation in Jamaica. There he had seen enough to become a lifelong enemy of slavery. Later he helped establish Sierra Leone, an African colony for liberated slaves, where he served as governor. When he left he traveled to the West Indies on a slave ship, so he could see with his own eyes the horror of a slave voyage. As the secretary of the African Institution he was now laboring tirelessly, without reward, to bring down slavery throughout the world.

Macaulay was also the editor of the *Christian Observer,* an influential journal with headquarters in Piccadilly. Going to and from his office, he had seen the posters advertising the naked African woman. South African natives, he knew, could leave the Cape Colony only with the British governor's permission. He also knew that the governor (a personal acquaintance) would never allow a native woman to be taken abroad for such an exhibition.

She must have been smuggled out of the colony, he thought. Or else, if they had permission, her exhibitors must have hidden their true purpose from the governor. However, suspicions don't make a case at law. Before he could file a complaint, Macaulay realized, he would have to get some evidence.

The hall at 225 Piccadilly is crowded and noisy when Zachary Macaulay enters. He notices to his surprise that there are some women in the audience. Up front he sees a stage raised about three feet from the floor, with a cage at one end. Inside it crouches or cowers the African woman.

Her keeper, Hendrick Cezar, strides up to the woman and says something to her in Dutch. Then he repeats it in English for the audience's benefit: "Come out!"

Slowly she rises to her feet. She seems to be ñaked, as in the posters. As she comes forward Macaulay realizes she isn't. She is dressed in a thin costume, the same color as her skin, designed to reveal every curve and cranny of her body.

"Go forward!" the keeper orders. "Go back!" She is being made to move up and down the stage to display her extraordinary form. "Go back into your cage! Sit down! Come out again!"

Macaulay feels a queasiness in his stomach. *Is this the way to treat a human being? Like a bear on a chain?*

Small wailing sounds come from the woman. The audience snickers and howls. The woman's face flushes. Heartsick, confused, she responds lamely to the commands. Cezar thrusts a jew's harp into her hand. She shakes her head, as much at the audience as at her keeper. Cezar growls at her in Dutch. Her face turns pale. The instrument moves to her lips and a sad little tune of her homeland vibrates through the hall. The audience applauds or makes grotesque noises.

The keeper orders her back into her cage. She obeys, slumping to the floor.

"Up and out!"

She doesn't seem to hear.

"Up and out!"

The woman doesn't budge.

Muttering to himself, Cezar lets down the curtain and steps behind it. The drop is flimsy and the light behind is strong. Macaulay can see the man's arm raised over the woman. He hisses like a snake. She cringes.

Cezar comes out, all smiles. He hoists the curtain. She steps forward obediently, terror in her reddened eyes.

"Come on up, ladies and gentlemen," Cezar barks. "Examine for yourselves the remarkable peculiarities of her form. Touch her."

They hurry forward. Eager, hungry hands reach toward her. A woman pinches her behind to see if it is real; a man pokes at it with his cane.

Macaulay waits for the right moment, approaches Cezar, and introduces himself. "Where did you get this woman?"

"From some Boers who brought her out of the bush."

"Did Lord Caledon give you permission to take her from the Cape?"

"Oh, yes. He agreed I could take her to Britain for two years and exhibit her." Wariness edges his hoarse voice. "Yes, sir. I have his permission in writing."

"I'd like to see it."

"No reason I should have it here. And if I did—no reason I should show it to you." He turns away.

Macaulay wants to question the African woman—but how can he, not speaking Dutch? Among his acquaintances is a native of Holland. He sends this man to Saartjie's exhibition with a friend. After the show they stay behind.

She looks at them.

"Saartjie, do you have any relations at the Cape?"

Cezar has come up. He mutters something in his Cape Dutch. She remains silent.

"Are you comfortable here?"

The sad lips say nothing.

"Would you like to go home to your own country?"

She looks at Cezar. After a few more futile efforts the visitors give up.

Macaulay now feels he has enough evidence to proceed.

He is soon closeted with the Attorney-General. He and his associates supply affidavits. One, interestingly enough, comes from William Bullock, the proprietor of the Liverpool Museum.

The hearing begins on November twenty-fourth in the Court of King's Bench, in London, Lord Ellenborough presiding.

"A female native of South Africa remarkable for the formation of her person," begins Mr. Attorney-General, adjusting his wig, "is being exhibited to the public under circumstances of peculiar disgrace to a civilized country." There is every reason to believe she was brought away from the Cape Colony without her consent and is being exhibited against her will. The Crown will ask, he says, for a writ of habeas corpus to produce the unfortunate female—but first he wants her to be examined in private by officers of the court through an interpreter, away from the intimidating presence of her exhibitors.

Lord Ellenborough grants his request.

That is on Saturday. On Monday the officers of the court call at the house in York Street with their interpreter.

The Saartjie who greets the court officers hardly seems to be the same woman Zachary Macaulay described in his complaint. She's respectably dressed. She's cheerful and smiling. She answers every question without hesitation, almost loquaciously.

Yes, *baas*, says Saartjie, she came to England of her own free will. No, nobody forces her to do anything. She's under no restraint.

She states that: On the Cape she worked for a Boer *baas*, Peter Cezar. She agreed with Hendrick Cezar to come to England for six years. *Baas* Dunlop promised to send her back rich.

Did she get Lord Caledon's permission to leave?

Yes, *baas*, she appeared before the governor. He gave his consent.

Is she well treated?

Oh yes, *baas*. She's very happy in England. She admires this country. She doesn't want to go back to the Cape. She doesn't miss her two brothers and three sisters at all. She has two black boys to attend her. And yesterday, on Sunday, she was taken out in a coach for two or three hours. It was wonderful.

Her keeper—does he treat her with respect?

Yes, yes, he's a good man. He doesn't make her do anything she doesn't want to do. He doesn't appear in her room until she's all dressed. Then all he does is tie a ribbon around her waist.

Does she have any complaint at all?

Only one. The English climate is terribly cold; can she have some warmer clothes?

The officers continue talking to Saartjie. After three hours they can't think of any more questions to ask and they take their leave.

On Tuesday the hearing resumes in court. Now Saartjie's exhibitors are represented by counsel—by no less a personage than Stephen Gazely, a barrister of some prestige and influence.

A report of Monday's interview with Saartjie is presented to the court. Lord Ellenborough is impressed. So is Mr. Attorney-General.

There is no ground, declares Mr. Gazely, for a writ of habeas corpus. Mr. Macaulay complained about the keeper Cezar. She has been removed from his care. Mr. Macaulay complained about the decency of her appearance. She is presently clothed in a dress of plain cloth as well as the silk.

The affidavit of a notary is introduced. The African woman, he says, has a contract which states she's to receive a share of the moneys earned by her appearance. The notary affirms he has read a copy of this contract to her in Dutch. She seemed, he says, to understand it perfectly; she was greatly pleased at the prospect of getting half of the profits from the exhibition.

"Those who show her," concludes Mr. Gazely, "are perfectly willing that the African Institution should appoint any sufficient person as trustee to take care of the property which is to be raised for her use....If the court should still think that this woman is treated with anything like cruelty, my clients are willing to give her up at once."

But Mr. Attorney-General doesn't want them to. "This woman is plainly not under restraint. The only effect of taking her from her keepers would be to let her loose to go back to them."

"A habeas corpus cannot be granted," agrees Lord Ellenborough. "Case discharged."

In the period between the time Zachary Macaulay first

saw Saartjie and the time the court officers visited her in York Street—an interval of several weeks—a remarkable change had come over her. How did it happen?

For the answer we must look at Saartjie's contract. The contract, written in Dutch, is preserved in Paris—along with Saartjie's bones. It is dated October 29, 1810—well after her London exhibition had opened, but less than four weeks before the court hearing.

This document is an agreement between Saartjie and Alexander Dunlop of St. James, Middlesex. It declares she agrees to be employed by him as a domestic servant for a period of five years, beginning the previous March 20 (when she presumably was still at the Cape). She also agrees to allow herself to be viewed by the public of England and Ireland "just as she is."

When Saartjie left South Africa in March this document didn't exist. The October date proves it was drawn up retroactively.

Why precisely at that time? We can guess that Macaulay's interview with Cezar at the theater in Piccadilly and his Dutch friend's visit must have given Saartjie's exhibitors clear warning there was a storm ahead. With the highly respected African Institution proceeding against them, they must have realized Saartjie could easily be snatched out of their hands and returned to the Cape. It was then that they must have called in Gazely. Apparently, on the barrister's advice they completely reversed their treatment of Saartjie and drew up the retroactive contract, offering her half the profit from her exhibition. With that and a promise to treat her better they had won back her friendship completely.

It is doubtful that Saartjie ever saw much—if any—of the money that was promised her. It would have been easy for Dunlop, later on, to tell her the money had been lost or stolen, or some other cock-and-bull story. Saartjie's people had lived with misfortune for centuries. Bad news was something they expected.

At the final hearing Zachary Macaulay was silent. But how could he complain when Saartjie herself refused to; when the court believed she was being handsomely paid; when her exhibitors offered to turn her money over to anyone the African Institution might name, or give her up altogether? Macaulay no longer had a legal leg to stand on.

* * *

"The Case of the Hottentot Venus" drew the eyes of the entire nation to Saartjie. Overnight she was playing to bigger crowds then ever. In March 1811 she was still exhibiting at the same address. Curiously, a print of her issued that month gives her name as publisher. (Dunlop and Cezar were doubtless trying to remain as inconspicuous as they could.) The picture does not, like earlier ones, show her nude. Instead we see her in a tight costume—like an old-fashioned suit of long winter underwear—with her African jewelry, her painted face, and her pipe. No question but that, like the print, the format of her show had changed.

Even before the trial brought Saartjie a national reputation, caricaturists had seized on her sensational figure as a springboard for their humor. One print after another poured from the presses. By modern standards these caricatures can all be considered racist. In November 1810 the most racist one of all was published. It shows Saartjie with two freaks—Miss Harvey, "the beautiful Albiness with Silk hair," and Miss Ridsdale, who was only thirty inches tall. "Vat uggerly tings," Saartjie is made to say. "No like a fine Voman, no grease about dem like I." The picture was called *The Three Graces*.

In March 1814, across the English Channel, Napoleon tottered and fell. The triumphant British and their allies marched into Paris. Soon afterward Saartjie was in the French capital. A Dutchman (Cezar?) had reportedly brought her over.

Saartjie's new impresario was the Frenchman Réaux. At a different address he was exhibiting another native of Africa. This one was a hippopotamus.

Saartjie caught on fast. Réaux exhibited her to the general public in his *baraque*, and to the rich and powerful in their mansions. A reporter from the *Journal des Dames et des Modes* wrote of one of her appearances: "The doors of the salon open and we see the Hottentot Venus come in....She's given some candies to induce her to cavort about and sing, and she's told she's the most attractive woman in society...." She was dressed in a skintight garment, all white, that covered her from neck to ankle. Perhaps it was in a salon like this that the great Cuvier first saw her and asked Réaux to bring her for examination to the Museum of Natural History.

In Paris Saartjie was soon a greater hit than in London.

Only professional boxers, it was said, could compete with her in popularity.

A one-act musical, *La Vénus Hottentote,* had been written almost overnight to cash in on Saartjie's success. The Théâtre de Vaudeville was jammed when the show opened on November 19, 1815. It would have done Saartjie good to see the play and learn she had made Hottentots so popular that a French-woman was pretending to be one to win a lover. But it is doubtful that Saartjie attended a performance. She was putting in a long day—from eleven in the morning to ten at night—working for Réaux. She had no time for recreation...and precious little time left to live.

She worked so long and so hard that wet, chilly Paris autumn that she fell ill. The illness became a raging fever that consumed her.

Réaux called in a doctor, who treated her for pleurisy, catarrh, and dropsy of the breast. His treatment didn't help. She had smallpox. She could not have been much more than twenty-seven on December 29, 1815, when she died.

Cuvier was informed immediately. Only he—driven by his scientist's curiosity—cared enough to ask for her body. The prefect of police readily granted the great man's request. Réaux no doubt drew some profit from the occasion.

No sooner was Saartjie's cold body stretched out on the dissection slab of the Museum of Natural History than Cuvier got to work.

A few years after Saartjie's death Geoffroy Saint-Hilaire and Frédéric Cuvier (Georges's younger brother) began to publish their *Histoire Naturelle des Mammifères,* a massive natural history destined to become a classic. The book describes many kinds of mammals—but just one type of human being, considered so important by the authors that the first chapter is given over to it.

The chapter was written and signed by Georges Cuvier. He called it "Woman of the Bushman Race," and it's about Saartjie. It opens with these remarkable words:

Nothing is more celebrated in natural history than the Hottentot apron, and at the same time nothing has been the subject of more controversy. For a long time some have completely denied it exists; others have insisted it was produced artificially or by caprice; and among those who have regarded it as a natural conformation there have been as many opinions as writers on the question of which of the female organs it developed from...

Our first examination [of the dead Saartjie] was bound to have as its object the extraordinary appendage that nature has made, we are told, a special attribute of her race.

We found it at once...In reality the apron is not, as Peron has claimed, an individual organ...it is a development of the nymphae.

Two pairs of lips, an inner and an outer one, protect the opening of the vagina in the human female. The nymphae are the inner pair. They're also known as the labia minora (smaller lips) because they're usually considerably smaller than the outer pair, the labia majora (larger lips).

In Saartjie, Cuvier reported, he found this situation reversed. The outer lips were almost unnoticeable. The inner lips, by contrast, hung down from the vulva. They were two and one-half inches long by about one inch wide.

"If one turns up these two appendages, together they make a heart-shaped form, with lobes that are long and narrow; the opening of the vulva is in the middle...."

(According to those who have studied the subject, the Hottentot apron may protrude as much as three and one-half inches or more. It is found in two forms. One is known as the butterfly, because it suggests a butterfly with wings outspread. The other is called the wattle; it resembles the wattle hanging from a turkey's neck. Khoisan men consider the apron attractive.)

"We know," Cuvier relates,

that the development of the nymphae varies a good deal in Europe; that, generally speaking, it becomes more sizable in warm countries; that Negresses and Abyssinians are inconvenienced by them to the point of being compelled to destroy these parts with fire and iron. This operation is performed in advance on all young girls in Abyssinia at the same age the boys are circumcised.

In the sixteenth century, he continues, the Portuguese Jesuits converted the King of Abyssinia and part of his people to Catholicism. When the missionaries observed the operation performed on the girls, they became convinced that, like the circumcision of the boys, it was a survival of Judaism, which had been practiced in Abyssinia, and they forbade it. "It turned out, however, that the Catholic girls no longer found husbands, because the men were unable to get used to what they considered a repulsive deformity." The Vatican sent a surgeon to Abyssinia to verify the facts. When the Pope read his report he told the Jesuits to allow the people to resume their ancient practice.

"As for the notion that these excrescences are produced artificially," Cuvier goes on, "it appears to be refuted today, if it is true that the Bushwomen have them in childhood. The woman that we have examined could hardly have taken any pleasure in procuring for herself an ornament that she was ashamed of and concealed with such care."

Physicians in later times, incidentally, have paid considerable attention to the Hottentot apron. The doctors Ploss and Bartels, in their monumental work *Das Weib,* quoted authorities who reported the apron was found throughout Europe. Dr. Robert Hartmann of Berlin declared he had observed it again and again in obstetrical examinations of German women. Dr. Max Bartels agreed it wasn't rare. He stated he occasionally found nymphae with just one lip overdeveloped; these cases, at least, he believed, were caused by masturbation.

But back to Cuvier. Proud of having pinned down the facts about the Hottentot apron, he took wax molds of Saartjie's genitals and anus. He also had several casts made of her cadaver. (One of these, it has been theorized, he gave to Réaux, who exhibited it.)

Next he proceeded to dissect Saartjie. He cut away her *tablier hottentot* and preserved it; this trophy of his science he later presented to the Académie Royale de Médecine. Sawing through her skull, he removed her brain and preserved it too.

In 1815 anthropology as a science was still to be born. The Bushman and the Hottentot were regarded as somewhat higher than the ape, somewhat lower than man. Examining Saartjie's skull Cuvier found characteristics that reminded him of both the black and the Mongol, but also of the animals. He dwelled upon the smallness of her nosebones. "In this last respect, especially, I have never seen a human head more like the ape's than hers." Her pelvic structure also reminded him of the apes. Her femurs too had a number of "characteristics of animality." He found the forward part of her brain was small because the skull was flat there, and he referred to the "cruel law that appears to have condemned races with flattened, compressed skulls to eternal inferiority." In the light of modern knowledge his observations seem biased and unscientific; but they were typical of his time and place.

About Saartjie's skin Cuvier made no special comment. The museum kept her skeleton, her brain, the wax molds, and one of the body casts, but not the skin. A South African professor has conjectured it was given to Réaux, who exhibited it. Dr. Robert Knox, the Scottish anatomist who played such a large role in the Burke and Hare story, reported in his *Races of Man* that he had seen "the stuffed skin of a Hottentot woman" in England. Perhaps it was Saartjie's.

Saartjie's remains became a permanent and highly valued feature of the museum's collection. Oddly, in 1827 her skull was reported stolen. Later that year it was mysteriously returned.

In time Saartjie's skeleton and cast passed into the possession of France's great anthropology museum, the Musée de l'Homme, which also inherited old documents and other Saartjie memorabilia.

In 1916 Professor R. Verneau of the natural history museum celebrated the one-hundredth anniversary of Saartjie's death with an article in the French journal *Anthropologie*. Among other things Verneau spoke of Saartjie's contract with Dunlop, the English surgeon, which mentioned she was to perform domestic duties for him.

I don't know if Dunlop required much domestic work of her, but she must have shown kindness to her numerous adorers; such was the claim of the scandalous gossip that has been handed down to us. Forty-three years ago, when I joined the museum, it was still being asserted she did not turn away those of her admirers who followed the ways of ancient Sodom. I am forced to admit that an examination of the wax casts we possess doesn't in any way contradict this gossip.

Saartjie, with her prognathism, big lips, broad nose, and prominent cheekbones, Verneau declared, had no proper claim to the title of Venus. "Her big backside, however, makes the day for our visitors."

But not for all. It certainly didn't for me on the day I went to see the Hottentot Venus.

I made my way through the crowded Paris streets to the Palais de Chaillot, which houses the Musée de l'Homme. Leaving the brilliant afternoon sunshine outside, I plunged into the recesses of the museum in search of Saartjie.

I found her eventually in an almost deserted hall. Standing in front of Case Number 33, I stared at Saartjie's bones, so carefully assembled and mounted more than a century and a half ago. Still I wasn't any closer to the real Saartjie. I was looking at only the framework that God the sculptor had used to hold one of his creations erect.

I saw Cuvier's painted plaster cast of her. Saartjie stands upright, balanced on her feet. Her eyes are shut tight. Her jaw is slack. Her body still shows the marks of the terrible malady that claimed her.

In life Saartjie, no matter what the professors said, had a sweet, feminine face and a winsome look that was captured by the artists who portrayed her. "Her character was gay," Cuvier said.

She was no Venus de Milo. But nature had endowed her with a great sexuality. To the men of her race and probably to many of the Europeans who saw her, the title of Hottentot Venus seemed fitting enough.

In death Saartjie is still a Venus, but a Venus of Sorrows. The plaster eloquently preserves her final agony. With her arms held slightly before her and a look of infinite woe on her face, she seems to be walking in a troubled sleep, groping her way out of the nightmare her life had become.

11   The Ugliest Woman in the World

A SAVAGE-LOOKING, weird little dwarf, she seems to be staring right into your eyes, holding you in a hypnotic spell.

She's dressed in a flashy red party frock that leaves bare her arms, her upper bosom, her legs. All are covered with hair. Her skin is yellow-brown and her apelike face is made more apelike still by an incredible growth of hair—soft, straight black hair that sprouts everywhere, almost burying her features. Hanging grotesquely from her chin is a black beard.

Her lips are huge and deformed. They thrust out from her face like the swollen borders of a great wound. Her nose is broad and squat, with big flat nostrils. Her ears are like strange tropical leaves; the earlobes are massive, and clumps of hair hang from them. Thick sideburns run across her lower cheeks and merge into a heavy mustache. Her large eyes, under bushy brows, are open wide in a glazed, unwavering stare. There is a kind of angry agony in them.

Only four-and-a-half feet tall, she looks like a giant next to her son. A tiny boy, he's dressed in boots, a white cloth around his loins, another over his shoulders. Most of his little body is bare so you won't overlook the heavy down that covers it. His baby face is hairy too. On a stand beside his mother he holds himself stiff and straight, like a lilliputian soldier.

Julia Pastrana's great twisted mouth is open. She seems about to tell you something—perhaps to reveal why she looks so agonized. If you want to hear her speak, however, you must be prepared for a long wait. An eternal wait. She and her little son were frozen forever in an almost perfect imitation of life by a Russian master embalmer one hundred and twenty years ago.

Maybe you have never heard of the hairy dwarf and her baby son before. But millions of people, all over Europe and the United States, have seen the two amazingly lifelike mummies at fairs, carnivals, and sideshows. And thousands, at least, have been moved to tears by their strange and terrible story.

Julia Pastrana, in her day, was one of the most sensational stars of the international stage and circus. Billed as The Bear Woman, The Ugliest Woman in the World, The Marvelous Hybrid, The Monster, or The Apewoman, she was exhibited from New Orleans to New York and Canada, from London to Berlin and Moscow. Her career was a brief candle. It flared up in 1854; it was snuffed out in 1860. In that short stretch of time—and after—she was so celebrated that reportedly she had up to fifty imitators, including some dead ones.

A lurid old leaflet, published in 1855 in Boston and sold in connection with her appearances, tells us as much about her origins as we're ever likely to know. P. T. Barnum, a contemporary showman, earned the title The Prince of Humbugs because he told such enormous lies to promote the attractions he featured. There's little reason to think Julia's manager, when he prepared his leaflet, was more scrupulous with the truth.

The leaflet was entitled *HYBRID INDIAN: The Misnomered Bear Woman, Julia Pastrana*. On its cover it bore a drawing of Julia, with her bizarre hairy face, arms, and shoulders, dressed in a broad-skirted gown, with pantalooned legs showing underneath. She was born, the leaflet relates, into a tribe of Root-Digger Indians living in the Sierra Madre Mountains in the state of Sinaloa, on the western coast of Mexico.

"Root Digger" was a term of contempt once used by whites to describe certain tribes of Indians supposedly too primitive to hunt or plant; their food was roots, locusts, bark, grubs, and anything else they could dig or catch. Anthropologists say these Indians lived in an environment so hostile that they had no choice.

The tribe that Julia belonged to, the leaflet tells us, looked just like her.

Their face and whole person is covered with a thick
black hair, and their features have a close resemblance to
those of a Bear and Orang Outang. Their mouths are elon-
gated with very thick lips. They have no front upper teeth,
but a strong jaw to masticate the food which they live on,
much like a brute.

All of this was somewhat easier to credit in 1855, when
Indians were little known and much hated. Representing
Julia as a member of a strange Indian tribe, perhaps a cross
between man and the animals, helped to make her seem more
exotic than she really was.

Today we know that her physical peculiarities—her dwarfed
stature, her extraordinary hairiness, and her abnormal
teeth—were the result of genetic mutation. It never rains but
it pours, the saying goes, and often an individual is born, like
Julia, not just with one, but with two or more birth defects.
Long after Julia's day there were two other famous human
oddities clothed with hair from head to foot, Jo-Jo the Dog-
Faced Boy and Lionel the Lion-Faced Man. Both were born
with just four teeth. Like these unusual individuals, Julia
was what is popularly called a freak.

At the edge of the mountains where Julia's tribe lived,
according to the leaflet, there was a small Mexican town
called Copala. Some of the women of the town used to go up
the mountainside to bathe in a lake there. One day, returning
home, they noticed that a Mrs. Espinosa who had gone up
with them had failed to return. A search party was organized,
but although they looked for her long and hard, not a trace
of her could be found. Deciding she must have drowned in the
lake, the party gave up the search.

"Six years afterward," the leaflet continues:

a Ranchero, who was hunting for his cattle on the mountain, heard a voice in a cave which he took to be a Mexican
woman. He went down to Copala and got a company of
men, who went up and surrounded the cave and by a great
stratagem succeeded in recovering Mrs. Espinosa.

Mrs. Espinosa had a curious story to tell. On the day she
had gone up the mountain to bathe, she wandered off from
her companions. Suddenly she found herself surrounded by
Indians. They took her to the top of the mountain and kept

her with them in a cavern in which they lived. Although the account doesn't mention it, she was probably adopted into the tribe and married to an Indian. This was the fate of thousands of white women (and men) who fell into the hands of the Indians in North America.

When Mrs. Espinosa was rescued she brought with her a two-year-old Indian girl. The mother of the girl had died when she was a few days old and the Indians placed the baby in the Mexican woman's arms. Mrs. Espinosa had cared for the infant and come to love her as her own.

In Copala Mrs. Espinosa took the child into her home. She had her christened, naming her Julia Pastrana, and she and her husband stood as godparents at the baptismal font.

After these convincing signs of affection, it's surprising to find that a few years later the Espinosas moved to Durango and didn't take Julia with them. Instead they left the child in the care of Pedro Sanchez, governor of the state of Sinaloa. What the governor's feelings were about Julia we don't know, but perhaps we can guess. Like other hairy children she probably already had a little beard and was quite a curiosity. Many kings and princes, especially in Spain, used to keep dwarfs as servants and entertainers in their households. The bearded girl dwarf must have been a source of considerable diversion in Governor Sanchez's palacio.

As Julia grew, so did her beard and her other abnormalities—the big nose, the protruding lips, the distorted ears, the glossy black hair that covered much of her face and the rest of her body. She was becoming a young woman, and no doubt she felt the normal desire of a woman for warmth, affection, love. But when she opened her great lips in an inviting smile, revealing her thick gums and malformed teeth, and her beard waggled, all she was likely to invite was laughter.

In April 1854 Julia ran away from the governor's palacio. Her reason, the leaflet states, was the "bad treatment" she had received.

What that treatment was, we can only imagine. Perhaps she had been taught to sing and dance for the entertainment of the governor's family and guests. She might have performed at fiestas for the assembled gentry, chanting a Spanish ballad of disappointed love in the sweet, sad voice that was to become famous, and clicking castanets in hands so small and delicate they seemed to belong to someone else.

And the listeners momentarily might have been carried away
by the pathos of the song, the weird appearance of the singer,
and the melancholy expression on her face. Then, after she
had stopped and the spell was shattered they would have
burst into laughter or jeers. Julia, while she shrank inside,
would have been obliged to smile and accept their derision
with grace. Then she would have turned and rushed back to
the kitchen—back to the piles of dishes and the mockery of
her fellow scullions.

But now she was twenty-two. She'd stood the ill treatment
of the Sanchez household as long as she could. And so, taking
her few belongings, she ran off into the night. She was returning to her people, the Indians of the mountains, although
she hadn't seen them since she was a child of two.

On the way, by a curious twist of chance Julia fell in with
a showman named Rates. He, it seems, instantly recognized
her possibilities. He persuaded the Indian girl to come to the
United States with him, where he assured her he would make
her fortune. In her troubled state of mind she wasn't hard to
convince. With Rates and a friend of his she set out for New
Orleans.

From New Orleans Julia was taken to New York City.
The heart of the city in those days centered around what is
the City Hall district today. The Astor House, Delmonico's,
the fashionable places of amusement were in that area.
Among them was P. T. Barnum's huge American Museum,
a five-floor emporium of entertainment. Just a few blocks
from Barnum's museum Julia was placed on exhibition at
Gothic Hall.

A bearded lady like Julia was a considerable novelty in
1854. Only the year before, Barnum had presented one from
Switzerland, Mme. Josephine Clofullia, who had drawn enormous crowds to his museum. There were some skeptics who
believed that only men properly had beards and that Madame
Clofullia just had to be a man masquerading in skirts. One
of these doubters, a William Charr, had brought a suit against
Barnum for fraud. In his defense at the trial in the Tombs
Court in July 1853 Barnum presented the testimony of well-
known physicians who said they had examined the Swiss
bearded lady and found incontrovertible proof that she was
a woman. The case was decided in Barnum's favor and his
museum was more crowded than ever.

Julia's manager decided that a little medical testimony

might help him sell his hairy protégée to the public. He wanted to verify not only that she was an authentic woman, but that she was one whose like had never been seen before. Why couldn't the certificate be worded to suggest, for example, that Julia was the offspring of a human and an ape?

For her medical examination Julia was taken to the office of a New York physician, Dr. Alex B. Mott. The certificate Mott gave Julia's manager was all he could have asked for. Among other things it declared:

> She is a perfect woman—a rational creature, endowed with speech, which no monster has ever possessed. She is therefore a HYBRID, wherein the nature of woman predominates over the brute—the Orang Outang. Altogether she is one of the most extraordinary beings of the present day.

When an entertainer gave a performance in those days it was called a levee. In preparation for her levees Julia had been given dancing lessons to expand her Mexican repertory. A quick learner with a natural grace startling in one so strangely formed, she soon was able to do the polka, the waltz, the schottische, the Highland fling, and other dances then in vogue. She also sang in Spanish. At her performances she answered questions about herself from the public; she was studying English but for the time being had to reply through an interpreter.

Julia's audiences were fascinated by her. They had seen one startling human oddity after another: Annie Swan, the Nova Scotia giantess, who stood seven feet five inches tall; Tom Thumb, the smallest man in the world, just twenty-five inches high; the Siamese twins, Chang and Eng, bound together by a ligament of flesh and blood; and others equally curious. Why shouldn't they take Dr. Mott's word that Julia was half woman, half orangutan? Theatrical reviewers encouraged the public's credulity. They referred to Julia as an "it." ("Its jaws, jagged fangs, and ears are terrifically hideous.... Nearly its whole frame is coated with long glossy hair. Its voice is harmonious, for this semi-human being is perfectly docile, and speaks the Spanish language.")

Julia's managers (they changed periodically) took her around the country. In February she was in New Orleans again. In August she was in Cleveland, in September in Boston, in November back in New York City.

Doctors and scientists around the country examined her. The charge had been raised that she was a black, and at her manager's request an Ohio physician declared he had compared her hair "with the hair of an African, under a high magnifying power, and from the comparison, [I] have no hesitation in saying that the individual in question possesses, by this test, NO TRACE OF NEGRO BLOOD." He decided that her other peculiarities "entitle her, I think, to the rank of a DISTINCT SPECIES." Samuel Kneeland, Jr., curator of comparative anatomy of the Boston Society of Natural History, examined her when she was in Boston, giving levees at the Horticultural Hall. He disagreed emphatically with the Ohio physician about her belonging to a separate species. To Mr. Kneeland she was "a perfect woman...she is certainly human." He said she was an Indian.

Later Julia toured Canada. Then, under the management of an American named Theodore Lent, who was to dominate the few tragic years she had left to live, she was taken to England in 1857.

Julia opened at the Regent Gallery in London in July. Lent invited members of the press for a special performance, and they were impressed. They had seen Mme. Clofullia in 1851, but that handsome lady, except for her beard, was like any other woman. By contrast Julia, dark, dwarfed, with her grotesque features and her hair-covered body, was like no one else they had ever encountered. She looked every bit the "wild girl" Lent said she was.

Julia had a good command of English now, and answered questions from the audience directly. The journalists commented on her lively sense of humor and the quickness with which she replied. She sang in English as well as Spanish. Her rendering of Tom Moore's "The Last Rose of Summer" brought tears to their eyes. (In the best tradition of the day she fondled a long-stemmed rose as she sang.) They were struck by the spirit and grace with which she danced, and didn't fail to observe how small and pretty her hands and feet were.

A photograph of Julia, in the possession of the Anthropological Institute of London, recalls this high moment of her success. She's wearing a gay, colorful frock that reaches just below her knees. It has a bouffant skirt that swirled as she danced; she wears no stockings, so the hairiness of her shapely legs can easily be seen. The frock is décolleté and armless, too, the better to show off the hair that covers her neck and arms. Fanciful appliquéed flowers, tendrils, leaves, and fruit curl over the dress like living things; the motif is repeated on her elegant little leather dancing shoes. Her hair is elaborately dressed, with long strands of curls thrusting out from her head, and a cross flashes on her bosom. With her chin high and her large sad eyes staring fixedly into the distance, she has the melancholy dignity of a tragic heroine.

Lancet, then as now the most respected medical journal in Great Britain, was curious about this strange apparition on its shores and decided she should be inspected. The magazine's representative, like everyone before him, was impressed by her remarkable hairiness. "Indeed, the whole of the body, excepting the palms of the hands and the soles of the feet, is more or less clothed with hairs." Yet her femaleness was unquestionable. "Her breasts are remarkably full and well-developed." The examiner found her nose peculiar; the nostrils "are remarkably flattened and expanded, and so soft as to seem to be destitute of cartilage." He commented on the large size of her mouth and the protrusion of her lips and asked her to open her mouth. Inside he was struck by the extraordinary thickening of the gum in front of the upper jaw; in front of the lower he saw a warty, hard growth.

Her teeth drew the examiner's special attention. "The lower set of teeth is perfect; but in the upper set the front teeth are all but deficient, the molars alone being properly developed."

Julia's teeth were always a subject of interest. A curiously different description of them was given by Alfred Russel Wallace to Charles Darwin, who with him developed the theory of evolution. Wallace's friend, Dr. T. Purland, a London dentist, reportedly had examined Julia's teeth and provided Wallace with the information.

"She had in the upper and lower jaw," wrote Darwin in his *Variations of Animals and Plants Under Domestication* some years later, "an irregular double set of teeth, one row being placed within the other, of which Dr. Purland took a cast. From the redundancy of teeth her mouth projected, and her face had a gorilla-like appearance."

The science of genetics hadn't yet been developed. Interestingly but mistakenly Darwin found a parallel between

Julia and other mammals, such as the whales and armadillos, that have both an unusual number of teeth and an unusual body covering.

When the season closed in London Lent took Julia to other English cities. Much of the bearded girl's life was a series of one-night stands. When she traveled by coach or train from one city to another or walked in the streets, she concealed her face under a heavy veil; if she hadn't she would have been constantly bothered by the curious. Lent obliged her to stay indoors as much as possible. He didn't want people to see for free what he expected them to pay up to three shillings' admission for.

It was a hard life for Julia. From eleven in the morning till nine at night, with a few hours out for meals, she appeared on the stage. But before? And after? On holidays? Often the only person she saw and spoke to was Lent. She cherished the hours she spent with him—he had taught her to read English, kept her supplied with novels, and showed her many kindnesses. But he was frequently away, making arrangements for her appearances. Her most constant companion was loneliness.

From England Lent took Julia to Germany. Their tour began in Berlin. The Germans were even more interested than the British in The Ugliest Woman in the World. Seeking to exploit her talents further, Lent decided to star her in a drama. Tom Thumb, Barnum's midget, had scored a great hit in a little play written especially for him during his French tour ten or twelve years earlier. The play had resorted to all sorts of tricks to emphasize the tiny stature of the miniature man. Why couldn't Julia's play make her out to be even more of a monster than she was?

Lent promptly found a German writer, and they dreamed up a plot for the play. When they arrived in Leipzig the piece was submitted to the police authorities. As soon as they gave their approval Lent went into rehearsal.

In late 1857 Julia opened in Leipzig. The play was called "The Farmer Cured." What the farmer was cured of is impossible now to say, but Julia's role must have been more appalling than appealing. After the second performance the authorities closed the show. For the rest of her stay in the city she performed her regular routine of songs and dances.

The editor of the *Gartenlaube,* a family magazine, decided that the furor Julia's play had aroused would make her a good subject for an interview. He wanted a picture of her, too, so he sent an artist as well as a reporter to her hotel. Lent received them warmly and presented them to "Miss Julia," as he called her.

"Since childhood," wrote the reporter, "neither of us had ever missed an opportunity to see any curiosity of this kind when one was shown in public. For sheer monstrosity, however, we can assure you that the creature that stood before us went far beyond anything we'd ever seen."

The writer described Julia's hairy, deformed face in detail. In her eyes he saw a kind of melancholy that aroused his sympathy.

When we entered, Miss Julia was occupied with preparations for her toilette. The interruption didn't seem to bother her a bit, and she greeted us with a friendly handshake. When she learned that my companion intended to conjure her lovely features onto his drawing pad with his pencil, she appeared very pleased and devoted most of her attention to him.

Our interview was conducted in English, and I must admit that she expressed herself with understanding and sureness on any subject we talked about.... In a pleased tone she told me about the triumphs of her American and English tours. She even claimed she'd received more than twenty offers of marriage. When I asked her why she hadn't bestowed her hand on any of these suitors she replied "they weren't rich enough." I strongly suspect her "guardian" had talked this nonsense into the poor creature. Still, I suppose many a money-minded Yankee might not be opposed to a union that assured him of a substantial income through the monstrosity of his bride.

Next Lent took Julia to Paris, where she was a sensation all over again. She appeared with the Renz Riding Troupe, one of the big equestrian attractions of the era. When the troupe went on tour Julia and Lent went with them. Her reputation had reached a peak. Lent became aware that rival managers were showing unusual interest in her. Several began to attend her performances and linger afterward to talk to her. Lent's canny showman's instinct told him they were trying to steal her away from him. When he asked her about it, her only reply was an embarrassed laugh.

If Julia were to leave him and go with one of his competitors, Lent realized, the consequences for him could be catastrophic. He had exhibited her for close to four years. Her reputation was international. Other bearded ladies there were, but he knew he could never find another to hold a candle to her.

What could he do to keep Julia from leaving? The solution to his quandary, when he found it, was so simple he was astonished he hadn't thought of it before.

For Julia Lent's proposal of marriage was the most wonderful surprise of her life. She had loved him almost since their first encounter. No other man had ever been so close to her. The flowers he had given her when she was sick or sad, the little presents—it would have taken a more worldly-wise person than Julia to perceive that such acts of kindness inspired her to give better performances; consequently more money flowed into Lent's pocket. But love-hungry Julia took his attentions as signs of genuine affection. How could she help but believe he loved her—especially after he had told her so himself?

On the morning of Julia's wedding her hairy face was radiant. It was touched, almost, with a kind of prettiness. "He loves me," she said to her friend Friederike Gossmann with a happy smile. "He loves me—for my own sake."

Without taking time out for a honeymoon the pair continued their tour. Before long Julia became pregnant. Lent, his detractors said, was hoping that Julia would have a baby that looked just like herself. Mme. Clofullia, Barnum's famous bearded lady, had given birth to a son who was covered with hair, and the boy had been an added attraction at her levees in New York City. Why couldn't Julia also have a hairy baby?

And what could be more understandable than that all Julia wanted was a normal-looking child who wouldn't have to suffer the way she did every day of her life?

Julia was appearing in Moscow, in 1860, when she felt her first labor pains. The birth was complicated and painful. She and the baby barely survived.

For most mothers, seeing their newborn child is a joyful moment. Not for Julia. The tiny boy the midwife placed by her side was sickly and covered with hair. He didn't even have the strength to nurse.

Nature has her own way of dealing with her blunders. Most infants with serious congenital defects are born dead or they die soon afterward. Thirty-six hours after Julia's baby came into the world he stopped breathing.

Three days later Julia, who had been tenuously holding on to life, let go. "I die happy," she said. "I know I have been loved for myself."

Almost overnight Lent's world disintegrated. He had been a husband and a father. Now he was neither. He had been the successful manager of one of the world's most celebrated human oddities. Now he had lost her forever.

Or had he?

At the University of Moscow, Lent had heard, a medical professor named Sokolov had developed a remarkable technique of embalming by injection. Not only did it preserve the deceased indefinitely, something beyond the powers of ordinary embalmers; it also made the dead person seem almost alive.

Lent called on Sokolov. The professor had heard of the strange bearded lady and declared he was eager to see what his art could accomplish with her. The bodies of Julia and her son had been autopsied at the Anatomical Institute. Sokolov embalmed them there.

When Lent viewed the two cadavers a few days later, he was astonished at how lifelike they appeared. The faces were especially striking. They looked like extraordinarily good portraits molded by a master craftsman in wax. Peering closer at Julia's face Lent was finally able to convince himself that it wasn't wax but her own skin, prepared in some wonderful way. The eyes were even more remarkable. They were wide open, and the eyeballs, of glass, had dark irises, just like Julia's real eyes. Somehow, unexplainably, they still seemed to express the agony he had so often seen in them when she was alive.

It was hard to believe the figures in front of him were really dead bodies. Lent was certain others would have doubts too. At his request Professor Sokolov gave him a document attesting that these were the authentic remains of Julia Pastrana and her son and that he had embalmed them in Moscow.

Lent had a cabinet made of wood and glass, placed the two mummies inside, and advertised that he had a more wonderful show than ever. And so after barely a week's vacation the dead woman was back on exhibition, coining money for her husband.

The American and his little family continued to travel.

Now he no longer had to fear that Julia would desert him—
nor she that he would ever stop loving her.

In London in 1862 the British nature writer Dr. Frank
Buckland was invited to view a great natural curiosity: a
creature, belonging to an unknown species, that had been
embalmed by a new process. Since he had an extensive knowledge of ancient mummies he was particularly eager to see
this modern one. When he entered the hall in Piccadilly he
saw a dark little figure standing erect and silent upon a table.

"Julia Pastrana!" he exclaimed.

Five years earlier, when Julia was being exhibited in Regent Street, Buckland had chatted with her. He remembered
her "exceedingly good figure" and noted how well it was preserved in the mummy. He recalled, too, her sweet voice, her
well-turned ankle, and her fine taste in music and dancing.

Lent took his mummified family to Sweden, France, Germany, and other countries. His exhibit was in great demand;
the tragic story and the macabre presence of the two mummies drew large crowds. His success inspired other exhibitors,
who obtained the remains of other ladies, had them embalmed, and added beards to them—or simply had figures
made of wax to look like the bearded dwarf. At one time,
reportedly, dozens of imitation Julia Pastranas, some with
mummified babies, were being shown.

These impostors must have been a serious threat to Lent.
What could he do to put them out of the running?

In his travels Lent came to Karlsbad, in Germany, where
he heard of a businessman named Bartels, a widower, who
had a bearded daughter named Marie. The girl, then eighteen, was never allowed out of the house by her father, who
was said to mistreat her. Marie, although she was a graceful
person with a full, womanly figure, had heavy masculine
features, and her entire body, except for her breasts, was
covered with hair. She had been shaving—several times a
day—since her confirmation.

After making the girl's acquaintance one day when her
father was away, Lent called again when he was in. Soon
afterward the showman declared that he wanted to marry
Marie. The proposal was agreeable to Bartels, but before giving his consent he made Lent promise he would never compel
the girl to appear on the stage as a bearded lady.

Marie's wedding day proved to be the last time a razor
touched her face. From then on Lent made her let her beard

grow. He gave her dancing lessons. He had her trained to ride a horse bareback and do tricks on it. He taught her English. And then he presented her in carnivals and circuses, along with his two mummies. He called her Zeñora—Miss Zeñora Pastrana.

In time Zeñora bore Lent a son. If he had hoped for a hairy addition to his family, he was disappointed again. The child was altogether normal.

Luck ran out on Lent in 1884 when he was touring Russia with his show. His son died. Soon thereafter Lent began to show alarming signs of mental disorder. He became manic; shouting with joy he tore up banknote after banknote and flung the pieces to the winds. He was taken to a mental hospital, where he died soon afterward.

As Lent's heir Zeñora was now the owner of the mummies of Julia and her baby. After a stay with her father, who treated her no better than before, she returned to show business, occasionally exhibiting with the mummies. She died in 1900.

The mummies subsequently came into the possession of a Norwegian showman named Castan, who exhibited them in Scandinavia with his Panoptikon, a wax museum. Later they were owned by another Norwegian, named Lund, the proprietor of a tivoli or amusement park at Oslo. (His son owns them today.)

In 1972 Lund sent the two mummies to the United States, where they were exhibited at county fairs by the Boston firm of Gooding's Million Dollar Midways. How the remains passed through Customs is a mystery, since dead bodies aren't usually allowed into the country unless they're being brought home for burial or are mummies destined for display in a museum. According to reports, American showmen offered large sums for the purchase of the two bodies. But the owner had them shipped back to Norway.

In 1973 Julia's owner was touring with the mummified "Apewoman," as he called her, in Sweden. There was a rising tide of protest against the exhibition. When the show got to a place called Hudiksvall, the authorities halted it and the mummies and their owner were sent back over the border to Norway. According to the Swedish press the bishop of Oslo was expected to arrange a cremation or burial. But neither ever occurred. Perhaps the property rights of Julia's owner took precedence.

At last report the two mummies were still in the hands of the Norwegian tivoli proprietor. He has said he might give them to a museum. Or, more likely, he might sell them to an American carnival operator if they could ever agree upon a price.

Perhaps they already have—and any day now you may see Julia Pastrana pull into town in her palace car, an elegant motorized caravan as big as a house, to hold her silent levees.

INSIDE the mausoleum the gloom, dense and ominous, weighed on the two men like a heavy black shroud. For Power, the custodian, it was indeed a dark hour, and even though the temperature in Memorial Hall was warm enough for November, he couldn't stop shivering. In the growing dimness—he could barely make out the face of Hay, the Pinkerton detective from Chicago—the minutes dragged by like hours.

Power finally broke the silence: "What time do you suppose it is?"

"Getting on toward seven, I would say." Neither man dared to strike a match to look at his timepiece. If the thieves came early, the light could warn them of the trap before it was fully set.

Minutes later they heard footsteps outside. Hay peered through the grillework of the door. "It's our boys."

Power opened up cautiously. Hay scrutinized each shadowy face as he identified the detectives one by one before letting them in. They were: Elmer Washburn, retired head of the United States Secret Service and former police chief of Chicago; English, his right-hand man; McDonald, a Chicago detective; McGinn, a Pinkerton detective; and Tyrrell, whom Power had met earlier....

Tyrrell, chief of the United States Secret Service office in Chicago, had shown up abruptly at the monument that morning. With him was old Major Stuart, Power's boss, chairman of the Monument Association.

When Tyrrell and Stuart informed Power of the plot, he was incredulous.

"Unbelievable?" Stuart shoved a telegram under his nose. Power read it in a daze. Lincoln's son had signed it himself.

The major sounded testy. "Show Tyrrell around the monument. There's very little time. The attempt will be made tonight."

Whenever Power escorted visitors through the mausoleum he always felt a swell of patriotism and pride, a keen sense of history. This time all he felt was horror.

The monument-tomb was built in the shape of a rectangle. At the south end was Memorial Hall, the museum room. Opposite it, at the north end, was the catacomb, with the sarcophagus of the great man. In between stretched a damp cellar. Here the supports for the terrace, the pedestals, and the massive obelisk on top of the monument formed a maze of passageways.

They were standing in Memorial Hall. "Show me the cellar," Tyrrell said.

Power lit two lamps and, keeping one for himself, gave the other to Tyrrell. He then led the Secret Service man into the cellar.

Holding their sputtering lamps, they walked through the winding black corridors. "I call this the labyrinth," Power said. They reached the alcove just in back of the catacomb. He paused. "There's no access to the catacomb from here. To get in there we have to go back out and around the monument. But from this point you can hear any sound that's made in the catacomb. Even though the wall is two feet thick."

"Really?" The Secret Service man's eyes narrowed. "If I stationed a man in this spot, he could hear any noises the thieves might make in there?"

"Absolutely. Would you like me to show you? Just wait here."

Power quickly retraced his steps to Memorial Hall. He emerged into the gray day, hurried around the base of the monument, and unlocked the catacomb door.

Inside, quite out of breath, he stopped by the gleaming sarcophagus. Only a few inches of marble separated him from the great man's broken body.

It felt like a sacrilege. He rapped smartly on the stone with his knuckles. "Did you hear that?"

Tyrrell's voice came to him through the wall. "I heard it fine. This spot will do fine. Thanks."

Power hastened back to Memorial Hall, where Tyrrell was already waiting. The custodian then led him out and around to the catacomb.

"You say this is the only entrance? Not much protection, this small door of metal rods. How is it locked at night?"

Power showed him the little padlock. "If only we had realized..."

They went inside. The Secret Service man stood for a moment by the sarcophagus, struck silent by the great name inside the funeral wreath of marble, and the immortal words etched above it: "With malice toward none; with charity for all." Then he was all business again as he examined the construction of the sarcophagus. "Let's get on with it."

Back outside, in gray daylight, they climbed up the steps to the terrace on top of the monument. They looked out over the grounds; Power pointed to the roads and explained where they led. Tyrrell kept checking his watch. He took a quick look at the statue, the empty pedestals, the tall marble-faced obelisk. Everywhere he asked about distances and wrote them down in a pocket notebook.

"Well, now I have to get back to town. I have a meeting with the detectives." He told the custodian he could expect a visit from the two thieves, Hughes and Mullen, that afternoon. "I know almost every move they're going to make." He smiled. "I have an undercover man planted in the gang. Swigles. Without him we never would have gotten wind of this business.... The blackguards would have pulled it off, Power, and you and I, we'd both be in the soup." He described the plotters so Power would recognize them, and then he rushed off.

At three P.M. the two men scrawled their names—false ones, to be sure—in the monument register. One of the visitors matched his description: Hughes, the villain with the long beard and the sorrowful, patient eyes. (The younger man, Power would learn later, was Louis Swigles, Tyrrell's undercover man.)

Hughes asked the questions. He pretended he was merely curious.

"How is the catacomb locked at night?"

"Is there a guard on duty?"

"How heavy is the casket?"

"Has it ever been opened?"

"Did you see the body?"

"What condition is it in?"

Power answered every question fully, naturally, as Tyrrell had directed: like ordinary questions from an ordinary visitor. It was not easy on Power's insides.

After the two men left the monument he watched as they made a sharp-eyed inspection of the grounds and headed back toward town.

Now, four hours later in the damp darkness of Memorial Hall, Tyrrell was hurrying through his final preparations. He gestured toward the labyrinth. "Lead the way, Power."

Power took up an unlit lamp in one hand. With the other he reached out for Tyrrell's hand. Tyrrell took another detective's hand, and that man another's. When they were all holding hands, like a line of nervous schoolboys, the custodian led them to the left, into the midnight of the labyrinth.

They reached a point in the corridor where no light could be seen from outside. Power lit the lamp and gave it to Tyrrell. As they started to move again, Power explained the layout. In the alcove close to the catacomb Tyrrell told them to stop.

"English, this is your post. Just wait here and listen. As soon as you hear them start to open up the sarcophagus, come and report to me. We'll leave a couple of lighted lamps in the corridor so you can find your way back to the hall."

English nodded and they left him. As they approached the hall again, Tyrrell blew out his lamp. "Take off your shoes, men. Make yourselves comfortable. And keep quiet. It may be a long wait."

It was. Ninety minutes went by before the detectives heard the sounds they were listening for.

Light poured through the grille in the door, washing away the darkness. The thieves were outside, holding up a lantern, trying to see into the hall. Tyrrell had expected that. The grille was covered with cloth on the inside.

The light disappeared. Apparently the thieves were satisfied. Footsteps crunched on the gravel, moving away toward the catacomb. Still nobody in the hall dared to move. The slightest sound could raise an echo in the monument.

Time passes slowly in the dark, and patience is its only measure.... Now light flooded through the grille once again. A voice whispered a password outside the door. Tyrrell opened up.

It was Swigles, the ex-con turned undercover man, who had duped the plotters into accepting him as one of their own.

"Hughes and Mullen are sawing away at the padlock on the catacomb door. Shouldn't take them long to get it off."

He padded off into the night, back to his companions.

Then: Footfalls murmuring toward them from the labyrinth. The detectives ran cold fingers over the heavy pistols in their pockets....

It was English, back from his post in the alcove. "They're working on the sarcophagus. I heard a grating noise through the wall. Like they were lifting the lid. Then some thuds...from a hammer, I guess."

Tyrrell nodded. "Stay here."

Well, the play is going into its last act, he thought. It was curious the way things had turned out—altogether bizarre. Because Tyrrell had put the cuffs on a man named Ben Boyd some thirteen months before, two crazy ghouls were now trying to steal the body of Abraham Lincoln....

Benjamin Boyd was one of the masters of American counterfeiting. Born in Cincinnati, Ohio, in 1834, Boyd was the son of an engraver. He made his first counterfeit plate, a note on the State Bank of Ohio, before he was twenty-one. From his versatile hands came one plate after another, producing bills so convincing, they were admired by the very banks they defrauded. In time he was said to be the best letterer on steel in the world.

The United States Secret Service came into existence in 1865. Its establishment was authorized, it is said, by President Lincoln on April 14—the very day he was assassinated. Its only purpose at the start was to fight counterfeiters. Undermanned and underfunded, it had an uphill struggle all the way.

In February 1875 Elmer Washburn, then chief of the Secret Service, set out to break up the syndicate of counterfeiters and passers of bogus currency allied with Boyd. In charge of the operation he placed his ace Midwestern operative, Patrick D. Tyrrell, chief of the Chicago office of the service.

In October 1875 Tyrrell swooped down on Boyd's headquarters in Fulton, Illinois. Boyd and his wife were captured, and so was a hoard of counterfeit money and plates. Convicted, Boyd was sentenced to ten years in Joliet Penitentiary in Illinois.

Big Jim Kneally was the boss of a ring of counterfeiters and "coneymen"—passers of counterfeit money—associated with Boyd. With his master engraver put away, Big Jim saw hard times ahead. He still had a store of Boyd's fake bills, and his ring continued to pass them. But when that money was gone, where could he hope to get anything nearly as good?

Meanwhile Boyd's counterfeit money kept turning up in the Chicago district. Tyrrell suspected it was coming from local members of Big Jim's ring. But suspicion is one thing, proof another. To get the evidence he needed, he called in Louis Swigles, a young ex-convict turned stool pigeon—in the language of that day, a "roper."

Swigles's assignment took him often to a dingy Chicago saloon called The Hub. A hangout of drifters and criminals, The Hub was owned by Big Jim but operated for him by Terrence Mullen. In the bar, liquor was sold honestly enough; the back room, however, was a meeting place for Big Jim's "shovers" of counterfeit. One of these was Jack Hughes, a fugitive from the law, who stood high on Tyrrell's "wanted" list.

To win the confidence of the coneymen Swigles saw to it that they learned about his criminal record. He also told them he was the Number One grave robber of the Chicago area. This daring and dangerous business made a big impression on them, and they looked on Swigles with favor. He, in turn, soon found out what they were up to.

The story he related to Tyrrell on October 27, 1876, was the most bizarre the Secret Service man had ever heard.

Big Jim Kneally had been trying to find an engraver who could provide him with counterfeit printing plates as good as those made by Ben Boyd. He hadn't succeeded.

Since Boyd was the only man able to do the job, Big Jim decided to get him out of Joliet. But not by a jailbreak—that might kill the goose that made the golden plates. Instead Big Jim planned to kidnap the body of Abraham Lincoln and trade him to the authorities in exchange for Boyd. Mullen and Hughes were picked to do the job.

"They're going to load it on a wagon and drive like the

dickens all the way to northern Indiana," Swigles said, rolling his eyes. "They're going to bury it there in the sand dunes. Then they'll open up negotiations with the authorities and offer to exchange Lincoln for a pardon for Ben Boyd.

"But wait till you hear this. Mullen and Hughes have never done anything like this before. They're impressed by my record as a body snatcher. They've invited me to come along and show them how. I'm also to provide a wagon and a teamster to carry away the body."

Tyrrell immediately got off a wire to his chief, James L. Brooks, in Washington, D.C., reporting what he had learned. The following day Tyrrell had his reply. He was to get in touch with Lincoln's only surviving son, Colonel Robert T. Lincoln, a prominent Chicago attorney, and talk the case over with him.

Tyrrell called on Colonel Lincoln. Appalled, the President's son said he wanted the Secret Service to do everything it could to protect his father's body. From the Secretary of the Treasury came special authorization for Tyrrell to move against the plotters.

On November 2 Tyrrell wired Washington again. Swigles had just been to see him. The gang had met in Swigles's place the night before and Mullen had revealed another angle of the plot. Besides demanding Boyd's freedom, the gang would ask that the indictment against Hughes be dropped—and a ransom of two hundred thousand dollars be paid—before they returned the President's body.

On November 6 Swigles reported that the gang would be going to Springfield that night on the nine o'clock train. They planned to break into Lincoln's tomb the next night. "That's Election Day," Swigles pointed out. "They figure everyone will be in town for the election. The cemetery and the monument will be deserted. No one will interfere while they're stealing the body."

With no time to lose, Tyrrell pinned down his strategy. He had no alternative but to let the plotters go ahead. Only if he caught them red-handed—in the act of removing the body—could he be sure of convincing a jury of their guilt.

No men of his own being available, he hurriedly borrowed a few. This operation was the biggest one of his career. He had planned it with meticulous care. Yet to carry it off he was depending on men whom, except for Chief Washburn, he barely knew.

In a pinch, could he really count on them?

As it turned out, he couldn't.

Half an hour after English had reported the plotters were working on the sarcophagus, Swigles was back at the door of Memorial Hall.

"They've lifted the marble cover and the end off the sarcophagus. And they've pulled the coffin partway out. They just sent me to fetch the wagon and teamster." He winked. There was no wagon, no teamster. "They're waiting for me at the catacomb door."

"You've done your part. The rest is up to us."

Tyrrell whispered to the detectives. Their pistols clicked as they cocked the hammers. Washburn, the retired chief of the Secret Service, was to stay behind; the others followed Tyrrell out the door.

Cautiously they skirted the east side of the monument, moving toward the catacomb. Tyrrell reached the catacomb door. It was shut. There was no one in sight. He pushed open the door. Inside, complete darkness.

"Hands up! Come out with your hands in the air!"

No answer.

"Throw down your guns and give yourselves up."

Still no answer.

He struck a match and stepped into the catacomb. Shadows leaped grotesquely around him. A loose marble slab lay across the sarcophagus; the marble top was propped against the back wall, where the President's young sons lay in the crypts. The front slab, with the great man's name, leaned against the side of the sarcophagus. The cedar coffin had been pulled out a foot or more. By the door lay the burglars' tools and the broken padlock.

"They must have gone off to hide nearby as a precaution while Swigles went to fetch the wagon," he said to the detectives. "They have to be somewhere around." And more urgently: "Get moving! We've got to find them."

As the detectives scattered, Tyrrell heard an explosion. One of the Pinkertons, Hay, had accidentally discharged his pistol.

"God, now we've lost them for sure!" Tyrrell moaned.

The moon had begun to rise. He raced desperately up the steps to the terrace on top of the mausoleum to get a look around the grounds.

Revolver in hand, Tyrrell walked swiftly around the terrace. Up ahead, close to one of the columns, he saw the form of a man. He raised his gun instantly and fired. The man dived behind the column, shooting as he moved.

He's going to try to escape down the other side of the terrace, Tyrrell thought. He ran to intercept him. He caught a glimpse of the man and fired.

Gunfire flashed at him from two different directions. Both of the body snatchers were on the terrace!

He raced to the head of the stairs. "Up here!" he called to the detectives below.

All at once a man stepped hesitantly from behind the column. "Tyrrell, for God's sake—is that you?" Another man came out and joined him.

The two on the terrace were not the body snatchers after all. They were the Pinkertons, McGinn and Hay, returned from where Tyrrell had sent them, sooner than he had expected. Only by the purest chance had they failed to blow each other's brains out.

Where had the ghouls gone—to Springfield? Tyrrell's old chief, Washburn, had hurt his foot and they needed to get a carriage for him. More time lost. When they got back to Springfield Tyrrell sent three of his party to search for the body snatchers.

But the ghouls might just as well have been on their way back to Chicago. With the two other detectives he rushed to make the midnight train. Swigles joined them.

They made it in time. Swigles left them as soon as they got on board. His cover had to be protected until the plotters were behind bars. The detectives combed the train from one end to the other. No Hughes. No Mullen.

Shocking as it was, the attempt to steal Lincoln's body on November 7 made few headlines, except in Illinois, Lincoln's home state, where the story became political fodder. Democrats charged that the Republicans had planned the kidnapping to make it look like a Democratic attempt to get even with Lincoln the Republican, and that the incident was intended to take place just before the election, but that the timing had misfired. Others asserted it was a hoax contrived by Elmer Washburn, hoping to cover himself with glory so he would win reappointment as Chicago's chief of police.

As for Hughes and Mullen, neither in Springfield nor Chicago could Tyrrell and his men find a trace of them. Fortunately he still had his ace in the hole, Swigles, whose standing with the Kneally ring hadn't been shaken by the fiasco in Oak Ridge Cemetery.

On November 17 Swigles reported that Hughes, after hiding out on his father's farm, had finally returned to Chicago. Should he be picked up? If he wasn't, he could get away. On the other hand, there was a good chance he would lead the Secret Service to Mullen. With three of his men Tyrrell immediately began tailing the body snatcher.

At eleven that night the detectives watched as Hughes approached a familiar address, 245 West Madison Street. It was Mullen's saloon, The Hub.

Peering through the window, Tyrrell saw his gamble was about to pay off. There was Mullen, standing near the bar, talking to Hughes as though nothing had happened.

One at a time Tyrrell's men entered the saloon. Each sat down close to an exit and ordered a drink. A few minutes later Tyrrell walked in. Hughes looked up. Instantly recognizing the newcomer as the Secret Service agent who had arrested him a few months earlier, he jumped to his feet and ran for the back door. A burly detective blocked his way. Another detective grabbed Mullen. The two men were shackled and carted off to Chicago's Central Police Station. Later Tyrrell took them back to Springfield.

Illinois at that time had no statute prohibiting body snatching. (One was passed three years later.) A special grand jury was convened. The charges it came up with were conspiracy and attempted theft of the President's coffin, valued at seventy-five dollars by its owner, the National Lincoln Monument Association. The defense argued that Mullen and Hughes were in Springfield on November 7 on lawful business; that they were the innocent victims of a plot engineered by Elmer Washburn so he could win back his old job as Chicago's police commissioner.

The jury wouldn't buy it. On May 31, 1877, the two would-be body snatchers were found guilty. They were sentenced to a year at hard labor at Joliet.

And what of the President's body and the broken sarcophagus?

For two days the catacomb remained just as the thieves

had left it, except for a shiny new padlock on the door. Then workmen pushed the red cedar coffin back into the sarcophagus and cemented the marble slabs in place.

Five nights later John T. Stuart, chairman of the Lincoln Monument Association and the President's first law partner, couldn't sleep. One obsessive thought kept running through his mind: What if another attempt were made and the thieves succeeded?

A more secure resting place had to be found for the remains of the Great Emancipator. Consequently the concrete seal was cracked open a second time, and off came the marble slabs. The casket was lifted out and the empty sarcophagus cemented shut. Stuart and a handful of his intimates—mostly elderly men who had known the President—wheezed and gasped as they moved the five-hundred-pound coffin through the catacomb door, outside into the black night, and around the mausoleum and into Memorial Hall. They swung around through the corridors of the labyrinth. They came to the point close to the middle of the monument that had been chosen for the reburial and set the coffin down on some planks.

"You fellows look exhausted," Power told them. "Leave the rest to me. I'll start digging the grave tomorrow. Go on home now."

During the following days, as the custodian dug he noticed the ground was sopping wet. There was a leak from the terrace above.

"It's unthinkable to bury the President's coffin in water," he complained to Stuart.

The lawyer nodded. "Cover the box with some of the planks and leave it above ground, just where it is. We'll have to work out something better."

And there the coffin remained, under its covering of planks, for two long years, while thousands and thousands of patriotic Americans continued to file into the catacomb and pause before the empty sarcophagus—completely convinced the martyred President lay right there beside them.

In 1878 the coffin was reburied in a dry area in another part of the labyrinth. And when Mary Todd Lincoln died four years later, she was laid to rest at the President's side. But such were the obsessions of the Great Emancipator's devotees that the Lincolns were reburied three more times before they acquired a final resting place. In 1887 a group calling itself the Lincoln Guard of Honor, dedicated to protecting the President's remains and celebrating his memory, secretly moved both coffins to a more secure spot, a vault of mortar and brick in the floor of the catacomb. By 1900 the monument had begun falling apart, and the state decided to tear it down and rebuild it from the ground up. With great secrecy, a few feet from the tomb a mass grave was excavated, and in it were buried the coffins of the President, Mrs. Lincoln, their three sons, and a grandson.

It took fifteen months to rebuild the monument. With relatives, dignitaries, and the Lincoln Guard of Honor looking on, the grave was opened up and a steam derrick raised the coffins. Lincoln's body was restored to its marble sarcophagus and the coffins of his family were placed in the crypts in the back wall of the catacomb. Remembering the attempted body snatching, Colonel Robert Lincoln ordered one of the new burglar alarms to be installed.

A month later Robert Lincoln visited the tomb and started to worry again. He was now the head of the Pullman train company. The company's founder, George M. Pullman, had made so many enemies in his money-centered life that it was thought necessary to protect his remains from them by burying his coffin in a new kind of vault—inside a steel cage that was then filled with Portland cement. The colonel wanted the same kind of security for his father, and he was ready to pay for it.

Thirty people came quietly to the monument for the President's reburial in the new ten-foot-deep grave: Illinois officials and members of the Lincoln Guard of Honor. There had been rumors that the body inside the President's casket wasn't Lincoln at all, or that it was a statue. Some of those who came insisted on making certain it was the President they were burying.

A plumber went into action with chisels and acetylene torch, working his way to the lead inner coffin. At last he was ready. A hush came over the witnesses as he began to lift up a square of lead. A strange, pungent odor rose from the opening, stinging people's nostrils and throats. The group pressed closer....

Abraham Lincoln's face was a powdered bronze. Someone remembered that after the assassination, when the President's body was making its seventeen-hundred-mile journey back to his hometown, Springfield, the skin had suddenly turned almost black. In Philadelphia an embalmer applied a heavy coating of white chalk to the face to make it more presentable. The chalk was still there.

The pillow on which the President's head rested had crumbled. The head had fallen back. The features that the whole world revered were shrunken but recognizable; who did not know the shock of black hair, the short black chin whiskers, the wart on the cheek, the strong nose? The arched, questioning eyebrows had disappeared, but the look of infinite sadness was still on his face. Small dots of yellow mold specked the black suit; it was the same one he had worn at his second inauguration. Vestiges of his white kid gloves—he disliked gloves but used to wear them to please Mrs. Lincoln, as long as she was looking—were still on his hands.

It was time for dust to return to dust. The piece of green-hued lead that had been lifted, was pressed down and soldered in place, and the coffin was closed. Awed, shaken, silent, the group watched the casket descending to the bottom of the steel cage. A gray tide of liquid cement washed over both casket and cage, and they were buried from sight forever.

CHARLOT. *You may not know him by that name—but I'm sure you've seen him sometime. More people have than any man that ever lived. In Tibetan monasteries, on the banks of the Ganges, in central Africa they adore him. His fans number more than a billion.*

"I'm known," Charlie Chaplin once said proudly, "in parts of the world by people who have never heard of Jesus Christ."

Corsier-sur-Vevey is a tiny, picturesque Swiss village perched halfway up the side of Mount Pèlerin. Below it sparkle the incredibly blue waters of Lake Geneva. Across the lake rise the Dents du Midi, rugged, snowy giants crowding one upon another.

Corsier is a quiet place. Vevey, on the lake below, is larger, livelier. Milk chocolate was invented there a hundred years ago and the town has never been the same since; today it is the headquarters of the huge Nestlé Corporation. But mostly this part of the Vaud Riviera is a haven for vacationers and retirees, a peaceful, orderly place, a place where hardly anything ever happens.

Until that day in March.

Mme. Erika Stirnimann lived in a house just fifty yards from Corsier's neat little cemetery. At 10 A.M. she locked the door to her apartment and headed for town to do some shopping.

Mme. Stirnimann's route took her past the cemetery.

187

Whenever she walked by she would look over the low stone wall. Charlot's grave was there and it was always covered with flowers. The sight of the colorful blooms never failed to lift her spirits. But not today. All she could see were disorderly piles of earth scattered over the plot.

Where are the flowers? she wondered. *Ah, the gardener must be getting ready to put in a fence. Or maybe he's just changing the flowers.*

She thought no further about what she had seen, nor did she consider it worth mentioning to anyone in the village as she went about her errands.

Much later, about 2 P.M., Etienne Buenzod came into the cemetery. Buenzod was the communal gravedigger. In a place as small as Corsier he seldom had much digging to do. It was just a tour of inspection.

Looking across the tiny graveyard Buenzod noticed the earth heaped about Charlot's plot. Like Mme. Stirnimann he promptly supplied himself with an explanation. *So the family is going to put up a monument,* he thought. Nothing very startling about that. Charlot had been Corsier's most celebrated resident, and probably its wealthiest.

Still Buenzod felt offended that, without his knowledge, outsiders had been puttering about in his cemetery. He walked toward Charlot's plot, close to the stone wall, to get a better look. At the head of the grave, he noted, the austere white cross was still in place. Then he stopped, stupefied.

At his feet gaped an enormous hole.

Buenzod stood for a moment, trying to make sense of the ugly wound in the earth, with the dirt scattered wantonly around it. Here and there a half-buried flower showed its bruised, soiled head.

A dog would have done a neater job, he told himself. *An exhumation? They would have asked me to do it.* The horror grew inside him. He hurried toward the exit.

As the gravedigger was running out, some people were coming in. Ever since Charlot had been laid to rest two months before, tourists had been visiting the cemetery in increasing numbers. Often as many as fifty in a single day. Like pilgrims to a holy place they came. To stand beside the grave and talk quietly about the wistful-faced little man who had charmed the whole world.

"Where is Charlot's grave?" asked one of them.

Buenzod's agitated hand waved them back. "The cemetery

is closed. Come back again another day." And he hastened off toward the town clerk's office.

They watched him disappear down the lane and then they went in. A handful of them and some of the townspeople were standing around the opening in the ground, arguing and gesticulating, when the police cars roared up. Politely but firmly gendarmes began shooing them out.

Jean-Paul Tenthorey was the *juge informateur*—the examining magistrate in charge. He sent inspectors of the Sûreté (the Swiss FBI) to comb the cemetery, the environs. Electronic flashes clicked as the identification squad photographed the hole, the disordered earth around it.

They saw the drag marks at once. They followed them from the hole and through the grass to the narrow lane. Across the lane, through the gouged grass on the other side. Around the gravestones. At the road that cut through the cemetery the trail ended.

Tenthorey squatted. The tire marks were clear and fresh. "A large vehicle. Like a van. I want casts of these tracks."

Down the lane outside the cemetery the investigators were already knocking on doors. "I didn't hear a sound all night," said Mme. Stirnimann. She told them how she had walked past the cemetery that morning and noticed the dug-up earth.

Mme. Virchaux, a neighbor, said her husband had come in at ten-thirty the night before. "Everything was quiet. He didn't see anything out of the ordinary."

"There must have been four of them," said another resident. "Otherwise they'd never have been able to move that coffin." He had helped at the funeral in December. "The box was solid oak. It must have weighed four hundred pounds."

News of the theft of Charlot's body blazed across Europe. Nowhere did it make more headlines than in Switzerland, where the great comedian had spent the last twenty-five years of his life.

"WHY DID THEY STEAL CHARLOT?" shouted a Swiss daily in nearby Lausanne, capital of Vaud canton.

"FANATICISM, GREED, MADNESS?" demanded another.

The papers had combed their morgues for earlier body snatches, and now they recounted them:

In 1946 the theft of Benito Mussolini's remains.

In 1973 Marshal Pétain, hero of Verdun.

In 1976 the coffin of the actress Martine Carol dug up.

In 1977 the attempt to steal the body of Elvis Presley. And now Charlot.

Fanaticism was the motive in the first two cases, greed in the next two. But in Charlot's case, who could say? Only the body snatchers.

When the news that Charlot had been stolen from his grave was flashed to America, it didn't take one film critic long to come up with a motive.

"The coffin will never be found," wrote Stanley Kauffmann.

It will not be put up for ransom. Some macabre maniac wanted possession of the remains as a holy relic.

This last madness, nauseating as it is, is still a kind of tribute. It's a demented obeisance to a world figure whose like the world had never seen before.

Wherever they speak French they call him Charlot. Just saying the name makes their faces light up. Whose face doesn't at the thought of the perky little fellow in the baggy trousers, the tight cutaway, the derby hat, ambling along in his enormous shoes, jauntily whirling his cane?

Clown and poet. Coward and hero. Pathetic outcast and would-be gentleman. In his scenarios life was always slapping him down. But always he picked himself up, brushed himself off, flipped his heels, and shuffled off toward the horizon.

He had lived it before he acted it. He was born in London in 1889. Only Charles Dickens could have imagined a childhood as abominable. Charlot's father, an alcoholic, deserted his mother when he was tiny. She sought shelter for herself and her two young sons in the Lambeth workhouse. The boys were shifted to an orphanage. For years the mother was in and out of mental institutions. In time the youngsters got out of the orphanage. Syd, the older brother, said they sometimes ate out of garbage pails. But by twelve Charlie was on the stage, playing small parts.

In his early twenties he had a growing reputation as a mime, dancer, comedian. He was touring the United States with an English troupe in 1913 when Mack Sennett, creator of the Keystone Comedies, hired him. For Sennett he invented the Little Tramp.

Two years on the screen and he was the best-known figure

in the budding motion-picture industry. In 1917 he signed a contract for a million dollars. It was an unheard-of sum.

He made dozens of short comedies that shine with life today just as brilliantly as they did sixty years ago. He made modern classics—*The Kid, The Gold Rush, Modern Times, The Great Dictator, Limelight....*

He wasn't as successful in his marriages. His friend Stan Laurel said Charlie was an incurable romantic—always looking for a beautiful fairy princess "who would fall in love with him as deeply as he fell in love with her and then they'd live happily ever after." He broke with one young wife after another. His liaisons shocked and tantalized America. Then, in 1943, at age fifty-four, he courted Oona O'Neill, a promising eighteen-year-old actress, and married her over the objections of her father, the playwright Eugene O'Neill. This fourth wife was, in Laurel's words, a true fairy princess; they did live happily ever after. The couple had eight children, the last born when Chaplin was seventy-three.

The bellowing of the House Un-American Activities Committee and Senator Joseph McCarthy was heard over the land. Chaplin aroused the fury of the superpatriots. He had never renounced his British citizenship. He lent his name to liberal and left-wing causes. He had tax troubles. In 1952, en route to Britain, he learned the Attorney General of the United States had announced his visa would not be renewed unless he could prove his "moral worth." "My prodigious sin was, and still is, being a nonconformist," he commented.

The comedian bought a thirty-seven-acre estate in Corsier-sur-Vevey and began a new life there. He continued to make movies. Twenty years later, in 1972, when America had outgrown the Red-under-the-bed hysterics of the McCarthy era, he was invited back to receive a special Oscar from the Motion Picture Academy. In 1975 Queen Elizabeth bestowed a knighthood on him. It was late in the day for the poor boy from Cockney Lambeth. He suffered a stroke. His sight, speech, hearing were failing.

Christmas Day, 1977. The children had come home to Corsier to celebrate the holiday with a rare father and mother. They would stay to mourn instead. As the day began, the comedian's life ended. Or rather, the mortal part of it. People live as long as they are remembered.

Two days later, with rain pattering on the tombstones of the mountainside cemetery and mist blurring the somber mountains, the actor was buried. An Anglican clergyman intoned a prayer. Attendants heaped flowers on the grave.

Now, sixty-five days later, the grave was empty.

By early afternoon the Sûreté had finished packing up its equipment and headed back to Lausanne. The gate of the cemetery stood wide open once more. Cars with license plates from all over Europe can always be seen in Corsier, but today they were more conspicuous than usual. The tiny graveyard overflowed with visitors.

At Chaplin's tomb, a kind of order. The gap had been filled in; gardeners had hidden it under fir boughs, tulips, daffodils. At the head of the grave something was missing. The cross. It had been removed by the Sûreté. One of the grave robbers might have touched it, leaving a fingerprint or some microscopic clue.

And Oona, Chaplin's lovely widow? How was she taking it? Had the body snatchers approached her? The press wanted to know. At the Manoir a tight-lipped butler answered the door. He had orders not to admit reporters. They tried the phone.

"No news. No ransom demand has reached us." Mme. de Monnet, Oona's secretary, repeated the words a hundred times. "For further information you must call Maître Jean-Félix Paschoud. The family lawyer. In Lausanne."

They did, but they learned nothing more.

From their spy posts around the estate, reporters saw young people arriving at the Manoir. The Chaplin children, no doubt, rallying to their mother's side.

During the day, peering through their binoculars, the newsmen spotted Oona Chaplin coming out of the house. With her was a woman in uniform. A nurse. Oona was leaning on her arm. Heavily.

Now they knew how she was taking it.

Headquarters had discovered few clues. It suspected the robbery was the work of a well-organized gang.

The famous actor, the police spokesman in Lausanne implied gloomily, had even made the gang's work easier. Although a wealthy man, he had insisted on the simplest of graves. No concrete reinforcement, nothing. An ordinary hole in the ground had been enough for him. His coffin wasn't lined with lead. He hadn't been embalmed.

"That," commented the spokesman, brightening a little, "could give the perpetrators some problems."

In the media world no news is never good news. News hawks plunged at any flicker of movement. Watching from their spy posts they saw the Corsier postman ride up to the Manoir and deliver a registered letter.

When facts are few a guess will do. Almost immediately the report was in the newsrooms. "The grave robbers have made their ransom demand."

One paper, in Stockholm, went further. It announced the sum: Two million Swiss francs.

In the Soviet Union Charlie Chaplin was a folk hero. A demand for ransom, Moscow was confident, would come at any moment. "This incident accurately reflects the everyday climate of criminality, blackmail, and violence that prevails in many countries of the West," snorted Tass, the Soviet news agency. "In life Charlie Chaplin ran away to a Swiss village to escape the irritations of the capitalist world, which hated him for his free spirit. Now, in death, he cannot escape its monstrous, perverse ways."

Later, when the facts became known, no one would be more surprised than the Communists.

Switzerland has its share of psychics, ever ready to help the baffled authorities. The radiesthesists are a special European breed; they use pendulums the way their counterparts in America use dowsing rods. They can even find a missing object or person with the help of a pendulum. It's not easy, they say. But, they explain, there's a close link between an actual place and the symbols that represent it on a map. The psychic holds his pendulum over the map and its gyrations show him where to find what he's looking for.

One celebrated radiesthesist told the police the coffin could be found across the Lake of Geneva, at Saint-Gingolph.

"No," said another. "Look for it near Rochers-de-Naye."

A third clairvoyant reported he had found some clumps of earth that had dropped from Chaplin's coffin while it was being removed from Corsier.

"Until we hear from the perpetrators," said the police spokesman at Lausanne, "we cannot afford to turn down any clues."

Grave robbing suddenly became big news. Now for the first time the public learned about a tomb that had been robbed in Aigle. The grave was an old one and there had never been any ransom demand. The bones were never recovered. The police had written it off as the work of medical students who needed a skeleton.

With Charlie Chaplin, of course, it would be different. At his death he had been worth, the papers said, one hundred million dollars. That sum was growing at the rate of more than forty thousand dollars a day.

When the thieves were finally heard from, the police spokesman declared, there would be a demand for a ransom.

A very stiff one.

At the Manoir, Geraldine Chaplin had taken over. Lovely, small, but not so frail as she looks. She has some of her father's talent as well as a good deal of her own. Her performances in pictures like *Dr. Zhivago, Nashville,* and *Cria* have impressed millions of moviegoers. She had left the film she was shooting in Spain to be with her mother.

Geraldine was answering calls for Oona. A well-placed Lausanne journalist managed to speak to her.

"Is there any news? Has there been a demand for a ransom?"

"No comment.... Please don't talk about this in the press. The more you write, the harder you make it for us."

From another person close to Oona: "She's gotten unsigned letters, insulting phone calls, threats.... It's terrible. Her attorney and the police have advised her to keep silent. The authorities are continuing to investigate. The less anybody knows, the less the police are likely to be interfered with."

And then, as if further explanation was needed: "The family could have worse to fear from the thieves. Remember, Mme. Chaplin has young children. Grandchildren too.... I'm sorry, I can't say any more."

In Lausanne Maître Paschoud, the attorney, would add only a little. Yes, there had been anonymous telephone callers. They had demanded enormous sums for the return of Charlot's coffin. No, they had not provided any proof that they had it.

Outside, on the streets, there seemed to be more policemen than usual. They stood around, often in pairs, chatting casually. But there was nothing casual about the sharp glances they shot after any stranger who lingered on a street corner, or in a telephone booth.

A report had come in over the wire. According to a newspaper in Los Angeles the body snatch had been engineered by anti-Semites. That called to mind an earlier report that vans with signs in Arabic had been seen in the cemetery at Corsier the night the coffin was stolen.

Was Chaplin Jewish? No one seemed to know for sure.

Chaplin himself had once commented that the Jews were a people of genius. "I'm sure there must be some Jewish blood somewhere in me," he had added. "I hope so." And once, when a movie company had proposed filming the life of Jesus Christ, Chaplin had asked for the leading role. "I'm a logical choice. I look the part. I'm a Jew."

But then sometimes he denied he was Jewish, pointing out he had been brought up a Protestant, like his father. But to add to the confusion, one source reported that his father was of French Jewish stock.

A journalist went to see Tenthorey, the examining magistrate. Could the theft be the work of anti-Semites? he asked.

Tenthorey shook his head. "No truth in that at all." The magistrate talked on with an air of repressed excitement. He hinted that he knew a good deal more about the case than he was free to say.

About a week after the grave was robbed, Geraldine received a phone call.

"Ici M. Rochat," the man's voice said over the crackle in the line. "This is Mr. Rochat."

The name was French-Swiss, but not the accent.

"Madame, how are you today? I am sorry to trouble you."

"Yes?"

"We have Charlot's coffin. If you want to get it back you must pay for it. Six hundred thousand dollars."

The words tumbled out in a hurry. As if he had kept them too long and couldn't wait to get rid of them.

"We've had a number of calls from people who say they have Father's coffin. None of them have given us any proof. Can you?"

"Yes, of course. Photographs. Shall I post them to you?" He paused for her reply. *"A bientôt. Merci, madame."* The phone clicked.

He had seemed terribly nervous. Eager to finish, to get off the line. And curiously polite.

A few days later, running through the mail for her mother,

she found the envelope. Some of the photographs were too dark and shadowy. Others were overexposed. But she could make out a coffin with metal handles. It was eight sided—the kind with sides that slant out from the head to the shoulders, then in toward the feet. Earth was scattered over it.

It looked like her father's. But she hadn't been at the funeral. She couldn't be sure.

Her mother was.

"Ici M. Rochat. Sorry to trouble you. The photographs—did they arrive? It is the coffin, no?" Hesitant. As though he wasn't entirely sure himself.

Keep him talking, the Sûreté had told her. The call was being monitored. At the telephone company, technicians, alerted, had begun to comb over the diagrams, the incredible network of wires that connected the Manoir to Vevey, to Lausanne, to the rest of the world. With some luck they would find the right circuit. If she could hold him on the phone long enough.

The daughter asked questions.

Long silences as Rochat pondered his replies. He seemed eager to satisfy her but afraid he might say too much, drop some clue the police might find useful. He was jumpy.

She was an actress, one of the finest. Maybe Rochat knew that. But maybe he believed she really needed the answers to all her questions; one coffin looks much like the next. But before long he was apologizing, stammering he had to hang up. The phone went dead.

She had done her best. But tracing calls is incredibly complicated; the police didn't end up with much. They needed more. "Try to keep him on the line longer the next time, madame."

He called several more times after that, but she could not stall him long enough. Finally she told him to call Maître Paschoud, the family lawyer, who would handle the actual negotiations.

The grave robber took down the phone number. *"Merci, madame.* I'll get in touch with him. *Au revoir."*

Maître Paschoud is one of the most respected members of the Vaud bar. Like any successful attorney he understands people at least as well as he understands the law.

"This is M. Rochat."

He had been expecting the call. Yes, he said, the negotiations were his department. Before they could begin, however, some questions had to be answered. (It was his way of taking his opponent's measure.)

He had it quickly. The man was riddled with insecurity. Young. Probably a neurotic. Certainly not a professional criminal.

Let's see what we can do with him, Paschoud told himself. *With luck we may be able to talk him out of it altogether.*

Soon Paschoud was proposing a lower sum than the six hundred thousand dollars Rochat had asked.

"Come down on my price?" The voice at the other end sounded shocked. "After so many risks? How can you talk like that?" Still the ghoul didn't reject the proposal out of hand. "I'll call you again next week."

To Paschoud it was like fishing. When Rochat called again the lawyer let out the line a little. The next time he pulled it in a little. Next he let it out again. He agreed. He disagreed. What was the hurry? The longer he drew out the negotiations, the better the chance Rochat would make some fatal slip that would lead the police to him. And the longer Paschoud kept him on the line, the more neurotic he seemed to get.

Rochat began to weaken. Paschoud had him discussing the ransom in terms of Swiss francs instead of dollars. That was a drop of almost 50 percent.

"I want half a million francs—in hundred-franc notes."

"Sorry. I just spoke to the Manoir. Mme. Chaplin is dead set against paying any ransom. Take my advice, Rochat. Give up this wretched business while you still can. You're not cut out for it. . . . Do you have any notion how many years you can get at hard labor for stealing a dead body? Especially such a famous one?"

"What are you saying, give it up? There are other people in this with me. They'll never stand for it." He was almost whining when he hung up.

"M. Paschoud, I do not like to be played with." The body snatcher was sounding edgy. "I've had enough. . . ."

Have I been dangling him on the line too long? Paschoud worried.

"I happen to know Mme. Chaplin has a young son up there. What's his name—Christopher?"

It was a new Rochat. He seemed dangerously distracted.

"Do you know I have a carbine...a Mauser...with telescopic lenses? At four hundred yards I never miss."

Later he repeated the threat.

Paschoud kept Oona Chaplin posted on the progress of the talks. His report of the latest conversations was hardly reassuring.

For Oona, the Manoir was no longer the haven it once had been. No more picnics on the lawn. No more tennis. No more puttering in the garden, where she had grown the vegetables Charlie loved. Policemen came every day. Armed guards patrolled the grounds at night. When a member of the family had to go somewhere, there was a guard in the car. For the first time in twenty-five years the gates to the estate were locked.

Hermann Brönnimann owns a farm in the fertile plain of the Rhône near Noville, about ten miles from Corsier-sur-Vevey. In April he was sowing his land with corn. He hadn't been able to finish one of his fields the previous week. On Monday the twenty-fourth he came back to it.

As Brönnimann moved along the edge of the field, close to the trees, he noticed something peculiar. The soil had been dug over recently. He remembered telling one of his hands to get the rocks out of a patch of soil. But this certainly wasn't the spot he had indicated. *He must have just dug up the wrong place,* he thought, and promptly forgot about the matter.

Maître Paschoud smiled. Things were looking up. The attorney and Rochat had agreed upon a price. Half a million francs. The body snatcher had told him how, when, and where he wanted the money delivered. The date was to be Monday, May 2. The place would be close to La Rosiaz. Where the Belmont Bridge passes over the expressway, near Lausanne. Rochat would pick up the money himself. (It was almost too good to be true.) He would be wearing a sports outfit. Like a cross-country runner. He would pass under the bridge. Above, the Chaplins' chauffeur was to be waiting, with the ransom in a bag. When he saw the cross-country runner passing beneath, he was to drop the money to him.

Inspector Jean Paccaud, working out the details, smiled too. Paccaud was the Sûreté officer at the Manoir. He had been there for days, wearing the uniform of Bovon, the Chaplins' chauffeur, keeping an eye on security. Now, as the chauffeur, he was to drop the ransom to Rochat from the bridge.

At strategic points all around, in discreet disguises, would be other officers of the Sûreté.

For two months the police had been scurrying all over the canton looking for the body snatcher of Corsier. Now, in a matter of hours, he was going to offer himself to them. It was almost too good to be true....

A telephone jangled.

It was Rochat, all nerves. "Sorry. I changed my mind. Call you again in a few days. Goodbye." Click.

It had been too good to be true.

Nine days later he called back. "We've put this off too long. Time to button it up. I'll call you again with final instructions. On Tuesday, May sixteenth. At nine-thirty in the morning. *A bientôt.*"

Now they knew the exact day he would make his next call. The exact time. And, more or less, from where. Having traced call after call, the police had determined that Rochat almost always telephoned from Lausanne. From a public pay phone booth. The question was: Which one? He kept changing them.

Lausanne is a good-sized city, sprawling outward kilometer after kilometer from its old center. It has two hundred telephone booths scattered through the city and suburbs.

Commissaire Cétou musters his forces. One hundred men are to cover two hundred phone booths.

Two to one, he reflects. *The ghoul can still slip through our fingers. Now, if we had a helicopter...*

They have one in Berne. "We'll send it over in plenty of time," they say.

On Tuesday the sixteenth, promptly at 9:30 A.M., Rochat rings up.

The Berne helicopter is sweeping the sky. Rising, dropping, hovering as police radios crackle and patrol cars wait.

Finally, over the static on the two-way radios: "This is Headquarters. The suspect has been located. In the public booth in the avenue de la Dôle. Take up designated positions. *Now.*"

In the patrol cars the officers check their maps. Tires screeching, the machines shoot toward their posts at the intersections. To bottle him in. To seal everyone else out.

*   *   *

9:45 A.M. In the avenue de la Dôle the first two police officers approach the phone booth. They look through the glass at the man in the booth.

Tall, young, slight of build, fair haired. Mustache. Glasses. He seems to be arguing with someone at the other end of the line.

One of the officers carefully pushes open the door.

"You are Rochat?"

His jaw drops.

They lead him unresisting to the police car.

His papers revealed that he was Roman Wardas, age twenty-four. A Pole, a refugee, residing in Switzerland since 1973. An auto mechanic, temporarily out of work.

The officers in charge played the tapes that had been recorded of his calls to the Manoir.

"Your voice, your accent are identical," they said. "Don't you agree?"

He nodded sadly.

"Where is the body?"

"At Noville. Buried in a field."

"You didn't pull off this job by yourself. You told Maître Paschoud you had accomplices."

"Accomplices? I had only one."

"Who is he? Where does he live?"

Wardas looked away. They asked again. He wouldn't answer.

They knew his address; they had his employment record. At his rooming house, in the places he had worked, the officers asked questions. Who does he spend his time with? Who are his friends? One was mentioned again and again. Gantscho Ganev. A Bulgarian refugee. An automobile mechanic like Wardas. A respectable man, married, with a child.

The next morning, in the small garage where he worked, they found Ganev. He raised his eyes from the engine he was adjusting, and the Sûreté card was held out for him to see.

"Your name is Gantscho Ganev? You are a friend of Roman Wardas?"

He was too surprised to reply. But on the way to headquarters he began to tell them everything.

A hundred yards past the Noville bridge the four cars swung off the road at the Brönnimann property. Mist swirled around them. The men piled out and began to tramp along the edge of the muddy field. Some were carrying spades. With the officers in the lead was a slender, nervous young man in handcuffs.

About thirty yards from the road the man in handcuffs gave a sign. The others gathered around him. Spades bit into the earth....

The heavy box that was removed from the hole had eight sides and metal handles. A man with a black bag stepped forward. Dr. Thélin, the canton's medical examiner, from the Institute of Forensic Medicine in Lausanne. Photographers of the police identification squad focused their cameras. The lid of the box creaked open.

The face inside had begun to blur. The way the face of the Little Tramp used to blur after he had shuffled down the road a stretch and turned to look back wistfully at The Girl. But they could still recognize him.

The body was in a twisted position. Had it been abused?

Dr. Thélin began his examination. He flexed the limbs and noted their suppleness. He studied the skin. "The remains are well preserved." He concluded the body hadn't been touched but had been shifted by the handling of the coffin. At his side M. Tenthorey, the examining magistrate, took notes. Willy Heim, attorney general of Vaud canton, looked on, stone-faced.

The police examined the interior of the coffin. Some objects of sentimental or monetary value might have been placed with the deceased, and they would have to be inventoried. They found nothing. It was recalled that Charlot had requested a simple, matter-of-fact burial. He was sentimental about many things, but not about death.

The coffin lid creaked shut. A hearse had arrived. The heavy oak box was loaded aboard.

The shovels were working again. The hole vanished. Only the marks of many feet showed where it had been. Officials climbed back into their cars with their prisoner.

Anyone in Noville can point the place out to you today. *"Le champ Charlot,"* they call it. "Charlie Chaplin Field."

He would sleep securely now.

The design for the underground vault in the cemetery at Corsier had been prepared by an expert. Trucks kept coming and going. A great rectangle was scooped out in the Chaplin plot. Masons worked steadily, lining it with massive concrete walls, installing heavy metal supports.

A week after the return from Noville everything was ready. To keep it from turning into a circus, they buried him early in the morning. The hearse pulled up at ten to six. Only a handful of mourners: Oona, her sons Michael and Eugene, her daughter Jeanne, a pair of faithful servants, the mayor. And a half-dozen policemen, just in case.

The coffin, covered with roses, disappeared into the darkness. Sealing it in was a great stone slab a foot thick, like a tabletop tombstone of the days of the resurrection men. Placed at the head of the grave, on a square of fresh earth, was the simple white cross with his name and dates. At the foot of the cross, two big bouquets of lilacs, white and purple.

It was just like the day of his first burial. Mist blotted out the mountaintops. The rain was falling steadily.

Attempted extortion. Disturbing the peace of the dead. Those would be the charges.

The penalty? That would depend on the court where the accused were brought to trial. If it was the Criminal Court in Lausanne, they could get as much as seven and one-half years' imprisonment. But the authorities could also try them right where it had all begun, in Vevey, at the Court of Petty Sessions. There the maximum penalty was six years.

Neither man had been arrested before. The public wouldn't learn their names until after their trial. In Switzerland first offenders, unless and until they are found guilty, can be identified in the media by their initials only.

Reporters interviewed people close to G. G.'s wife. He was, the public soon read, a hard-working man of steady habits. He was thirty-eight, fourteen years older than his accomplice, R. W. "Gentle and reserved," said some. "A bit naïve," according to others.

G. G.'s earnings were small and there was a child to support. Mme. G. G., a Swiss, had taken a job. She worked two weeks a month in a psychiatric hospital. Nights. To rob the cemetery the two men had chosen one of her nights on duty. That way she couldn't notice how late G. G. came in.

But she had noticed something. "My husband has changed," she had told a friend. "He's gotten irritable. Awfully irritable."

He was devoted to her, to their son. Like the self-respecting

Swiss, he wanted to be in business for himself. "If I had a garage of my own," he had told the police, "my wife could give up her job and stay at home with the boy." During the weeks after the body snatch he had gone about inspecting small garages; looking for one he could make a down payment on with his share of the ransom money.

"Because he wanted to be happy," concluded *Le Nouvel Illustré* of Lausanne sympathetically, "he has destroyed his home."

And the younger man, R. W., who had played the leading role? Quiet. Polite. Inoffensive. Hardly the "criminal type." He had gotten the idea for the grave robbery from the newspapers. Body snatching, he had read, was common across the border in Italy. If you chose the right victim the ransom could be enormous.

In December news of the death of Charlie Chaplin and his burial at Corsier had filled the Swiss newspapers. Only twelve miles from Lausanne, reflected R. W.

The Pole made several trips to Corsier. He looked at the cemetery and the Chaplin plot. Could he swing the job by himself? Too hard, he decided. He needed a helper, a man with muscle. If the helper had a van, so much the better.

His friend G. G. had both. In addition he had an instant camera. R. W. broached the subject to G. G. The Bulgarian saw his garage coming closer. He began to nod. "But there's one condition. No violence."

After the robbery they saw each other only a few times. G. G. was happy to stay in the background. R. W. started the negotiations. As he read in the newspapers of the furor unleashed by the body snatch he was terrified. Whenever he heard footsteps behind him he trembled. For days at a time he was afraid to enter a telephone booth to call his victims. He began having nightmares. In two months he had lost thirteen pounds. He wanted to give up the extortion attempt, the press said, but he felt he had gone too far to turn back.

Somehow the two grave robbers—bumbling, confused, amateurish—had awakened the sympathy of the media. With Chaplin's body recovered, with no ransom paid, the ghouls suddenly seemed pathetic rather than dangerous.

Jacques Chessex is a prominent Swiss poet-professor who writes for the newspapers. Chessex found something bizarrely amusing, a kind of Chaplinesque black humor, in the incident.

"I envy and admire the posthumous fate of M. Chaplin," he wrote.

There is a fable in that horror. Look. I began very small. A Jew. An orphan. Ridiculous, ridiculed, turned out, beaten. But look. I wore frock coats full of holes, a workhouse uniform, the derby hat of the ghetto. I carried a cane like some preposterous weapon. I had a mustache that underscored the sadness of my smile.

O.K. So it's not the king, the dictator, or the old genius of *Limelight* that you dug up and took on a journey. It's not the patriarch or the lord of the manor of Vevey.

Just remember the spaghetti shoelaces in *The Gold Rush,* the miserable slum in *The Kid*. . . the lonesome road, the shattered hopes, the blows.

Now do you know whom you dug up and planted once more in scandal? It's nothing to worry about. Relax. It's only the immigrant, Charlot. The real one.

He's been through worse before.

The morning was cold. Outside the court, news photographers, television cameramen, reporters, curiosity seekers jostled for position, stamped their feet to warm them, or drank from steaming thermoses. When the police van pulled up they surged forward. Gendarmes waved them back.

Handcuffed together, Ganev and Wardas edged out. They tried to shield their faces from the lenses. Ganev, the large, athletic one, raised both his hands in front of his anxious face, jerking Wardas's manacled hand up with his own. The Pole's face, pale and drawn, caught the glare of the flashes.

Both men had been sitting in Bois-Mermet Prison in Lausanne for seven months while the government interrogated them, sifted the evidence, polished its case against them.

Maître Pidoux, Maître Burnand, their young attorneys, court appointed, looked more cheerful. All of Switzerland was going to hear about them and how they pleaded for their clients. It couldn't hurt.

The small hall at Vevey, redecorated for the occasion, was jammed. Not everyone who wanted to get in had been able to; only about sixty could be accommodated. About a third of them, on the seats in front, were journalists. The rest were local people or those who took a special interest in the case.

One of these, an attorney, greeted a Lausanne reporter he knew.

"You're going to see some real theatrics here." He grinned wickedly.

The jury of four took their places. Two were engineers, one a teacher, one a housewife. Promptly at 9 A.M. the judge, M. Roland Châtelain, opened the trial.

The official report of the case was read to the court. Step by step it spun the story, a tragic web of greed and stupidity. The reporters scribbled away, noting such curious details as that the Chaplin coffin weighed 182 pounds and his body only 81, and that Wardas had made 27 telephone calls to the Manoir and to Maître Paschoud during the bungling, erratic course of his negotiations.

The mood in the court was distinctly good-natured. Judge Châtelain interrupted the reading with humorous sallies from time to time. Dour-faced Willy Heim, the prosecutor, permitted himself an occasional smile or an ironic comment. The spectators chuckled.

Ganev was sworn in. He was a round-faced man, dark haired, with long sideburns. He leaned forward to catch every word as Châtelain questioned him about his past, occasionally with the help of an interpreter.

As a child, Ganev said, he had suffered at the hands of a sadistic stepmother. As a young man he had lived in grinding poverty. If only he could escape to the West, he had thought. It sounded like paradise to him.

He had tried. He made one attempt after another to reach the border. Each time they caught him and threw him in jail. He served three years at forced labor. In the uranium mines. Then a daring, dangerous escape. A long, fierce swim across the Danube. And, finally, freedom.

The court was visibly impressed.

Bulgaria was behind him, but not the scars, the insecurity that life there had gouged into him. And Switzerland—Switzerland hadn't turned out to be exactly heaven. From time to time he was out of work. His wife had to take a job. He felt demeaned. He wanted something better for her, for his son. If he could only get a little garage of his own.... And then along came Wardas with his plan.

"Tell me, how does a man like you come to take part in such a crime?" asked Judge Châtelain. "Didn't you get any religious training as a child?"

"No, sir. They gave us lessons in . . . morality. Carrying off a dead body—that didn't seem so terrible. I didn't think it would hurt anybody."

"A dead body is just an object to you Bulgarians?"

"Yes, sir."

Now Wardas was on the stand.

"You didn't realize you would hurt Mme. Chaplin by stealing her husband's body?"

"No, sir. It wasn't like kidnapping a living person."

"A coffin is only a thing to you?"

"Yes, sir. An object without any value."

"Not for Mme. Chaplin," the judge snapped. "And if you thought she'd pay a huge sum of money to get back her husband's body, doesn't it follow that you believed your action would cause her pain?"

Wardas hesitated. "I only thought the Chaplins were very rich."

Châtelain asked about the night of the grave robbery.

Haltingly Wardas told how he and Ganev had driven to Corsier in Ganev's van. Ganev had dropped him inside the cemetery with two stolen spades, then gone off to park the van outside so it wouldn't attract attention. Wardas began to dig.

It started to rain. Light from nearby houses cast frightening shadows on the flower-covered tomb, the white cross.

Ganev returned. He looked scared.

"We must get going!" Wardas whispered.

Ganev took up a spade. They worked steadily in the rain. Mud stained their trousers, covered their shoes.

After two hours of digging, one of them jumped down into the hole, while the other remained on the surface. The coffin was incredibly heavy. Panic gave them strength. With enormous effort they lifted it out of the grave.

"My first plan wasn't to steal the coffin at all. I simply intended to make the hole deeper, put the box back in, and cover it up. We wouldn't even have taken it away . . . we would only have pretended to. People would see the hole we left and believe the coffin was gone."

"Why didn't you do that?"

"The ground was too hard. There were too many rocks."

Ganev went out of the cemetery and drove back the van. The thirty yards they had to drag the coffin seemed like a mile. At last they got it to the van and pushed it in.

Wardas had chosen the field at Noville to hide the coffin; he knew the area because he had fished there a number of times. He had already dug a shallow hole. The pair unloaded the weighty coffin. They saw at once that the hole was too narrow, and they made it wider. They shoved the coffin down inside, and had almost refilled the hole when Wardas remembered what they had forgotten to do. It was one of the most important steps in his plan.

They dug out the box again. Ganev got his instant camera and shot one picture after another. Now they could give Mme. Chaplin proof that they actually had the coffin.

Maître Paschoud was called into the hall.

"Did you ever meet the man you dealt with on the telephone, counselor?"

"No, never, Your Honor."

"Well, there he is." Châtelain gestured to Wardas to stand up.

Awkwardly Wardas rose to his feet. Paschoud turned to look at him.

"So you're Rochat?" The attorney smiled. "Hello there!"

Wardas bowed stiffly. Laughter rippled through the small hall.

Paschoud had never allowed the police to monitor his telephone conversations, claiming they were privileged. Now he gave an account of them, consulting his notes. Although the Pole had lowered his demands, the lawyer said, he had never given them up altogether. At one point in the negotiations, in fact, the lawyer had offered him one hundred thousand francs, with his personal assurance the Chaplins wouldn't prosecute, if the grave robber would tell him where the body was hidden. Wardas had refused.

A key point in the government's case was the threats that Wardas had allegedly made against Christopher Chaplin. Paschoud gave an account of them.

Wardas, on the stand, denied he had been in earnest. "I didn't even have a rifle." He admitted mentioning the Mauser. "But it was only because of Maître Paschoud's attitude. He refused to take me seriously. I had to convince him I meant business."

At the time of his last telephone conversation with Paschoud, Wardas said, he had made up his mind to abandon the extortion attempt.

"Then why didn't you?" The judge was annoyed. "All you

had to do was send a sketch of the Noville field, with a cross marked on it to show where the coffin was buried. That could have been the end of it."

The young Pole flushed. "I didn't think of it."

A Bulgarian refugee, a Dr. Todolov, was called. He sketched a picture of the political repression in Bulgaria, of the hard lot of the people. Of how the Communist system drained traditional religious beliefs out of children's minds and crammed them with Marxist materialism.

Châtelain asked Todolov about grave robbing in Bulgaria.

"It happens every day. The dead are buried in their best clothes, good shoes. The poor dig them up and take what they need."

"Isn't robbing the dead punishable by law?"

"Absolutely not. There's nothing sacred about the dead in Bulgaria."

In the afternoon Geraldine Chaplin entered the court. She was to testify in place of her mother, who wouldn't be called.

A star of the screen is a star everywhere. Every pair of eyes in the room followed her as she walked to the witness chair. Small, slender, with delicate, sensitive features, she bore a striking resemblance to her father in his youth. She wore her hair in a ponytail. She was dressed in blue jeans, a purple-red sweater, knitted coat.

She described the hail of telephone calls that pelted the Manoir in March and April.

"Why was it you who answered so many of them?"

"Because I wanted to take the pressure off my mother. This awful business left her in a state of shock. And I had better control of myself than my brothers and sisters. I'm the oldest....

"The whole thing was hard for us to understand. During all his years at Corsier my father was respected . . . loved. And then, all of a sudden, this . . . violence. To think that someone could hate him so much. . . . Why? It made no sense. And then we heard about that rifle with the telescopic lens. We had to take the children out of school. Right at examination time."

Talk of the ransom had fed their fright. What if thieves thought there was a large sum of money in the house to pay the body snatchers—and broke in, ready to kill to get it?

Coolly, clearly, her voice unwavering, she answered the judge's questions. Her testimony finished, she declined his invitation to remain. It wasn't hard to understand why. The eyes of the court followed her slender form as she left. The parade of witnesses continued. But it was as if, on a stage, the lights had gone out.

Evening was coming on. The last witness was heard. Châtelain adjourned the court until Thursday, when Prosecutor Heim would make his indictment. The youthful attorneys would plead for their clients.

And the jury would decide their fate.

It was, people were saying, just like a scenario by Charlie Chaplin.

It had sighs and tears, but it had some smiles too.

The characters: Two malcontents who run away from Communist countries because they want to be capitalists. To get to be a capitalist you only need one thing: capital. They decide to imitate the latest style in Italy—steal a rich man's body and hold it for ransom.

Teeth chattering, the amateur ghouls dig up the coffin and bury it somewhere else. Then they have to dig it up again because they have forgotten to take pictures.

Is that—or isn't it—pure Chaplin?

Keystone Kops? Lots of them. Police, gendarmes, the Sûreté, dashing all over the lovely Swiss scenery, hunting down false clues, chasing up false trails.

The main character even has a mustache. He's a bumbling fellow but his manners are good; he wouldn't think of starting a telephone conversation with his victims without a "How are you today?" (If Charlie had played the role he would have lifted his derby to the phone when he began and ended each call.)

Our grave robber may be down at the heels but he always (almost always) remembers he's a gentleman. When the victims complain he's putting them under a strain he's very understanding. He's only too happy to suspend the ransom negotiations for a couple of weeks.

Next the fiasco of the ransom drop. But that's good Chaplin too. Can't you see Charlie, in T-shirt and runner's shorts, hotfooting it along the road in his oversized shoes—dashing up to position himself under the bag of money that the Sûreté inspector, disguised as the family chauffeur, is about to drop?

(Sure, the scene never took place. But you know how Charlie would have filmed it: A dream sequence in the inspector's mind, with the crook running in to catch the falling bag like a ballplayer after a fly ball, while a crowd of Keystone Kops runs in to catch him.)

The climax: The gentle crook yakking away in a phone booth, too absorbed to see the helicopter buzzing around and the Keystone Kops pouring in like the horde of Genghis Khan. The crook finally seeing them and meekly holding out his hands for the cuffs. Just like Charlie in his old escaped-convict roles: a little relieved or maybe a little absent-minded.

No—that's not the climax. Not quite.

The last day of the trial. Thursday, December 14.

Willy Heim, the prosecutor, walked on like a heavy of the old school.

"It was cold and gray that morning," he intoned, glasses perched low on his nose. "A flock of crows rose screeching and quarreling as we drew near. Mud clung to our boots. The men opened the coffin. I looked down at the face of the great actor." He paused.

The spectators leaned forward, intent on his words.

Suddenly he was no longer speaking French. English, accented English, was coming from his lips.

"Alas, poor Yorick! I knew him, Horatio."

The Swiss in the courtroom who didn't understand English looked puzzled. Those who did—not to mention the British and Americans among the reporters—grimaced.

The histrionics over, Heim demanded a stiff penalty. An example had to be set. Otherwise other graves would be robbed, other families tormented.

For Wardas, the brain of the affair, the prosecutor asked the maximum penalty, six years. For Ganev, the assistant gravedigger, four years. In addition both men should be expelled from Switzerland for fifteen years.

Judge Châtelain called on the defense attorneys to make their pleas.

Maître Burnand, for Ganev:

"Great artists never die. We shall go on forever enjoying Charlie Chaplin on film. Laughing when he laughs. Crying when he cries....

"Charlie Chaplin is every one of us. He is Roman Wardas.... He is Gantscho Ganev....

"Ganev doesn't deny he did wrong. He made a mistake and he regrets it. He's written to Mme. Chaplin, begging her forgiveness. She, by refusing to appear against the accused, has shown she feels pity for him....

"Give him back to his family. They need him desperately."

Maître Pidoux, for Roman Wardas:

"Is this gentle young man, a refugee from the country of Paderewski and Chopin, an extortionist? Or is he a lonely stranger in an alien land, driven by hardship and suffering to surrender to the temptation to get money in an unlawful way?...

"He never directly threatened the Chaplins. He never intended to shoot anyone. Maître Paschod—a colonel in the reserves, mind you—was playing with him like a cat plays with a mouse. The threats, if they were ever uttered—and we have nothing but Maître Paschoud's word for them—were intended only to get the lawyer to take him seriously. And remember, Wardas says that at the very end he decided to give up the demand for a ransom....

"Let his sentence be a fine. Set him free tomorrow."

Even the sober-faced jurors looked shocked.

In the afternoon they presented their verdict.

Both men were guilty as charged.

Gantscho Ganev: sentenced to eighteen months in prison, sentence suspended. A fine, and parole for five years.

Roman Wardas: sentenced to four and one-half years in prison and a fine.

Neither man would be expelled from Switzerland. Switzerland doesn't expel political refugees.

Wardas appealed. In May 1979 he appeared before the Court of Appeals in Lausanne. He had a new, more experienced attorney.

The court listened to Maître Lob's plea, then turned it down. The Vevey judgment, the magistrates explained, was just right. The heavy sentence would help to keep out of peaceful little Switzerland this custom of trying to get rich by digging up the dead. Would keep it, added one of the magistrates, where it came from, in that boot-shaped country to the south.

Wardas was carted off to prison.

The gentle ghoul wouldn't have to wear one of those old-fashioned black-and-white striped uniforms, the kind the Little Tramp used to in his prison comedies. He wouldn't be chained by his ankle to a big ball of iron. But he would have to stay on ice for a while.

Not too long a while at that. He had already been locked up a year. Good behavior could knock a third off his sentence. He could be out in two and a half.

The lonely Refugee was still very lonely. His family lived in far-off Poland. His friends had deserted him. On visiting day no one came to see him...

...Except the Girl.

Her parents had forbidden her to visit him. They didn't want any daughter of theirs keeping company with a jailbird.

But did that stop the Girl?

Never.

She came to the prison on every visiting day.

She brought the jailbird gifts.

She kissed him through the barrier.

She looked deep into his eyes.

Her own eyes shone as she talked about the future, and she fumbled in her bag for a tissue.

Some tears, yes.

But some smiles too.

Just like in the old Charlie Chaplin movies.

Hommage à Mlle. Mireille Schnorf de Vevey

Acknowledgments

A CONSIDERABLE amount of time was necessary to research the book. I have followed up these stories not only in the United States but in Britain, France, Scandinavia, and elsewhere. I could have accomplished little without the assistance of many fine people, whose contribution I would like to acknowledge here.

First, as ever, my wife, Evelyn, who helped me unstintingly with the problems that arose during the research and the writing and, as reference librarian of the Norwalk Public Library, Norwalk, Connecticut, furnished me with an endless stream of detail and books. My son, John, was a wise editorial counselor, reading the manuscript critically and making many valuable editorial suggestions. My daughter, Jean, worked long hours typing and retyping the manuscript and raising pertinent questions. For their aid and encouragement I am under a significant obligation to these three, as well as to my agent, Scott Meredith, Elliot Ravetz of his staff, and Maureen Baron, executive editor of Fawcett Books.

For important information about the status of anatomy studies today and yesterday I owe a special debt of gratitude to Dr. John E. Pauly of the Department of Anatomy, University of Arkansas for Medical Sciences, Little Rock, Arkansas; Dr. Thomas R. Forbes, E. K. Hunt Professor of Anatomy, School of Medicine, Yale University, New Haven, Connecticut; Whitfield J. Bell, Jr., executive officer of the American Philosophical Society, Philadelphia, Pennsylvania;

and Dr. A. J. Ladman of the Anatomy Department, University of New Mexico, Albuquerque, New Mexico.

Mireille Schnorf of Vevey, Switzerland, a journalist on the staff of the *Feuille d'Avis de Vevey,* generously provided a wealth of material about *l'affaire Chaplin* for which I can never thank her enough. E. H. Bovay, Swiss consul, New York City, also helped, and so did Elinor Green, counselor for public affairs, United States Embassy, Bern, Switzerland.

Fred Olds, director of the Oklahoma Territorial Museum of the Oklahoma Historical Society, Guthrie, Oklahoma, not only answered all of my questions and generously provided leads and photographs of Elmer McCurdy, but illustrated his envelopes with drawings that made my day and the postman's.

Jorn Wounlund, of Gothenburg, Sweden, aided greatly by ferreting out background material and photographs of Julia Pastrana. Mr. and Mrs. Björn Lund also helped. Miss L. Kennedy, city librarian of Johannesburg, South Africa, supplied new facts about the Hottentot Venus, and Mrs. L. J. DeWet and Mrs. E. B. Nagelgast of the library's Africana Museum supplied pictures. The staff of the Prints Department of the British Museum made available old prints for study. Y. Azoulay of the Laboratoire d'Anthropologie of the Musée National d'Histoire Naturelle and the Musée de l'Homme of Paris furnished photographs and documents.

I am also indebted to Dr. Caroline Grigson and Professor A. E. W. Miles, honorary curator of the Odontological Museum, and L. Allen, curator of the Hunterian Museum, of the Royal College of Surgeons of England, and E. H. Cornelius, librarian, the Royal College; also to Eric J. Freeman, librarian, the Wellcome Institute for the History of Medicine, London; Representative John Moss, United States House of Representatives, and William Shook, subcommittee on oversight and investigations of the Committee on Interstate and Foreign Commerce, United States House of Representatives, Washington, D.C.

Also James T. Hickey, curator, Lincoln Collection, Illinois State Historical Library, Springfield, Illinois; Dr. B. J. Mack, assistant keeper, Museum of Mankind, London; James L. Murphy, reference librarian, Ohio Historical Society, Columbus, Ohio; John Melville Jennings, director, Virginia Historical Society, Richmond, Virginia; Sally Morgenstern and Marilyn Gardner of the Rare Book Room and Denis Gaffney of the Public Service Department of the New York Academy of Medicine, New York City, for assistance above and beyond the call of duty; the staff of the library of the New York Historical Society, New York City; Arthur Horan, special assistant to Senator Abraham Ribicoff; Miss Roth of the Prints Department of the New York Public Library; the ever-resourceful Mrs. Walter Pitkin and Ruth Adams of the Westport Public Library, Westport, Connecticut; Mrs. Trudi O'Donohue and Mrs. Miriam Tamsky of the Norwalk Public Library; Jean Botts, medical librarian, Wiggans Library, Norwalk Hospital, and Dr. Roy Barnett, chief of pathology of Norwalk Hospital; Thomas G. Falco, assistant historical librarian, Yale Medical Library, Yale University; Ingeborg Glier, chairperson, Department of Germanic Languages, Yale University; the Office of the District Attorney, Queens, New York; and the knowledgeable DeWitt Bodeen of Woodland Hills, California, and Rosaria Koñstantiñ of Norwalk, Connecticut.

Bibliography

THIS bibliography is suggestive rather than complete. The author has consulted other books, pamphlets, manuscripts, and periodicals, as well as newspapers too numerous to mention.

BOOKS, PAMPHLETS, AND MANUSCRIPTS

Adams, Norman. *Dead and Buried?* Aberdeen, Scotland: Impulse Books, 1972.

Altick, Richard D. *The Shows of London.* Cambridge, Mass.: Harvard University Press, 1978.

Ashton, John. *Social Life in the Reign of Queen Anne.* New York: Charles Scribner's Sons, 1925.

Bailey, James Blake, ed. *The Diary of a Resurrectionist.* London: Swan Sonnenschein & Co., Ltd., 1891.

Baker, William Spohn. *Washington After the Revolution.* Philadelphia: J. B. Lippincott Company, 1898.

Ball, James Moores. *Lectures on the History of Medicine.* Philadelphia: W. B. Saunders Company, 1933.

———.*The Sack-'em-Up Men.* London: Oliver and Boyd, 1928.

Baartman, Saartjie. Baptismal certificate. Archive of the Musée de l'Homme, Paris.

———. Prints depicting her. Department of Prints and Drawings of the British Museum, London.

Bernard, Hugh Y. *The Law of Death and Disposal of the Dead.* Dobbs Ferry, N.Y.: Oceana Publications, Inc., 1966.

Biography of Madame Fortune Clofullia, the Bearded Lady. New York: Baker, Godwin and Company, 1854.

Blackwell, Earl, ed. *Celebrity Register*. New York: Simon and Schuster, Inc., 1974.

Blanton, Wyndham. *Medicine in Virginia in the Nineteenth Century*. Richmond: Garrett & Massie, Inc., 1931.

Bowen, Walter S., and Neal, Harry Edward. *The United States Secret Service*. Radnor, Pa.: Chilton Book Company, 1960.

Buckland, Frank T. *Curiosities of Natural History*. London: Macmillan Company, 1900.

Burking the Italian Boy. Fairburn's Edition of the Trial of John Bishop, Thomas Williams, and James May. London: John Fairburn, 1831.

Carrington, Hereward. *Death: Its Causes and Phenomena*. New York: Arno Press, Inc., 1977.

Castiglioni, A. *History of Medicine*. New York: Alfred A. Knopf, Inc., 1947.

Chambers, R., ed. *The Book of Days*. London: W. & R. Chambers, Ltd., 1879.

Chaplin, Charles. *My Autobiography*. New York: Simon & Schuster, Inc., 1964.

Chapman, Carleton, B. *Dartmouth Medical School*. Hanover, N.H.: University Press of New England, 1973.

Clarke, Joseph Henry. *Reminiscences of Early Embalming*. New York: The Sunnyside, 1917.

Clendenning, Logan. *The Romance of Medicine: Behind the Doctor*. Garden City, N.Y.: Garden City Publishing Company, 1933.

Coffin, Margaret M. *Death in Early America*. Nashville, Tenn.: Thomas Nelson, Inc., 1976.

Cohen, Daniel. *The Body Snatchers*. Philadelphia: J. B. Lippincott Company, 1975.

Cole, G. D. H., and Postgate, Raymond. *The British People 1746–1946*. New York: Alfred A. Knopf, Inc., 1947.

Cole, Hubert. *Things for the Surgeon*. London: William Heinemann, Ltd., 1964.

Committee on Interstate and Foreign Commerce, House of Representatives, Ninety-Fifth Congress. *Use of Human Cadavers in Automobile Crash Testing*. Washington, D.C.: U.S. Government Printing Office, 1978.

Cooke, Alistair. *Six Men*. New York: Alfred A. Knopf, Inc., 1977.

Cooper, Bransby Blake. *The Life of Sir Ashley Cooper, Bart*. London: John W. Parker, 1843.

Cope, Zachary. *The Royal College of Surgeons of England. A History*. Springfield, Ill.: Charles C. Thomas Publisher, 1959.

Crowell, Robert. *Interment of the Dead. A Sermon*. Andover, Mass.: Flagg and Gould, 1818.

Cuvier, Frédéric, and Geoffroy Saint-Hilaire, Etienne, *Histoire Naturelle des Mammifères*. Paris: Chez A. Belin Librairie-Editeurs, 1824.

Darwin, Charles. *The Variations of Plants and Animals Under Domestication*. London: John Murray, 1868.

Dobson, Jesse. *John Hunter*. Edinburgh: E & S Livingstone Ltd., 1969.

The Doctors' Riot. Jersey City, N.J.: Reed and Cornrick, 1913.

Dorman, Michael. *The Secret Service Story*. New York: Delacorte Press, 1967.

Drimmer, Frederick. *Very Special People*. New York: Bantam Books, 1976.

———, ed. *The Animal Kingdom*. New York: Greystone Press, 1954.

———. *Scalps and Tomahawks: True Eyewitness Adventures of Indian Captives Who Lived to Tell Their Tales (1750–1870)*. New York: Coward-McCann, Inc., 1961.

Duffy, John. *The Healers*. New York: McGraw-Hill, Inc., 1976.

Fischer, Eugen. *Begegnungen mit Toten*. Freiburg, Germany: H. F. Schulz Verlag, 1959.

Flexner, James Thomas. *Doctors on Horseback: Pioneers of American Medicine*. New York: The Viking Press, 1937.

———. *George Washington and the New Nation (1783–1793)*. Boston: Little, Brown & Company, 1970.

Foot, Jesse. *The Life of John Hunter*. London: T. Becket, 1794.

Frey, Jacob. *Reminiscences of Baltimore*. Baltimore: Maryland Book Concern, 1893.

Gallagher, T. M. *The Doctors' Story*. New York: Harcourt, Brace & World, 1967.

Geoffroy Saint-Hilaire, Etienne. Description of the Hottentot Venus. Manuscript. Archive of the Musée de l'Homme, Paris.

George, Daniel. *A Book of Characters*. London: Edward Hulton, 1959.

George, Mary Dorothy. *Catalogue of Political and Personal Satires in the Department of Prints and Drawings in the British Museum*. London: Printed by order of the Trustees, 1947.

Goff, John S. *Robert Todd Lincoln*. Norman, Okla.: University of Oklahoma Press, 1969.

The Great and Eccentric Characters of the World, Their Lives and Their Deeds. New York: Hurst & Company, 1877.

Habenstein, Robert W., and Lamers, William M. *Funeral Customs the World Over*. Milwaukee: Bulfin Printers, 1963.

———. *The History of American Funeral Directing*. Milwaukee, Wisc.: Bulfin Printers, Inc., 1955.

Haestier, Richard Emile. *Dead Men Tell Tales*. London: J. Long, 1934.

Harrah, Barbara K., and Harrah, David, R. *Funeral Service*. Metuchen, N.J.: Scarecrow Press, Inc., 1971.

Harrington, Thomas Francis. *The Harvard Medical School*. New York: St. Lewis Publishing Co., 1906.

Headley, J. T. *Great Riots of New York*. New York: E. B. Treat, 1873.

The History of the London Burkers. London: T. Kelly, 1832.

Huff, Theodore. *Charlie Chaplin*. New York: H. Schuman, 1951.

Hunter, John. Embalming. Manuscript. Royal College of Surgeons of England.

Hybrid Indian! The Misnomered Bear Woman, Julia Pastrana. (Boston?): 1855.

Jackson, Percival E. *The Law of Cadavers and of Burial and Burial Places*. New York: Prentice-Hall, Inc., 1936.

Jameson, Eric. *The Natural History of Quackery*. London: Michael Joseph, 1961.

Journal and Certificates on the 4th Voyage of Mr. Blanchard...the 16th of October, 1784...accompanied by John Sheldon, Esq. London: Baker and Galabin, 1784.

King, Bess. *The Tomb of Abraham Lincoln*. Springfield, Ill.: Lincoln Souvenir and Gift Shop [n.d.].

Kobler, John. *The Reluctant Surgeon*. New York: Doubleday & Co., Inc., 1960.

Kutscher, A. H. *Death and Bereavement*. Springfield, Ill.: Charles C. Thomas, 1969.

Lamb, Arthur H. *Tragedies of the Osage Hills*. Pawhuska, Okla.: 1935.

Leavitt, Andrew J. *The Body Snatchers. A Negro Sketch*. New York: DeWitt Publishing House, 1879.

LeFanu, William. *A Catalogue of the Portraits and Other Paintings, Drawings and Sculpture in the Royal College of Surgeons of England*. London: E & S Livingstone Ltd, 1960.

Lehmann, Alfred. *Zwischen Schaubuden und Karussells*. Frankfurt: Verlag Dr. Paul Schöp, 1952.

Lewis, Lloyd. *Myths after Lincoln*. New York: Harcourt, Brace and Company, 1929.

MacGregor, George. *History of Burke and Hare*. London: Hamilton, Adams, and Co., 1884.

Marks, Geoffrey, and Beatty, William K. *The Story of Medicine in America*. New York: Charles Scribner's Sons, 1973.

Mathews, Anne. *Memoirs of Charles Mathews, Comedian*. London: E. R. Bentley, 1839.

McCabe, John. *Charlie Chaplin*. New York: Doubleday & Co., Inc., 1978.

McWhirter, Norris, and McWhirter, Ross. *Guinness Book of World Records*. New York: Sterling Publishing Co., Inc., 1974.

Odell, George C. D. *Annals of the New York Stage*. New York: Columbia University Press, 1927–1949.

Oppenheimer, Jane M. *New Aspects of John and William Hunter*. New York: Henry Schuman, 1946.

Otto, Hermann, W. ["Signor Saltarino"]. *Fahrend Volk*. Düsseldorf: E. Lintz, 1900.

The People's Natural History. New York: E. R. Dumont, 1902.

The People vs Joseph Brower. An Indictment for the crime of body stealing, 13 April 1788, in New York City. MS 969. New York Academy of Medicine.

Pettigrew, Thomas Joseph. *A History of Egyptian Mummies*. London: Longman, Rees, Orme, Brown, Green, and Longman, 1834.

Ploss, H. H., Bartels, Max, and Bartels, Paul. *Das Weib in der Natur- und Völkerkunde*. Berlin: Neufeld & Hening, 1927.

Polson, C. J., and Marshall, T. K. *The Disposal of the Dead*. London: English Universities Press Ltd., 1975.

Power, John Carroll. *History of an Attempt to Steal the Body of Abraham Lincoln*. Springfield, Ill.: H. W. Rokker Printing & Publishing House, 1890.

Puckle, Bertram S. *Funeral Customs*. Detroit: Singing Tree Press, 1968.

Roughead, William. *Burke and Hare*. Notable British Trials. London: William Hodge, 1948.

———. *The Murderer's Companion*. New York: Reader's Club, 1941.

Schapera, I. *The Khoisan Peoples of South Africa*. New York: Humanities Press, 1951.

Sievers, H. J. *The Harrison Horror*. Fort Wayne, Ind.: Public Library of Fort Wayne and Allen Co., 1956.

Sitwell, Edith. *English Eccentrics*. New York: Vanguard Press, Inc., 1957.

Snow, Clyde, and Reyman, Theodore A. *The Life and Afterlife of Elmer J. McCurdy*. Detroit: Paleopathology Association, 1977.

South Africa 1977. Official Yearbook of the Republic of South Africa. Johannesburg: South African Department of Information.

Stannard, David E., ed., *Death in America*. Philadelphia: University of Pennsylvania, 1975.

Swinton, W. E. *Giants Past and Present*. London: Robert Hale Ltd, 1966.

Taylor, Tom. *Leicester Square*. London: Bickers & Son, 1874.

Thétard, Henri. *La Merveilleuse Histoire du Cirque*. Paris: Prisma, 1947.

Thompson, C. J. S. *The Mystery and Lore of Monsters*. New Hyde Park, N.Y.: University Books, Inc., 1968.

———. *Quacks of Old London*. London: Brentano's Ltd, 1938.

Toole-Stott, R. *Circus and Allied Arts World Bibliography*. Derby, England: Harpur & Sons, 1967.

Truax, R. *The Doctors Warren of Boston*. Boston: Houghton Mifflin Company, 1968.

Turner, Cecil Howard. *The Inhumanists*. London: Alexander Ouseley Ltd, 1932.

Van Butchell, Martin. Collection of articles about Martin Van Butchell. London: Royal College of Surgeons of England.

Wickes, Stephen. *History of Sepulture*. Philadelphia: Blakiston, 1884.

Wood, E. J. *Giants and Dwarfs*. London: Richard Bentley, 1868.

Young, Agatha. *Scalpel*. New York: Random House, Inc., 1956.

Wiley, N. P. Letter to I. B. Van Schaick about a body snatcher. MS 1121. New York Academy of Medicine.

PERIODICALS

Aesculape. November 1926 and November 1930 (articles by Jean Avalon); January 1952 (an article by P. R. Kirby); and May-June 1961 (an article by Jean Boullet).

Africana Notes and News, June 1949 and September 1953 (articles by P. R. Kirby).

Amusement Business Magazine, October 14, 1972.

Annals of Anatomy and Surgery, 1881 (an article by E. M. Hartwell).

British Medical Journal, June 3, 1899 (an article about John Sheldon).

Bulletin of the Medical Library Association, July 1934 (an article by F. C. Waite).

Bulletin of the New York Academy of Medicine, September 1973 (an article by David C. Humphrey).

Bulletin of the Society of Medical History of Chicago, January 1935 (an article by Alan F. Guttmacher).

Ciba Symposia, May 1944 (articles by Simon Mendelsohn).

Examiner of London, November 25 and December 2, 1810.

Forum, December 1896 (an article by Thomas Dwight).

Die Gartenlaube, No, 48, 1857.

Illustrated London News, July 4 and July 11, 1857.

Journal of the American Medical Association, February 16, 1963 (an article by the Committee on Medicolegal Problems).

Journal des Dames et des Modes, February 12, 1815.

Journal of the History of Medicine, October 1953 (an article by Jessie Dobson) and January 1968 (an article by Whitfield J. Bell).

Journal of the History of Medicine and Allied Sciences, 1950 (an article by J. C. Ladenheim) and 1966 (an article by Horace Montgomery).

Life, September 15, 1952 and February 9, 1953.

New England Journal of Medicine, February 9, 1939 (an article by Frederick C. Waite).

New York State Journal of Medicine, October 1, 1943 (an article by Claude Heaton).

Ohio State Archaeological and Historical Quarterly, October 1950 (an article by L. F. Edwards).

Oklahoma Monthly, January 1977 (an article by Glenn Shirley).

Proceedings of the Royal Society of Medicine, February 1974.

Quarterly Review, January 1933 (an article by S. Wood).

Society of Antiquaries of Scotland. Proceedings. Series 4, 1912 (an article by James Ritchie).

South African Journal of Science, July 1954 (an article by P. R. Kirby).

Theatrical Observer and Musical Review, London, July 20, 1857.

Westminster Review, July 1824 (an article by Southwood Smith).

Yale Journal of Biology and Medicine, Vol. 7, No. 4 (an article by Hannibal Hamlin).

Zeitschrift für Ethnologie, January 4, 1876 (an article by Max Bartels).

ABOUT THE AUTHOR

FREDERICK DRIMMER became interested in the strange and bizarre adventures of the dead when research on another project brought him in contact with showmen who exhibit the embalmed cadavers of freaks and criminals. It was a natural jump from tracing the lives and afterlives of these individuals to delving into the little-known story of body snatching. In researching the unusual events narrated in this book he traveled thousands of miles to view preserved bodies and skeletons and interview their custodians.

Mr. Drimmer is perhaps best known for his bestseller *Very Special People: The Struggles, Loves, and Triumphs of Human Oddities* and for his lectures on this subject before college audiences. His most recent book is *The Elephant Man*, a fictional biography. He wrote the script for the Home Box Office movie, *Some Call Them Freaks*, which ran for five years. He has a broad background in scientific and historic subjects. He edited the monumental three-volume *The Animal Kingdom*, an authoritative work of natural history, and *Captured by the Indians*. He wrote over 100,000 words for the *Reader's Digest Family Health Guide and Medical Encyclopedia* and contributed numerous articles to *Funk and Wagnalls Encyclopedia* and other publications. He holds a Master of Arts degree from Columbia University and has taught at the City College of New York and Norwalk (Connecticut) Community College. For many years he was editorial head of Famous Artists School and the Greystone Press.